The Last Straight Woman

Also by Phoebe Maltz Bovy

THE PERILS OF "PRIVILEGE"

The Last Straight Woman

On Desiring Men

Phoebe Maltz Bovy

Hardcover edition published 2026

Library and Archives Canada Cataloguing in Publication

Title: The last straight woman : on desiring men / Phoebe Maltz Bovy.
Names: Maltz Bovy, Phoebe, author
Identifiers: Canadiana (print) 20250335433 | Canadiana (ebook) 20250335441 | ISBN 9780771013027 (hardcover) | ISBN 9780771013034 (EPUB)
Subjects: LCSH: Heterosexual women—Social conditions. | LCSH: Heterosexual women—Sexual behavior. | LCSH: Heterosexual women—History. | LCSH: Heterosexuality—Social aspects. | LCSH: Man-woman relationships. | LCSH: Feminism.
Classification: LCC HQ23 .M35 2026 | DDC 306.7—dc23

Cover design and art by Kate Sinclair
Typeset in Dante MT Pro by Erin Cooper and Six Red Marbles
Printed in Canada

Signal, an imprint of McClelland & Stewart
Penguin Random House Canada
320 Front Street West, Suite 1400
Toronto, Ontario, M5V 3B6, Canada
penguinrandomhouse.ca

1 2 3 4 5 30 29 28 27 26

To Baba

PENNY (Moyra Fraser): They get to an age, don't they, men.

JEAN (Judi Dench): Oh, we all get to an age, Penny.

PENNY: Yes, but we don't have yearnings for young men, do we?

JEAN *tilts her head, as if to contradict, but stops herself.*

—*As Time Goes By*[1]

FREDA: Wear your baggy Y fronts with the loose elastic.

—Victoria Wood, "The Ballad of Barry and Freda (Let's Do It)"[2]

CONTENTS

INTRODUCTION

Mrs. Slocombe's Pussy

Miss Brahms and Mrs. Slocombe work together at a fictional London department store on the 1970s–80s British sitcom *Are You Being Served?* In the ample downtime between customers, they gossip about their off-duty lives. On one such occasion, Miss Brahms tells Mrs. Slocombe about a Greek town that is, per a friend who's vacationed there, filled with bottom-pinching men. Miss Brahms—played by a young, gorgeous Wendy Richard—recounts this in a disgusted tone, and assumes Mrs. Slocombe (Mollie Sugden)—a fellow woman, after all—will share her preference for a holiday locale where she'd just be left alone.

Mrs. Slocombe has a rather different response: "Really? Where exactly was that?"[1] She asks this in a hushed, husky tone that's a little knowing, a little camp, and rife with the innuendo that characterizes the show. Mrs. Slocombe travels the world without fear of unwanted male attention. She suggests this is because she's more upscale than her colleague's friend. The audience knows to laugh, because the issue is certainly not that Mrs. Slocombe is posh. She's just . . . old. Not elderly, but middle-aged, plain, and whatever the opposite is of demure. Mrs. Slocombe's vanity prevents her from admitting that she moves unmolested through public spaces, but she nevertheless lets it slip that she wishes she did not.

Miss Brahms likes men. She gives no indication of preferring women (not inconceivable, on a show with an unstated but unambiguously gay male character, John Inman's iconic Mr. Humphries), or of being asexual. But hers is a tepid heterosexuality, and a pragmatic one. Men take her out to nice dinners and complain when she fails to sleep with them as thanks. She is not above noticing a movie star—Burt Reynolds's 1972 *Cosmopolitan* centrefold makes an impression—but is more typically on the receiving end of lustful gazes. Men, for Miss Brahms, are a little useful, a little frightening.

Mrs. Slocombe, for her part, *adores* men, but they don't usually find her worth pursuing. She's a little lonely, and a lot horny. Whether in the store, in the presence of a male customer, or in the stories she tells of her pub outings with an off-screen best friend, she's game. *Her* complaint about the iconic Reynolds photo is that the pose obscures a key part of the actor's anatomy, although she only admits as much after first pretending to find the nude photo revolting. It is once Miss Brahms cops to appreciating it that Mrs. Slocombe speaks her own unvarnished truth.

If Miss Brahms is a working-class everywoman, Mrs. Slocombe is the show's comic relief. She wears her hair in a matronly, proto–Marge Simpson beehive in rotating shades of pastel—a look more commonly associated with drag queens—and is regularly referred to as fat, in the way that unremarkably sized women so often are in mid-twentieth-century sitcoms. Despite the "Mrs.," there's no Mr. Slocombe at home. She lives alone with a cat she refers to—with one double entendre along these lines per episode—as her "pussy." On hiring movers: "Well, you know how clumsy those removal men are, I'm not having them handling my pussy."[2] Except we all know that, if given the opportunity, she would.

Female heterosexuality has been understood almost exclusively as the experiences of women like Miss Brahms. Women, that is, who may be nominally straight, but whose relations with men are mainly about deflecting their advances. I'm here to make the case for a concept of straight womanhood that includes, even prioritizes, the Mrs. Slocombes of the world. By "the Mrs. Slocombes of the world," I do not literally mean women who resemble Mrs. Slocombe, although given how riled some today are by the mere thought of "cat ladies" and women with unnatural hair colours, I could see a feminist case for this as well. But no, what I mean are women whose interest *in* men is stronger than their interest *to* men, rather than the other way around.

In terms of sheer numbers, the Mrs. Slocombe experience is closer to where most straight women and girls find themselves at any point in time. Most women—most people—are not remarkable-looking, in either direction, but are, as the kids say, *mid*. The women whose physical presence screams *female sexuality*, whose physiques are referenced by the expression *sex sells*, are the exception. Yet very few women are asexual. Contrary to the images the expression *a sexual woman* might summon, most female sexuality is happening in the minds and bodies not of lingerie models but of women whose general-interest sex appeal is nil.

A typical straight female life cycle goes surprisingly quickly from an awkward youth unsure if any of the boys you like will ever reciprocate, to an adulthood where men compare you unfavourably with eighteen-year-olds.[3] Life expectancy for Canadian women is over eighty. This means of approximately seventy man-liking years, a woman may spend ten of them in love-interest mode herself. And that's the women who get a prime to begin with. Yes, there are a handful of women—Naomi Campbell, Isabelle Huppert, Helen Mirren—who spend a half-century turning heads. Most do not. (By the later seasons, even Miss Brahms doesn't look like Miss Brahms, something the show has the gallantry not to acknowledge.)

Roughly half the world is female, and most women are straight. On one level, straight women are hyper-visible, saturating the landscape heteronormatively from billboards and sitcoms, in novels and social media posts, holding forth about husbands and boyfriends and let us not forget fiancés. On another, they're shockingly underexplored. What is female heterosexuality, anyway? Is it a gender and sexual orientation combo like any other? Or is it a social role, one held by women with no great interest in men, but who lack the courage or sense of adventure for other paths? At a moment when women are succeeding like never before in education and professional life, do men still hold any interest for women? Would all women be gay if they could, and if they say they can't, what's stopping them? Isn't female sexuality fluid? Didn't they do that study where women were equally aroused by hetero porn, lesbian porn, and monkey sex? *Do* women even desire men, or have we merely been socialized over millennia to put up with them?

Straight women today are at a crossroads. Not obsolete, exactly, but on the decline. Straight women are, going by survey data, a smaller percentage of the population than ever before. A 2022 Gallup polling of more than ten thousand adult Americans shows that 19.7 per cent of Gen Z identifies as "something other than heterosexual," compared with 7.2 per cent of the overall population,[4] and women are more likely than men to identify as bisexual.[5] Some theorize that women are inherently sexually fluid, capable of sexual and romantic feelings for men and women,[6] and that binary sexual orientation is a man thing. Moreover, "women" is itself a category in some degree of flux, and sometimes deemed exclusionary. People assigned female at birth are now more likely than those assigned male to medically transition as adolescents.[7] And more people—in Gen Z, mainly uterus-having sorts—now identify as non-binary.[8] Together, this means that there are fewer people inhabiting that bit of the Venn diagram where "straight" meets "woman."

Much of this shift can be attributed to people feeling freer to come out than in previous generations. But there is also a sense, in some quarters, that *straight woman* is a bit ick as an identity, that it sounds reactionary or conventional, that it comes across as staid or unadventurous. Prudish. While there are absolutely trans women who date men, and are therefore among the ranks of straight women, all told this is a small demographic, one that faces a very different set of obstacles and stereotypes than the bulk of straightwomankind. If you're a trans straight woman, you still fall under the queer umbrella, and no one thinks you're a bore for liking men. Not so for the overwhelming majority of straight women. In her 2022 memoir *Bad Sex*, writer Nona Willis Aronowitz recounts coming to terms with her own heterosexuality, but only after a valiant effort at being the sexually omnivorous person she felt she ought to be. She gave other demographics a go and found "cis men" were the only ones who did it for her after all. Realizing she was straight, she writes, "made me feel shamed. Exposed and uncool."[9]

Is it *men* that women have gone off, or just the confining role of boring straight lady? It would seem, at least from the countless magazine and newspaper features on gender and sexual politics, that straight women are passé. In the world of actual people, this indifference has yet to manifest, at least in the aggregate. Well-intended efforts to counter the assumption that all women are straight give the equally misleading impression that it's a fifty-fifty shot whether any given woman will like men, something even the Gen Z stats don't claim. Young women are approximately as into men as ever before, but less into the whole straight *thing* than in previous generations. Here is where new identity categories come to the rescue.

There are now a plethora of ways to identify into queerness that don't require such drastic measures as having sex with women or transitioning to become a man. A woman doesn't even need to claim bi-curiosity to find her way under the LGBTQIA umbrella, when the "Q" is right there. The amorphous, all-encompassing term "queer," the reclaimed slur, allows people to gesture at being sexual minorities without specifying which sort. Someone who's by all accounts straight can correct the record and insist she's "queer" without anyone asking her what she means by this, lest they be accused of nosiness or gatekeeping. Or rather, people (often, gay people) *do* have some questions but the polite thing is to take people at their word when they assert their queerness. Even if there is much private, backchannel discussion of how we all know that lady with a husband is as queer as Hugh Hefner. (A derisive term exists for this: *spicy straights*.)

If you're a young woman who likes men, but whose interest in sex is perhaps less than your boyfriend's, you *could* cop to fulfilling a stereotype about women having lower libidos than men. Or you could do something more modern and situate yourself on the asexuality spectrum. You can call yourself a "demisexual"—a type of asexual—and have people anxiously googling what you are, lest they offend a marginalized minority, only to learn that demisexuals are people who only have sex once they've formed an emotional bond. Conversely, if you're a promiscuous woman whose many partners are all men, you can climb under the queer umbrella via self-identification as kinky, polyamorous, or even hypersexual.

The obvious way out of the gloom and doom of the straight woman label is by chucking "straight." The less-commonplace involves abandoning the stodgy "woman." By this I don't mean the phenomenon of gender dysphoria, wherein a small number of people assigned female at birth know that not to be who they are, and face substantial social and potentially legal obstacles just trying to lead their lives. I mean that it is now possible to identify out of womanhood without presenting as male or even androgynous. *Teen Vogue* assures that no matter your appearance and your pronouns, you can call yourself non-binary.[10] (And . . . you can! But if you present entirely as a cisgender man or woman, you can only do so much when it comes to others' perceptions.) A CBC personal essay insists you can have long hair, wear dresses, and go by your birth name of Julia and still be done wrong if someone refers to you, however innocently, with she / her pronouns.[11] Unlike race and ethnicity, where self-identifying into a marginalized group is very frowned upon (see: "pretendians"), sexuality is this realm where gatekeeping has become incredibly taboo. What this means is that there are a certain number of people—few on the whole, but more in some circles—who come across as straight women, who present as women and only date men, but who, because they don't entirely identify as women, therefore wouldn't consider themselves straight, either.

While there have been major shifts in how dress-wearing vagina-havers attracted to slacks-wearing penis-havers describe themselves, the material facts on the ground haven't much changed. Underneath the labels, the same people are, on the whole, into the same other people. So is it simply a matter of straight women rebranding? If so, who cares?

It matters more than one might think. If we imagine straight women to be a dying breed, then feminism can be about bringing on that man-optional Utopia. Women who continue to partner with men can be dismissed as out-of-it conservatives, or simply as fools. Man-wanting can be viewed as a weakness to be overcome, an inability to resist social conditioning. If, however, we accept that the thing once called female heterosexuality remains by far the predominant experience among the population feminism occupies itself with, then we need to be looking for feminist approaches to female heterosexuality. We need to be taking women's desire for men as a given—as no less real than any other deeply ingrained urge—and working with that, rather than wishing it away. We need to be doing this even if the numbers *are* shrinking. Even if there's just the one straight woman left. But it's all the more important given what the numbers actually are.

My aim here is not to insist that heteroflexible women with husbands, or assigned-female-at-birth non-binary people with high heels and boyfriends, are in some definitive sense straight women in denial about their true selves. Sexual orientation and gender identity are socially constructed categories, so there is no such thing as digging deep and unearthing official truths in these areas. If, in an everyday situation, a woman tells you she's queer, and then introduces her male partner, no *gotcha* is in order. Maybe, if she expanded upon what she meant by "queer," you wouldn't think she was, but politeness dictates nodding along respectfully. If you feel moved to call her a *straight woman who thinks she's interesting*, have the decency to wait until she's left the room. But I'd also urge some sympathy for the spicy straights. If you get some straight women claiming to be queer, this is because . . . straight women have internalized the idea that straight womanhood is a bit ridiculous.

But it does not make a woman frivolous or conventional to like men. To land on that idea via progressive ideology is to sort of horseshoe-theory yourself into a regressive misogyny wherein you're only a full human being if you're male and if you're attracted to women. It is commonplace to be a straight woman, this I'll grant, but it's no more *basic* than any of the other ways a person can be. There are boring people of all genders and sexual orientations. Do we imagine the people with fifty identity-signalling emojis in a social media bio are the world's most captivating? It's a matter of taste, I suppose, but I for one do not. All straight women have inner lives, because everyone's got one of those. That you're a straight woman and *unique* doesn't make you queer; it makes you like everyone else, of every gender and sexual orientation.

But I have spent too much time on the edge cases and not dealt with the everyday scenario of straight women lamenting their heterosexuality. The phenomenon I have called Ban Men feminism[12] is best understood as a reaction to #MeToo awareness-raising, following the 2017 exposés about abusive men in Hollywood and beyond, and the gender disparities in household labour during the pandemic lockdowns. Young women, per the discourse, see men as a threat, not as a source of enjoyment. Middle-aged women, already saddled with male partners from the era when women felt they needed to have those, have had a mass epiphany that these men are worthless. It has become a given in progressive media and posts that marriage is good for men but bad for women. Everyone knows that the women in opposite-sex households are pulling more than their weight. There are memes about how a woman should throw out the whole entire man. When they aren't outright abusing women, one learns, men are mistreating them in subtle but no less nefarious ways, undermining their careers and failing to recognize their brilliance. The shortcut to improving your life, as a woman, is meant to be simple: rid your life of men.

When I was in college, in the early 2000s, conservatives were the ones pearl-clutching about campus hookup culture. If you were at all panicked about young women having casual sex, you were a reactionary, a slut-shamer, an enforcer of the double standard. This started changing around 2011, when the Obama administration applied Title IX, a U.S. law against sex-based discrimination, to campus sexual assault, and, more broadly, when progressives started talking a bit more about male sexual violence and stopped emphasizing that women were just as down for casual sex as men. With #MeToo and the ensuing reckoning, sex negativity could also function as a progressive stance. Suddenly, it started to look like the belief that women are capable of authentic sexual desire—and, more generally, that the differences between men and women had long been overstated—had been a blip, and that we were right back to the idea that sex is something men demand and women are forced to put up with.

In following all the bad-men news cycles, all the viral posts about layabout husbands, you wouldn't know that women get anything positive from interactions with men. There's been no real reckoning with the fact that women fantasize about men they have no future with or may never meet. Heteronormativity makes no such demands, and yet straight women do plenty of this. But mainstream feminist culture of the last few years never lets on. Instead, men are discussed like they're a dangerous drug, and like what's needed is the most effective harm-reduction strategy. A drug, moreover, that women only tried in the first place out of peer pressure but would never have arrived at unprompted.

It would be inaccurate to say that Ban Men feminism has gone unchallenged. Anti-feminists on the right are certainly not on board, arguing, as they do, that men have it worse. In terms of who has political power at this moment in time (I'm typing this in February 2025), it would be those fellas. Meanwhile, some on the left spent the immediate post-#MeToo moment reminding that prioritizing sexism above all other discrimination ignores the complexities of power and oppression. First it was about intersectionality, or differences in privilege among women. But soon enough, it was about the iffiness of speaking of *women* as victims in a society that included white women and Black men. Indeed, the did-you-know-how-hard-it-is-to-be-a-woman-*did-you?* of 2017–18 gave way to a 2020–21 spent learning that women could be awful, too—maybe even worse than men. There was Covid, with its myriad "Karens"—middle-aged white women who either insisted everyone around them wear a mask or spread anti-vax messages on Facebook. There were influencer *mea culpas* (all the white women lifestyle bloggers promising to Do Better and posting about reading Robin DiAngelo) and girlboss downfalls. While a trickle of feminist complaints continued during the pandemic, the principle #MeToo concerns—office sexual misconduct and inappropriate behaviour on dates—suddenly seemed a bunch less urgent, what with lockdowns, and quite possibly racist, given the implications of encouraging women to go on high alert and maybe call the cops if a man to whom they have not been introduced enters their line of vision. Young women weren't dating, and the middle-aged women staying home 24/7 with their kids were too worn out from that reality to be producing much discourse on the experience.

Feminism went out of style . . . only to return, in 2023, more youth-centric and Ban Men than ever. Even grown women were now identifying as "girls," in some convoluted attempt at aligning themselves with the unproblematic children who are our future, and to distance themselves symbolically from housework and childcare.

"Woman" just has too much baggage.[13] The second election of Donald Trump in 2024 brought with it, among so many other things, a new round of calls to boycott men.

While Ban Men feminism is (obviously) not a genocidal program to rid the world of men, it nevertheless posits manlessness as the solution to women's woes. It insists that female friends are more reliable than male partners and declares that every woman's dream is to be in women-only spaces as much of the time as possible. Much virtual ink is spilled over how "woman" is to be defined in such spaces (that is, over trans-inclusivity), but rarely is consideration given to how deeply unappealing an all-female-however-defined space is for most women. Ban men, and you ban sex and romance for the vast majority of us.

Here is the moment to reveal that I am a straight woman. (Shocking information, I realize. If you need to take a moment to collect yourself . . .) This makes me unusual—not in the world at large, where it is *extremely* usual, but rather within the narrow field of people analyzing straight womanhood as such. The typical commentator is a mystified outside onlooker. The two best-known works in this area—Asa Seresin's 2019 "On Heteropessimism" and Jane Ward's 2020 *The Tragedy of Heterosexuality*—fit that mould, as do lesser-known articles and forum threads where heads shake about what the women who exclusively date men could *possibly* be thinking. It can be illuminating to see how you look to others, but there are things missed when you're not hearing from someone who speaks from personal experience.

It seems a bit silly to even point this out, given the sheer number of people we're talking about, but let it be known, I could not possibly speak for all straight women. Even the ones who share my other demographic categories have their own subjectivity, their own manner of being interested in men. My being a straight woman does however give me the ability to know when a sweeping assertion of what we are about is missing the mark. When I hear that straight women are thus because society demands heterosexuality of us, because the patriarchy has coerced us into allying with men, I know to be skeptical. I'm immediately reminded of the times when my own guy-liking was *not* convenient.

No one can *come out* as straight, because it's what's assumed of everyone. But it is entirely possible to become aware of your own heterosexuality, and here is what first alerted me to mine: There was a *Wayne's World* poster up in my summer camp cabin when I was eight years old, and Dana Carvey as shaggy-haired (wigged) rock superfan Garth in that photo made an impression on me. I don't see it now. In fact, it strikes me as borderline unhinged. (Why Carvey as Garth and not just as himself? Why not Carvey's other recurring *Saturday Night Live* characters, such as George H.W. Bush or the Church Lady? Questions that gesture at a central premise of this book, which is that desire cannot really be interrogated.) Another impression-leaver of that part of my life, Timothy Dalton in *The Lion in Winter*, shown to us in a history class, holds up better. My tastes weren't uniformly unconventional, just all over the place, coalescing around this one consistent trait: maleness. I had a picture of Keanu Reeves up in my childhood bedroom, but I also have a like-it-was-yesterday memory of being ten and daydreaming about Graham Chapman, fit and (fleetingly) naked, as the Jesus-type figure in Monty Python's *Life of Brian*.

I attended an all-girls school until I was fourteen, so celebrities and passersby would play a key role in awakenings. There was this element of scarcity where real-life, same-age boys were concerned. I had fun with my school friends, and had the usual tempestuous clique drama with them, but it was clear that something was missing, for me, in this environment. In fourth grade, a French teacher once brought her teenage son to class. Once. I remember this better than I do the subjunctive, and I have *taught* French.

During these same tween years, I dealt with the unsolicited attentions of grown men, at a level far exceeding anything I would encounter even in my twenties. Head-swivelling, the hurling of marriage proposals at me at a farmer's market with my mother, a man sidling up inappropriately on a bus. Things like this existed in an entirely different universe from my liking of boys or whichever crushes on grown men. I was an ordinary-looking child, but New York's catcallers were not discerning. I once had knee scrapes from rollerblading and a man on the street yelled to me—I was probably about eleven at the time: "You've been spending too much time on your *knees*."

I was in middle school during the Bill Clinton administration and, more specifically, the Monica Lewinsky scandal. The knee-chafing sex act dominated the public consciousness. According to school gossip, some of my classmates had not only located boys but were giving them blowjobs. I had only the most abstract idea of what "blowjob" meant. I had a proto-feminist sense that it was wrong that the boys were not reciprocating, though the reciprocal act seemed even more confusing, containing, as it did, the word "eating" in the expression. What I'm saying is that I imagined actual food was involved. My misconceptions were not helped by a rumour involving this one girl's older sister, her boyfriend, and some tuna salad.

In time, like most adults, I progressed from crushes to the real thing. The reason I cut off this story before the actual-relationships portion of my life is partly a matter of discretion. But it's also that sexual orientation is about who you *want* to be having relationships with, whether or not that pans out. Plenty of lesbians marry men and have "straight" sex for decades, only to realize that the reason they were repulsed by sex with their husbands wasn't because that's just how women feel. It is how *some* women feel. But it is, to put it mildly, far from the universal female condition.

The dwindling space taken up by straight womanhood could be viewed as obsolescence. Or you could view it in a positive light, as presenting an opportunity for those who remain. What does it mean to be a straight woman at a moment when other options abound? If what the feminist thinker Adrienne Rich called "compulsory heterosexuality" is fading, what remains, heterosexuality-wise, is the *voluntary* variety. Perhaps the time has finally come to understand female heterosexuality as what it is, at its core: women sexually and romantically desiring men.

The Last Straight Woman is not a defence of men. I'm not saying that women should like men, but that most do. The ubiquitous notion of women *going off men* is at once descriptive and prescriptive. Indeed, the idea that women could deem men unworthy and therefore give them up rests on a belief that female sexuality is weaker or more fluid than male, such that shunning men indefinitely is a viable option for us. As such, these "new" ideas about who women are and who we should be are not as new as all that. Rather, they build on a long-standing myth: that men possess a general lust for life that includes sexual appetites, whereas women choose between ambition and romance.

Underpinning the divergence is this notion that male sexuality is a natural and near-unstoppable force, whereas women can take it or leave it, and will, if serious people, do the latter. Straight women's need for men is not understood as a mirror image of straight men's need for women, but rather as an entirely different category of requirement. The woman-needing man is someone who *has needs*, as in, for sex. He needs, effectively, a parking spot for his penis. This is the implication of the phrase *He needs a woman*. If he required partnership more generally (or his ironing done), he might instead be said to want *a girlfriend* or *a wife*. If it's about needing a "woman," the expression implies a kind of primal urgency. An implicit *I need a woman* TONIGHT.

The woman who says *I need a man* is saying what, exactly? Because it's not a request for sex, or even fully-clothed flirtation. She's announcing that she doesn't think she's complete unless she has a male partner. That she subscribes to outdated ideas about women needing husbands for us to count as full-fledged adults. Or she's saying she's weak, physically, and needs *a man about the place*, someone to be home with her at night to fend off intruders. She is just asking to be fed, as a corrective, the classic feminist line about a woman needing a man like a fish needs a bicycle.

The idea that men have *needs* and women *neediness* is built into the supposed science of these matters.[14] Appetites are thought to be gendered, which I suppose makes sense at a moment in time when people talk of something called "girl dinner"—which is, best as I can understand, not eating dinner at all.

A woman who says she needs a man has as good as declared herself plain, desperate, and also a bad feminist. No one is impressed by the woman who thinks she needs a man. And that is how this gets expressed, that a woman *thinks* she needs one. The implication is that she has thought wrong. That there's some greater truth, according to which the man is not necessary. No one speaks of men *thinking* they need women. There is, it's understood, no thinking involved.

So here I am, reclaiming man-needing as a feminist pursuit. How so? For a woman to announce a sexual orientation—*any* sexual orientation—is an assertion of autonomy. Saying *I'm straight* conveys your need not for one specific man, but for *men*. It's an expression of need, and therefore vulnerability. But if anything, it's a way of pushing back against the role of dependent wife or girlfriend. What *I like men* means is: *If it doesn't work out with you, I could make it work with someone else*. If a specific man disappoints, there are many billion other possibilities. With male desire, this is understood. Everyone gets that a man does not lose his pre-existing sexual orientation upon making a commitment, and that the most that can be asked of him is that he not be too careless with his web browser.

I'm not saying that we women with boyfriends or husbands or out on a first date need to ramp up our own conspicuous head-swivelling. Or maybe, on some level, I am saying exactly that. We do need to remember, and remind, that it is *men* we like, and that we do not cease to exist as sexual and romantic beings outside the context of a particular relationship. Women are people, people who *want*. Maybe we shouldn't like men, but on the whole, we do. That needs to be our starting point.

ONE

Sex After Trump

BOYDRUNK

In 2024, the dating app Bumble found itself under fire for the marketing campaign slogan "A vow of celibacy is not the answer." A billboard bore that message, along with a photo of a man and woman happily canoodling, representing the satisfied customers. It seems an unremarkable message for an app whose target audience is people looking to have sex. What's interesting is not that some people were offended, because someone's always offended, but rather *why*: Bumble had failed to read the room, which is a problem if you're trying to sell a service to people in that room. Many young women were still hoping to meet men, as they always were and likely always will be. But times were such that openly admitting to such interests was simply not done. Just as dieting was being euphemistically referred to as "wellness," man-seeking was something young, aspirational-type women still did, but discreetly, and with hand-wringing.

Didn't Bumble realize that young straight women find dating a nightmare and have had it with men—the loser men of their generation and the creepy old men their senior? Had they missed that *needing a man* had become an embarrassingly dated pursuit? The change was abrupt, all right. As recently as 2010, *Harper's Bazaar* had run a humour essay by *Man Repeller* blogger Leandra Medine Cohen called "Can You Be in Fashion and Still Get a Man?" But to speak in such terms in 2024 would mark you as a relic. The thing is, Bumble rather obviously did know about this shift, as it's the discourse the ad was referencing. Why else mention vows of celibacy to begin with?

Bumble trotted out the inevitable woke-corporate apology,[1] vowing to do better on behalf of those who'd educated them on such things as "celibacy is the only answer when reproductive rights are continuously restricted," and that "for many, celibacy may be brought on by harm or trauma." There are some, they now realized, "for whom celibacy is a choice, one that we respect." Bumble had also heard "from the asexual community, for whom celibacy can have a particular meaning and importance, which should not be diminished." Definitely crucial for an app where people meet for sex and romance to keep the needs of asexuals front and centre. The whole thing amounted to a long-winded (this is a mere snippet) *mea culpa*, from a dating app, for . . . being a dating app.

Given how of-the-moment and therefore fashionable the Bumble stumble was, it's no surprise the *New York Times* Style section covered it.[2] Writer Gina Cherelus gestured at young women's reasons for (apparently) embracing celibacy, at least in principle: "Perhaps it's one way women are searching for peace within themselves after one too many situationships, ghostings and other romantic hardships." Human beings have always disappointed one another, but there *is* something different afoot. Something where all-the-women have had it with all-the-men. Thus the seemingly counterintuitive "trend of choosing to abstain from sex, decentering men or going 'boy sober.'"

"Boysober," itself the subject of its own *Times* Style section coverage,[3] is, per the then-twenty-seven-year-old comedian Hope Woodard, who coined it, "an all-encompassing term, one that meant abstaining from romantic relationships with people of any gender." Except that it is about women who date men. There's a nod to inclusivity—anyone *could* be dating anyone; someone who comes across as a she/her *might* use they/them pronouns—when everyone kinda-sorta knows what this is all in reference to. The boysober Brooklyn comedy show had, per reporter Marisa Charpentier, an "audience of mostly women and nonbinary people," there to receive Woodard's message of don't-need-a-man empowerment: "'Maybe we are one of the first generations of women where we don't actually have to plug into a man for, like, energy and power and whatever.'" Liberation not through having all the casual sex you want, but through retreating from that realm entirely.

A *Times* online headline reads "'Boysober' Is Celibacy with a Rebrand," and the *rebranding* angle here is key. This amalgam of assigned-female-at-birth young adults—some women-identified, some not—who date terrible men (but would, in theory, date non-men, but often only in theory) is how Gen Z has rebranded straight women. It's not that all the boysober women are straight. A twenty-five-year-old audience member told Charpentier that she emerged from her own stretch of boysobriety to realize guys weren't for her. But one gets the distinct sense that most of the boysober masses will be riding the man wagon again soon enough. Boysobriety is a way of announcing that you don't need a man, in a way that makes you seem like yeah, you kind of do, or else you wouldn't be using the language of addiction to describe them.

THE FIRST BANNED MAN

Ban Men feminism, in its current incarnation, owes everything to Donald Trump. Since he came on the political scene in 2015, the U.S. president has served as an avatar for bad men of a certain type: the abusive husband, the bullying boss, the daddy with whom there were *many* issues. Prior to that, Trump had been an entertainment figure as much as a businessman, a personal brand whose name was on gaudy buildings, with cameos in everything from *The Nanny* to *Home Alone 2*, and referenced sarcastically everywhere from *The Golden Girls* to early-aughts Britcom *Benidorm*. His tabloid-fodder personal life involved three successive wives, each of whom looked the part, and an id-fuelled tendency to hold forth about how sexy his own daughter was. The *Access Hollywood* tape, where "when you're a star, they let you do it," the "it" in question turning out to be "Grab 'em by the pussy," inspired all the "pussy hats" at the Women's March. Sexual misconduct accusations rain down on him pretty much continuously—one such brush with controversy was a felony conviction for sending hush money to a porn star—which seems not to tarnish his brand. If anything, it gives him cred in the corners where caddishness is viewed as an asset.

Trump owned the Miss Universe pageant, positioning himself as a kind of Hugh Hefner figure, but with 1980s gilded ostentatiousness instead of 1950s clubbiness as the aesthetic. He was not simply a bon vivant who couldn't help himself, like the A-list men who periodically lunge at nannies or chambermaids, women who—for obvious socio-economic reasons—tend not to resemble pageant queens. No, Trump was a *judge*. He presented himself as the ultimate arbiter of female beauty and therefore worthiness. Whether a woman was hot-or-not to Trump personally was meant to align with her objective appeal.

And Trump's first presidential term, while less drama-filled than his second (as I type, a mere month into it), did wind up having a measurable impact on American women. Thanks to his Supreme Court appointees, the U.S. Supreme Court overturned *Roe v. Wade*, which had recognized American women's right to abortion. While this would have been true of any Republican president, it came as a lower blow, coming as it did from a man not exactly known for reticence himself. The second Trump term has already seen such developments as (some) American women joining a South Korea–based movement to boycott sex and relationships with men, and a *New York Times* fashion article, "Hefty Sweaters for Heavy Times," attributing the trend of women wearing massive, chunky sweaters to an interest in protecting oneself from some mix of right-wing policies and the men emboldened by the same.

The 2016 election felt like being jolted back to an era before anyone outside niche feminist circles cared about sexual harassment or taking women seriously as human beings. It seemed like a harbinger of a new era of handsy bosses and decorative bimbo secretaries, different from the previous such ages only in that everything was now dumber and more online. And the setback seemed to have come out of the blue. Hillary Clinton was supposed to win! Clinton—or whoever was managing her social media at the time—tweeted, on October 26, 2016, "Happy birthday to this future president," accompanied by a headshot of Hillary as a girl. I think every culture has a proverb for why you should never post along those lines.

Hillary Clinton's loss was widely interpreted as a blow not just to the Democrats but also to an entire gender. Women in the U.S. and beyond donned pussy hats in mass protest. Feminism itself leapt from a fringe preoccupation of students and bloggers to the default assumed position of women—maybe even of people generally—whatever their politics or place in the world. To convey that you thought a woman was racist or classist, you could call her a *white feminist*, regardless of her own race. Along similar lines, TERF (trans-exclusionary radical feminist) became shorthand for *transphobe*, as though most anti-trans bigots could be classified as any kind of feminist, radical or otherwise. But it adds up if you remember that everyone was now some kind of feminist. Anti-feminism became tantamount to expressing sympathy for rampage-prone incels. Whether this shift constituted a victory for feminism or a dilution of the term to the point of meaninglessness, who can say?

It is Donald Trump's political and visceral repulsiveness to so many women that makes him so important to our story. From the time he became the Republican nominee in 2016, Trump was the subtext, and often the text, of Ban Men feminism. He was not merely a much-despised politician but a figure onto whom all male unpleasantness could be projected. The march to "resist" him was, remember, a *Women's March*. Journalists and comedians likened Trump to "bad boyfriends." Although many women (if not as many as sometimes claimed; the ubiquitous 53-per-cent-of-white-women stat turned out to be an overestimate[4]) did vote for Trump, and the world is wide enough to contain women who think he's attractive, his fan base skewed male, and opposition to him was even more closely associated with feminism than one would expect with a Republican president. The first Trump era marked the beginning of a pronounced (and surprisingly international[5]) political gender divide, with young women far to the left of their male counterparts.

To hate Trump was to be so done with men and their BS. Blythe Roberson's quasi-satirical 2019 *How to Date Men When You Hate Men*, a centrepiece in the Ban Men literary canon, opens as follows: "I think about men all the time. About how they, individually (Donald Trump) and as a group, are oppressing me. And about how they, individually (Timothée Chalamet) and as a group are very hot."[6] Nona Willis Aronowitz's 2022 memoir *Bad Sex* begins with an allusion to the same catastrophe: "In the last few days of 2016, everything in my life and in America was in extreme disarray." Trump is more than subtext in E. Jean Carroll's 2019 *What Do We Need Men For?*, a tongue-in-cheek anti-man tirade by the former *Elle* magazine advice columnist whom Trump was eventually convicted of sexually abusing and defaming. Carroll wrote that Trump assaulting her put her off men entirely, such that she hadn't had sex at all since the incident in question.

Trumpian awfulness extended to those in his orbit. In a 2019 *Paris Review* essay, "On Being a Woman in America While Trying to Avoid Being Assaulted,"[7] novelist R.O. Kwon describes her reaction to a Trump Supreme Court then-nominee who was not-un-Trumpian in his alleged personal history: "On the day Brett Kavanaugh was voted into the Supreme Court despite multiple, very credible accusations of sexual misconduct . . . A man catcalled me. 'Are you fucking kidding me,' I said, flaring brave, for once, with fury. 'Today, of all days.'" The catcaller, a man with the power to intimidate but (one suspects) little sway in society at large, felt somehow connected to a Supreme Court justice who would, in 2022, vote to curtail American women's reproductive rights.

#METOO AND THE END OF SEX POSITIVITY

In October 2017, *The New York Times* and *The New Yorker* published Pulitzer Prize–winning exposés about the many allegations of sexual misconduct, including rape, against Hollywood producer Harvey Weinstein. Many of the accusers were famous actresses. Weinstein, along with being objectively bad news, was the perfect villain for the moment. The template for addressing sexism was in place: identify a powerful man with a *pattern* and mobilize women to take him down. Weinstein—another heavy-set man from Queens a few years Trump's junior—harnessed a pre-existing fury, one retroactively applied to bad men of yore and used as a lens for understanding the modern-day ones. Soon enough, young women—and formerly young women, and the occasional man—were revealing that beloved male celebrities, academics, and media personalities were terrible people, entitled blowhards whose sense that they could get away with anything had long gone unchallenged. The timing here was not incidental. #MeToo functioned as shorthand, connecting Trump with ordinary women's bad experiences with men.

Anti-creep feminism was already a movement prior to 2017. There's of course a longer history of feminists (and not just feminists!) viewing rape as abhorrent, but I'm talking about an early-2000s feminist mood. Hollaback!, rebranded Right to Be, was founded in 2005 to combat such things as men jerking off at women on the subway. The activist Tarana Burke, credited with coining the phrase "me too" in the context of sexual abuse, did so in 2006. In 2011, the Obama administration took on campus sexual assault, applying the Title IX anti-sex-discrimination statute to that which was previously brushed off as date rape and swept under the rug. That same year, Canada held its own with the inaugural SlutWalk, a march of scantily clad women insisting on their right to wear whatever they'd like without men taking advantage, inspired by a cop with some victim-blaming clothing advice. *The New Yorker* covered the #YesAllWomen hashtag—its meaning virtually identical to that of #MeToo, though instigated by an incel mass shooter and not a gross mogul—in 2014.[8] #MeToo galvanized existing sentiment, making sex pests the topic of the moment for an impressive two-plus years, with waves of renewed interest whenever another bad-man news cycle surfaces. It emerged from the part of the feminist movement devoted to women's right to sleep around without being shamed or assaulted, but changed the narrative to one dubious that women even wanted to be having all that sex to begin with.

This is not the place for a full assessment of #MeToo and its impact on society, mostly because it's off topic but also because it's still ongoing. People will sometimes point to instances of sexual misconduct and say something like, *and people say #MeToo went too far*. I take their point, but I also think it's worth asking whether #MeToo was ever structured in a way to address concrete problems. Some of what are called failings of #MeToo (things like male employers now being wary of hiring women lest "issues" arise) are better interpreted as backlash. The cancellations felt momentous at the time but didn't all stick.[9] Most obviously, Donald Trump was not actually banned or cancelled or anything of the kind. He simply took four years off from being president, then resurfaced tanned, rested, ready, and with a vice-president known for speaking derisively of Democrats as "childless cat ladies."

#MeToo went too far *and* not far enough. It certainly raised awareness of male sexual misconduct, a real and entrenched problem, and for this alone, it deserves some credit for cases of justice-served since the campaigns began. There was also a too-wide net-casting element that saw a great many men labelled "problematic" for anything from being rude to co-workers to standing credibly accused of rape. This bit was rather less helpful, but again, not our focus here.

The impact of #MeToo that's relevant for our purposes is its profound shift in what it meant to be a socially liberal feminist. In the decade or so prior, the party line was that women were at least as sexually voracious as men. To suggest otherwise was to out yourself as a gender essentialist and a conservative. If you pooh-poohed hookup culture, this was because you were a shaming pearl-clutcher opposed to premarital sex, or at least to women's participation therein. Whereas after 2017, the sexists were the people who refused to acknowledge that a woman *risks her life* going on a date with a man. That Margaret Atwood–attributed quote was ubiquitous: "Men are afraid that women will laugh at them. Women are afraid that men will kill them." Ubiquitous, and taken as a literal comment on how women feel in ordinary everyday interactions with men.

Prior to #MeToo, you could demonstrate progressive and feminist credentials with the expression *consenting adults*. As in, if adults freely agreed to a sexual encounter, this was all that mattered. This was how you differentiated yourself from the people who disapproved of same-sex or casual relationships. #MeToo-era feminism questioned whether women were on enough of a level playing field to consent to much of anything. Suddenly, in the name of social justice, young people were flagging power imbalances, however minuscule, between lovers or anyone so much as contemplating a move in that direction. This meant that "actually women like sex" became . . . not a conservative position, but a heterodox one. A Gen X provocateuse might say something about how women *love* flirting at the office or admit to missing the days when she was catcalled, and everyone would groan. She would be branded a #MeToo skeptic from the left, a libertine from the right, but mostly just ignored for being a dinosaur.

HOT GIRL FEMINISM

Forgive me for stating the obvious, but #MeToo invites women to say: "me, too." The phrase itself elicits a coming-forward with shared experiences, and an expectation of respectful silence from any women who do not relate to the stories others are recounting. Insofar as #MeToo is about how women are judged on sex appeal, this is true of all women, whether or not the judgment is favourable. Some women get hired only to be lunged at, while others are passed over because they're deemed unworthy of a lunge; neither situation is optimal. The journalist Marie Le Conte has pointed out that the same women are, in different contexts, leered at and ignored. These are two sides of the same unpleasant coin.[10] #MeToo, however, had little interest in the plight of the overlooked. To be a woman was to be relentlessly pursued by men.

Prior to #MeToo, beauty standards discourse was a bit part of feminism. The world was so cruel to plain or older women, or simply ignored them. Feminists recognized that it was both a problem that women (but not men) were judged on sex appeal even in non-sexual contexts and a bummer for women trying to date that men wouldn't date them if they didn't meet conventional definitions of hotness. Such concerns didn't really fit in the new framework. I mean they did, if what was up for discussion was the racism of *Western* beauty standards, but this was more a matter of the injustice in play when certain beautiful young women are valorized over others. But the plight of the mid was so last season. Why would being less sought-after by men be a *bad* thing? Bemoaning the fact that people *didn't* want to sleep with you became male-coded, incel-coded. The woman who men *didn't* hassle was now effectively a logical impossibility, because to be a woman was, everyone solemnly agreed, to face a barrage of unwanted male attention. *That* was the universal female experience.

Similarly, in the before-times, feminism prioritized women asking men out, women proposing to men, things of that nature. I don't mean *prioritized* as in considered these things more important than the pay gap. But it was understood that cultural factors siloed women into a passive role when it came to getting relationships started. Post-#MeToo, none of this resonated. Women were organizing to stop unwanted advances, not fighting to make ones of our own! Insofar as

#MeToo had a pragmatic plan for stopping male sexual misconduct, it pretty much consisted of making the public sphere a flirtation-free zone. The baby (women asking men out) was therefore disposed of along with the bathwater (men asking women out).

To speak of relationship dynamics in this way is to assume that the default woman is someone whose interest *to* men far exceeds any she has in them. There's a name for women like this: hot.

As a PR move for feminism, a hot-girl turn couldn't have been more brilliant. Suddenly, feminists were stereotyped not as women too ugly to get a man, but rather as women so inundated with male attention that they needed to mobilize to deflect it. The popular image of a feminist went from Andrea Dworkin to Emily Ratajkowski or, better yet, a Barbie doll. It's convenient when the women whose rights are up for discussion physically resemble the ones in lingerie ads. Stories of beautiful actresses chased around the room by powerful old men functioned two ways at once: as the legitimate feminist grievance they were and as lowest-common-denominator entertainment. #MeToo as *The Benny Hill Show*. I'm reminded of what Greta Gerwig said of her blockbuster 2023 *Barbie* movie: "I'm doing the thing and subverting the thing."[11] It's not that there's some auteur of #MeToo pulling the strings, but rather that #MeToo narratives themselves serve this dual purpose.

BAN KEN FEMINISM

The *Barbie* movie ostensibly offered up a feminist message. After all, it got conservatives hot and bothered, with its girl-power messaging and talk of "patriarchy." And it *did* embody what has come of feminism, but not in a way I'd celebrate.

Much is made, in *Barbie*, about the dolls' noted absence of genitals. But Barbie World isn't a romance-free zone. The main Ken's unrequited love for the main Barbie (played convincingly by Margot Robbie) announces itself early on, before there's any talk of dolls entering the real world. This affection mismatch is in keeping with the overall girl-power (or buy-dolls) message of the movie, whose tagline is "She's everything. He's just Ken." In Barbie World, Barbies have all the possible professions, while Kens can only do something called "Beach," which is like being a lifeguard without the lifeguarding. This is meant to mirror how it goes in the real world, where women are only allowed to be decorative. Barbie World is as misandrist as the real world is misogynist. Ken is a layabout loser who doesn't deserve Barbie but who annoyingly pesters her throughout the film, first like a sad puppy, then like a disgruntled incel.

All of this was meant to be a maximally relatable *comment on our times*. Ken is all men, Barbie all women. Ken is the crisis of masculinity personified, the proverbial fallen-behind young man, without purpose, not in employment or education or training; a NEET. If Ken didn't exist, Richard V. Reeves would have had to invent him.

For all the script-flipping—women presidents! women authors, even, can you imagine?!—it's striking that Barbie World permits only men to experience sexual or romantic desire. Early in the film, Ken asks Barbie to spend the night with him. This prompts some knowing humour about these dolls' anatomical deficiencies, but the fact remains that he does want this. When Barbie and Ken enter the real world, she responds to catcallers at a construction site by pointing out that she doesn't have a vagina, that neither of them has anything going on downstairs, while Ken anxiously fibs that actually he does have genitals. A man—even a doll that vaguely represents one—has his pride.

Also: a clichéd construction-worker harassment scene serves as shorthand for *how it goes for women* in the real world. Barbie goes from a land where she's admired by a chivalrous Ken to one where she's objectified for looking like, well, Barbie. Or, really, for being a woman, because this is what women must deal with.

In neither universe does Barbie herself appear to like-like anybody. The only reference to a man's desirability in the entire movie (unless you count two men briefly checking out Ken on the real-world boardwalk) comes from Weird Barbie, played by Kate McKinnon, a lesbian actress playing a vaguely queer-coded character. When she makes a remark to Stereotypical Barbie about how hot her boyfriend is, this is stated more as a matter of fact (he is played by Ryan Gosling) than as anything resembling thirst. Robbie's Barbie is hyperfeminine but—or more accurately, *and therefore*—without any discernable sexual orientation. Men either respectfully worship her or ogle her, or they pretend not to like her because they actually love her. She views men first with disdain, and eventually chaste affection, like a sea of bratty little brothers.

Every night in Barbie World is girls' night (literally), not because the Barbies are lesbians, but because they live in blissful non-sexuality. They, with their smooth Barbie-doll crotches, never get *distracted by boys*. This is their superpower, the reason they have such ample . . . cvs. Whose fantasy is this? Because there *are* women who seek out all-female environments, but—with all due respect to queer femmes—the aesthetic overlap between the Playboy Mansion and a womyn's music festival is minimal. This sort of "girls' night" is only feminist in the sense that sorority houses are feminist, announcing, as they do, that a given society allows women to gather and enjoy themselves. But the movie can't make Barbie World a fully unsexed universe, because we need to understand that the Barbies are *hot*. Stereotypical Barbie in particular. And how would we know this were it not for Ken courting her? Men, even anthropomorphized Ken dolls, are inconceivable except as testosterone-fuelled desirers. Where the testosterone comes from, anatomically speaking, is not addressed. But only Ken gets to yearn. When Barbie does wind up opting for womanhood over Barbiedom, this manifests itself as her going for a gynecologist's appointment. It's a funny ending line (the way she's dressed, you imagine she's headed for a job interview), but so . . . clinical. She's having her bits examined before she's even had a chance to do anything with them.

At first, Barbie-as-feminism seemed like a strange throwback to five–ten years prior. To the so-unfashionable-these-days liberal, capitalist, girlboss feminism. The sort associated with Hillary Clinton or Amy Schumer and mocked with the expression *yas queen*. But then I realized that no, *Barbie* picked her moment. She is the bimbo, reclaimed, like in all those think pieces and posts about women reclaiming "bimbo" in the name of feminism. A girly-girl who is intentionally embracing a performance of frivolity. The bimbo is an unbothered, inadvertent tormentor of men. The bimbo, at least in her 2.0 form, is not catering to the male gaze, but rather manipulating it. She's all hair, heels, and cleavage but as a power move. She is *playing with* femininity, not a conventionally feminine woman mindlessly being herself, or doing anything so pathetic as trying to get a boyfriend. It's all really subversive and very possibly—because what isn't?—queer. *Of course* Barbie is aloof where Ken's concerned. She is too cool for man-liking, and too hot to ever find herself, even for a millisecond, in the role of desirer.

As someone whose idea of feminism is women getting to look like crap while admiring good-looking men, I cannot say that bimbo feminism—*Barbie* feminism—speaks to me. I did however enjoy watching Simu Liu as one of the Kens.

E PLURIBUS UNUM

The #MeToo moment allowed women to speak out in new ways but also flattened the female experience. To be a woman was to be young, gorgeous, and terrified. Typical content online in those years was stuff like an attractive American woman's ukulele video about how she "can't use public transportation after seven pm," because, it is implied, men on it will attack her.[12] Seven!

A counterpart to that lyric exists in R.O. Kwon's 2019 *The Paris Review* essay "On Being a Woman in America While Trying to Avoid Being Assaulted." I am a woman, I think, and I lived in America until my early thirties, so I was, presumably, the target audience. Here is how Kwon describes riding an elevator: "The elevator doors slide open, and there's one man inside: I evaluate his size against mine, calculating how well I could fight him off, if I had to." She writes about entering her own hotel room afraid that as she had accidentally left it unlocked, a man will have snuck in with intent to assault her. She checks, and there is no man. I have been in elevators once or twice in my life but, barring other cues, have never reacted this way to sharing one with a strange man. A man would need motive, not just opportunity, and for reasons doubtless as particular to myself as Kwon's are to hers, I do not assume a man would find proximity to me a source of such temptation. As for the hotel room scenario, I've seen *Psycho* and can kind of see where she's coming from. But it has never occured to me to imagine there are random men everywhere waiting for me to appear and thinking, *finally, now's my chance*. I nevertheless take Kwon at her word that this is how she experiences elevators and hotel rooms. And it would seem she has her reasons.

Kwon arrives at the topic with her own history as the victim of "gropings" and things of that nature. What she describes seems unpleasant but not necessarily at the level where someone would be this on edge. I don't think personal essayists owe readers full accounts of everything they've dealt with in life and can only consider that someone as frightened as she describes being may have faced more than she's mentioning.

In one sense, you could credit #MeToo for creating an environment that allowed women to speak honestly about the threat of male violence. But it's also deeply #MeToo that Kwon presents her reaction to everyday life not as her subjective experience but as *how it goes for women*. If you're a woman, you relate. The corollary being that if you don't relate, you're something else. I will not dwell overmuch on the headline, which writers don't generally choose, and will return instead to the essay itself: "Sometimes, I'll read a novel written by a man in which a woman walks home alone, late at night, in America, without having a single thought about her physical safety, and it's so implausible that I'll put the book down."

The scenario Kwon describes as "implausible" is one *I have experienced*. Maybe I move through public spaces—in America, even—with a false sense of security. Or maybe it's that I know that men in women's lives—relatives, partners, or vengeful exes—are more likely to pose a danger. This could be what permits me to walk down the street without assuming that behind every hedge is a man about to pounce. Maybe I've just been lucky, at least in the narrow sense of the hedge thing having never happened to me.

Another possibility here is that I'm grotesque. I feel like an asshole for even wondering this, but it strikes me as possible that R.O. Kwon is just prettier than I am, and that this explains at least some of our diverging experiences. An asshole, that is, because I should just feel grateful that I have been spared whatever would give a woman these fears, but also an asshole for imagining looks in any way enter into it. But they kind of do. It's my plainness privilege that allows me to get into an elevator and not only feel confident he's not going to lunge but also take a crafty peek at the man in it and size *him* up.

Nowhere is the shift within feminism away from angst at being passed over and towards the plight of the too-sought-after more visible than in model and actress Emily Ratajkowski's 2021 memoir *My Body*. R.O. Kwon *might* be better looking than I am. With Ratajkowski, there is no question, for she is better looking than everybody. Most fashion models are either ethereally beautiful in a way that registers as high fashion or sexy in a way that catches male attention. Ratajkowski has the professional if not necessarily personal fortune of being both. This is another way of saying that, despite being otherwise quite slim, she has large breasts. I know this both because I have seen photos of her and because she writes about it at length.

Emily Ratajkowski came into the public eye with her appearance in the 2017—but crucially, *May* 2017, so pre-#MeToo—Robin Thicke and Pharrell Williams "Blurred Lines" music video, in which she writhed around seductively to lyrics like "you a good girl / I know you want it." In subsequent years, Ratajkowski made a name for herself as the politically engaged model, an engagement that ranged from support for Bernie Sanders's 2020 presidential campaign to statements to the effect of: a woman should not be taken less seriously on account of being spectacularly good-looking. *My Body* leans heavily into that second thought, but with a more serious twist. She writes about the men who've creeped on her or worse over the years, and there have been many. (She would later accuse Thicke of groping her on set.)

In the book, Ratajkowski describes a life of being hollered at by men non-stop even before she was famous. She recounts being assaulted by a fashion photographer who then profited from the photos he took during that photo session. Awful things are regularly happening to her, and they're wrapped up in her profession as the model known for being particularly pleasing to the male gaze. Most women attract less attention, to put it mildly, but also most women can state, correctly, that their boobs aren't relevant at the workplace. If your job involves being photographed in a bra, this has to make *eyes up here, boys* more of a challenge.

The book is titillating in that extremely #MeToo double-register way, where the sexiness is wrapped up in the kale of feminist good intentions. But for a book that's so steeped in sex, it's not particularly sexy, at least if you're not of an orientation that finds endless discussions of exactly *how* big her breasts are, relative to how small her waist is, arousing. For me it's a mix of envy-inspiring and dull.

What, I wanted to know, is it like to date men if you're a woman universally considered desirable? Is it fun to be able to get nearly any man you'd want? Do you get hung up on the "nearly" and fixate on the few you don't impress? Or is the attention *from* men so overwhelming that you never stop and look at them? I can only assume it's the latter. What made *My Body* such a perfect fit for its moment was the way it distilled the role of woman as gazed-at, with hardly a pause on woman as gazer. While boyfriends and a husband are mentioned, there's exceedingly little about Ratajkowski herself desiring men—or anyone, for that matter. (She would later come out as bisexual.[13]) She refers to her now ex-husband as "handsome," in a nod to men as embodied creatures as well, but it is *her* body that is the centre of the book: "I'm one with my body only during sex," she writes. "When my husband and I fuck, I like to look in the mirror so I can see that I'm real." Given what she looks like, who can blame her for mounting a mirror?

I appreciated *My Body*, illustrating, as it does, a life so unlike my own. The phrase "my body" appears ninety-four times in the book, not counting the acknowledgements, whereas I'm not sure I've thought about my own body ninety-four times. The significance of

Ratajkowski's memoir here is where it fit in the publishing landscape. Times were such that an unusual personal narrative was presented *and received* as testimony about how it goes not for models but for *women*. A blurb from Lena Dunham, who canonically does not resemble Ratajkowski, reads, "She knows the pain that lives in every woman and she isn't afraid to link arms and say she's been there, and that it hurts." This assessment was in line with the book's marketing materials as well as the author's own understandings. Ratajkowski spelled out as much in an interview with *The New York Times*, that what she'd written was "not just about modeling. 'Every woman I know—doesn't matter what they look like, or if they've commodified their image or not—knows what it feels like to be looked at, to be rejected, to get attention for how they look.'"[14]

A consensus has formed, in recent years, that womanhood consists of fending off suitors. This shared belief extends beyond #MeToo feminism and into broader commentary on gender relations. Resentful men, perhaps hearing one narrative after the next of how to be a woman is to be drooled over, accept the priors (namely that women all experience this) but see this as a form of female privilege. "Any young woman who is even moderately attractive," wrote critic William Deresiewicz in a 2023 *Tablet* essay,[15] "will be courted, complimented, paid attention to, by women as well as men. Older men will buy them things. People will hang on their words even when they aren't interesting and laugh at their jokes even when they aren't funny. They will have entry into places—private clubs, backstage after a show—young men can only press their noses against. They will be able to advance professionally by batting their eyelashes at powerful men."

It was an entertainingly written essay but one that bore no relation to how I experienced my twenties. Where were these flirtation-based promotions? *William*, I wanted to tell him (if he would register my middle-aged presence), *what you are describing is not how it goes for young women, but what it is to be Emily Ratajkowski*. The misconception is not unique to Deresiewicz. If anything, he gets points for at least specifying that he meant *young* women, and past a certain attractiveness threshold.

The #MeToo definition of "woman" as this lusted-after entity is ostensibly about finding common ground. After all, women of all classes, races, nationalities, and so forth have dealt with lechery or worse. But it amounts to feminism embracing the same definition of "woman" as does the proverbial incel, the sort who insists that no woman would have him, but if you press him on this, by "woman" he means a category limited to head cheerleaders, prom queens, and women in his preferred porn. The remaining 99.999 per cent of the female population—doubtless containing *some* women who'd have him—simply doesn't register. It's not that he sees them as women who aren't his type. It is that they *do not register as "women" to him*, thereby allowing him to insist in good faith that not a woman in the world would give him a chance.

There's a 1964 episode of *The Dick Van Dyke Show*,[16] where Laura (Mary Tyler Moore), a stay-at-home mom and wife of Rob, a comedy writer, is taking a writing class on a lark. The teacher decides Laura "showed promise" before the class has even begun. (She had given as her reason for taking the class, "The Spanish class was full.") A friend of Laura also takes the class, but as this woman does not resemble a young Mary Tyler Moore, the teacher hardly notices her. Things eventually go where the viewer knows they will, and the teacher confesses his love to Laura. This happens in a disturbing scene—played for laughs, as attempted rapes in old sitcoms so often are—in which the teacher is on the cusp of trapping her behind a desk chair, only for her to be saved when Rob enters the classroom.

The episode ends with Rob and Laura recounting the debacle to his colleagues Buddy and Sally. Laura, indignant, asks, "Can you imagine, a man who was hired to teach housewives creative writing has the nerve to come right out and flirt shamelessly?" Sally, perennially single, says, in a sarcastic voice: "Shocking." Sally starts getting up, and Rob asks where she's going. "To see if there's an opening in that rat's class." Sally then does a little bow, making it clear that this was a comedic bit, and returns to the couch.

In that gesture, Sally reminds Laura—and by extension, the viewer—that there are women who'd *love* to have an adult-ed teacher with ulterior motives. The episode is written with enough precision that the thing Sally regrets not experiencing isn't the attempted assault (there's no reason to think Sally knows about that part), but what Laura describes as flirtation. There's also a writers'-room exchange between Buddy and Sally in which he casts doubt on Sally's femininity. Buddy says it doesn't matter if Laura's creative writing stinks because "women writers never amount to anything anyway." Sally pokes him and asks, "What am I, a duck?"

MY LIFE AS A DUCK

It would have been roughly 2007. The place: New York University's Institute of French Studies, where I had recently started a doctoral program. I was chatting with fellow female grad students. All of us were in our early twenties. The other two were both gorgeous, one a former professional model. I looked like a pre-kids, pre-forehead-wrinkles version of my current self. The women complained that men were hitting on them constantly, it was *too much*. I felt as though I was meant to nod along, but how? My own lived experience wasn't theirs. I don't want to overstate my plainness. I was slim, clear-skinned, and did not have trouble getting boyfriends. But I was, even at my peak, readily able to move through the glamorous part of New York where NYU is located without the eyes of male passersby popping out of their sockets like in a cartoon. There was *the time* a guy hit on me in a campus coffee shop. This did not happen every time I got a between-classes mocha.

In retrospect—and I was less generous in my thoughts at the moment—I don't think my classmates were trying to boast. They really did contend with more than their share of unwanted male attention. What I realize now is that I felt like a hideous loser during this conversation. What, if anything, did I say in response? I would have maintained my dignity had I responded in kind. And that's probably what I did. I can't imagine I told my statuesque classmates point-blank that I simply wasn't as popular as they were and thus couldn't relate. If you say anything that indicates you do not experience the same, you've announced you're ugly, which comes across as fishing for compliments, or somehow *makes the ugliness official*.

I share this story, one that makes me look bad physically as well as metaphorically, to get at what I think is a real phenomenon out there in the world: women feeling pressure to exaggerate their unsolicited male attention. Two things can be true at the same time: women fear sexual violence, and women's value, in our society, remains deeply connected with our perceived ability to inspire sexual thoughts in men. And with #MeToo, launched a decade after that interaction, participating in *feminist* conversations started being contingent on nodding along to other women's stories about how men keep whistling at them. If you want to see yourself as a good-looking woman and a good feminist—and who wouldn't want both those things?—this is where you're left.

There can also be—and here's where things get *really* awkward—a wishful-thinking element to women's discussions of men's forwardness. How could there not be, when the expectation is that a man makes the first move? To say that you want male attention you're not getting is to announce that you *want for male attention*. It's socially acceptable to say *ugh he's all over me* but reeks of desperation to say *aaah I wish I could be all over him*, unless the *him* in question is some heartthrob male celebrity. So the latter sentiment sometimes expresses itself as the former. I don't dare bring up real-life instances of this but will do the discreet thing of pointing you instead to a 1991 episode of Britcom *Waiting for God* ("Young People"). In it, a married woman in her late thirties expresses her lust for a male college student who has tapped her on the shoulder, with an elaborate fear-fantasy of him dragging her into the countryside. (The episode ends with them off-screen, consummating that which she has instigated.)

But the all-time greatest instance of this phenomenon is in a 1979 *Fawlty Towers* episode, "The Kipper and the Corpse." A very elderly Miss Tibbs is, because farces demand this, stuck in a cupboard with a recently deceased middle-aged man, a fellow hotel guest. Recounting this experience to hotel owner Sybil Fawlty, Miss Tibbs says, "*Anything* could have happened." Sybil is skeptical: "Well he *was* dead, dear." This prompts Miss Tibbs to say, woman to woman: "A man is a man, Mrs. Fawlty." Sybil replies, "Oh, I know," graciously allowing Miss Tibbs to believe that a dead man could have made a pass at her.

It can be frightening, as a woman, to get hit on. It can also be validating, a sign that you've still got it, that you're still *alive*. Even if, as was the case for poor Miss Tibbs, your imagined suitor is not.

YES, ALL WOMEN?

Hyacinth Bucket-pronounced-"Bouquet" of the 1990s Britcom *Keeping Up Appearances*, Patricia Routledge's rightfully internationally renowned protagonist, is a post-menopausal fuss-maker extraordinaire, a Karen *avant la lettre*, a henpecking wife from before the trope became too passé to put in sitcoms. Hyacinth is often found at her landline (the show's final episode presents her with a mobile phone), asking to speak to a manager. The gist of the show is that Hyacinth is unbearable to be around. Someone—a fellow parishioner or volunteer; she is a proper Midlands housewife—hears her voice, cries, "It's the Bucket woman!" and the room clears.

But one group of people cannot get enough of Hyacinth: posh men. Along with being generally objectionable, Hyacinth is a social climber. She's forever trying to insinuate herself with people she views as her betters, men and women alike. This is all snobbery, without a hint of flirtation. The women just do their best to avoid her, but the men regularly mistake her attentions for something else. And if you think about it for a moment, it's no mystery why: These are objectively ordinary middle- or upper-class men whom Hyacinth has convinced herself are basically royalty. An entire episode revolves around how impressed she is by a local man for owning a garden supply store. Another has her fawning over a woman in her parish whose only notable attribute is that she lives in a house that is called "the Grange." But if Hyacinth has clocked you as someone to impress, she is hurling herself in your direction. This gets perhaps wilfully misinterpreted in respective episodes by a lord, a commodore, and a country squire.

But it's a recurring character, the Major, whose pursuit of Hyacinth crosses into the most disturbing territory. He chases her around gardens, paws at her, tries to get her alone. The episode "Golfing with the Major" is the extended version, for the Major has lured Hyacinth and her husband to a hotel under false pretenses. She thinks it's a couple's outing on which the men will be playing golf, when in fact his wife isn't joining them and the Major's plan is to send her husband off and get Hyacinth to himself. He takes her for a drive in the country in his flashy convertible and things take a distinctly #MeToo turn. She struggles to get out of the car, but he pins her in, kissing her, informing her she's just his type. "Mature, matronly ladies have always been my problem," he tells her as she's attempting to shove him off her with words and force.[17] She finally breaks free and is seen readjusting the rear of her outfit, implicitly her undergarments.

The audience is meant to find it hilarious (laugh tracks spell out what would have been clear without them, plus it's acted as farce) that she emerges from these situations dishevelled. The joke is, in part, that she's let things get out of hand because she so desperately wants to impress her social betters, that after all those efforts to have every hair in place, she's all mussed. It's her comeuppance. The contrast between how proper she wants to be and the awkwardness of finding herself in such a mammalian situation plays into it as well. But it's mostly that Hyacinth—the least sexy woman imaginable, as well as the least pleasant company—seems like the last person on Earth a man would seek out for a good time.

The relationship between how pretty a woman is and how much male aggressiveness she must endure is complicated and fraught. One is meant to say that no relationship exists between hotness and victimhood, and in a limited sense, one would be correct. Sexual abuse occurs in nursing homes. Domestic violence impacts women of all physiques. How much day-to-day hassling a woman encounters will be partly a matter of the catcalling culture or lack thereof where she lives. Lecherous bosses have been known to care more about proximity than whether the woman at arm's reach would win a beauty contest.

And yet. We all know that a gorgeous twenty-five-year-old is hollered at more often than a little old lady, but also more than her homely nineteen-year-old friend. We *know* this. If you're hot, you get more of the good sort of attention—easier to get dates and jobs, to find flattering clothes—but also more of the bad.

THE POST-#METOO DATING LANDSCAPE

In 2023, a journalist named Ashley Hupfl, responding to New York City mayor Eric Adams making some offhand remarks about how outdoor dining was a good setting for flirtation, posted to X, "Fact: Women do not want to be 'eye candy' and have weird creeps 'slip them their number' while grabbing food with friends."[18] While Hupfl received no shortage of pushback—from women who do like getting asked out, and from people who (they phrased it less delicately) did not believe Hupfl was inundated with offers—the fact remains that this sort of statement has become normal. It is taboo these days to hit on people in public settings, in a way that would have been unthinkable even fifteen years ago.

Dating and hookup apps are the backdrop to this shift. Without them, the expectation of a just-business-ma'am public sphere is incomprehensible. Technology has made it possible to compartmentalize: Real-life spaces are for work or hobbies, while this special online zone is for *that* stuff. The existence of apps was I guess supposed to liberate in-person interactions from any sort of sexual charge. How exactly this was meant to work, I have no idea. Had the people coming up with these theories never been in a room with other people before? But this seems to have been the thinking. If only everyone could keep their urges on the urge-specific websites and direct all their sexual interest towards people they'd only seen on screens, this would make it possible for women to participate fully in the rest of life: working, commuting on public transit, or hanging out with friends. This was *what women wanted*. All of life could now at long last be a zone safe from . . . well, from what, exactly?

As overwrought as a lot of this has been—and as mystifying as it feels to many Gen X and old-millennial women, who equate feminism with sexual autonomy—pushback was needed in response to gender-neutral sex positivity. Men and women are *not* on an equal playing field, where playing the field is concerned. But instead of a more nuanced conversation about who has which options and faces which risks, what ensued was a proliferation of taboos. Missing from all these conversations was any sense that women might not just consent to but seek out sexually charged situations with men. The #MeToo-era straight woman is defined by what she *doesn't* want. Even female pursuit is framed as a safety measure, a way of keeping the lustful males at bay.

It still amazes me that the idea could have caught on that women *want* daily lives devoid of even the potential for sex. I don't think female heterosexuality is centrally about women enjoying men hitting on us; I think it's far more about us noticing the men *we* want, and hoping something comes of it. But someone has to initiate, and in this new order, female initiation became illogical to contemplate. The de-sexualizing of public spaces was not the only feminist path possible. There might have been, instead, more meaningful attempts at liberating women to pursue men. Instead, we got messaging about how frightened women are by men at all times, how if you smile at a man he'll assault you, the implication being that with men on the *hunt* as they are, women are only ever playing defence. To me, at least, it has never added up that women, all-the-women, prefer to go to a park, a coffee shop, or even an office where they can be sure that they will not have a sexually charged interaction with a man. The unpleasantness of a respectful but unsolicited come-on is the price one must pay for the profound joys of what happens when interest *is* reciprocated.

What began as a kind of cross-industry workplace audit, sniffing out lecherous bosses, soon extended beyond HR territory, morphing into the unofficial framework for understanding power relations in male-female relationships more broadly. Suddenly it seemed like everyone had an opinion on whether a professor could date a former student who had since graduated, or whether this was basically child abuse, even if the "child" in the scenario was on the far side of thirty. Couples seemingly composed of what five minutes earlier would have been called *consenting adults* were now under the microscope. Someone on then-Twitter claiming to be a nineteen-year-old libertarian journalist in Virginia (which seems a bit specific to invent, but who knows) posted her(?) objections to actors Al Pacino and Robert De Niro having decades-younger (but unambiguously adult; the younger was twenty-nine at the time) female partners. "We need to talk about how age gaps like this are legal. The difference in lived life experiences and wealth strips away any facade of consent, this is borderline p*dophilia."[19] Posts like that epitomize what is now referred to as *age-gap discourse*. The brain only stops developing when you're in your twenties! Romantic relationships with any age or power differential (a.k.a. all relationships, and not just straight ones) were now suspect. All offline attempts at initiation suddenly had predatory vibes.

Looking back at some of the #MeToo news stories, one sees . . . not a sex panic, exactly, but interpretations of events that only made sense within that hyper-specific climate. Readers were hungry for tales of male sexual misconduct, and the bar for what counted as such just kept dropping. A woman claimed she'd been forcibly kissed, as a "wide-eyed 26-year-old," by the author Junot Díaz.[20] The story was presented at the time as basically a man assaulting a child (a child of twenty-six), eliding both the age of the supposed victim and the absence, it turned out, of any kind of assault.

Fandom, or a fame differential, could now render consent questionable. (R.I.P. the idea of groupies.) In 2015, comedian Aziz Ansari, a cozy early-2000s sitcom presence from *The Office* and *Parks and Recreation*, had made it big with his very own show, *Master of None*, for which he was the first Asian American to win a best-actor Golden Globe. Not only did it have an impeccably diverse cast—an Indian-American man with a Black lesbian best friend—but there was a very special episode ("Ladies and Gentlemen") devoted to what a scary world it is for women. He had off-screen feminist credentials. So what could possibly be juicier or more worthy of joyless condemnation than the revelation that Ansari himself had . . . well, that he had what, exactly?

A clickbait website called Babe interviewed[21] the pseudonymous "Grace," who had gone on a date with Ansari where the sex had been at his instigation and not pleasurable for her. The woman "compare[d] Ansari's sexual mannerisms to those of a horny, rough, entitled 18-year-old."

The trouble is, it wasn't clear from the story that Ansari had even *allegedly* assaulted Grace. His violation seemed to have consisted of failing to be his comedic persona in real life. Arguably his fame was significant, not because fans can't consent but because a close read of the piece suggests Grace agreed to a date with a man she was not attracted to sexually simply because he was a household name.

The story was a bit of a watershed, though, because it prompted a conversation about which bad-boyfriend-type behaviours merited news coverage. Publications with more gravitas than Babe ran articles questioning whether what Ansari did belonged in the category of sexual misconduct. Suddenly, the ethics of publicizing what a celebrity is like in bed weren't so straightforward. There are feminist interpretations of why mediocre sex happens, but does this mean that naming and shaming individual men for alleged sexual ineptitude constitutes a public service? But the mood of the moment was that anyone with any kind of public-facing role was fair game, as long as the reveal was done in the name of women's safety. Any male-feminist hypocrisy angle was a bonus.

Qualms remain, but the toothpaste has left the tube, and we now live in a world where there are hundreds of location-specific Facebook groups called "Are We Dating The Same Guy?" Started in 2022 as a way for women to see if their boyfriends were claiming to be exclusive with them while doing the same with other women, it morphed into a way for women to "review" the men they went on online dates with. A *Glamour* article about the groups calls it, in the subtitle, "the whisper network women have been using for centuries, just amplified."[22] The article itself, by Jamie Kahn, is more circumspect. Sharing a lover or prospect's dating profile, photos, or private messages is an ethically and potentially legally dubious proposition, one best reserved for cases where women's well-being is at risk, and where no other channel can get the message across. (Local groups periodically get shut down for this reason.) As Kahn put it, "Most would appreciate a heads-up about a serial cheater, but does it also make sense to 'warn' the women of your community about a guy who Venmo-requested you to split drinks after the date? What about someone who ghosted you?"

I suppose ghosting—passively ending a flirtation or relationship by just not contacting the person again, nor responding to their messages—would belong on a "whisper network" website if you viewed it as a violation of consent. But no one would do that, right?

Courtney Sender's 2018 *New York Times* Modern Love column, "He Asked Permission to Touch, but Not to Ghost," made the case for rejection as akin to consent violation.[23] Sender, then in her late twenties, met a younger man online. They had tender, deeply respectful sex, and he even spoke about a meal he planned to cook for her on what would have been their third date. In what was either the act of a sadistic abuser or the unremarkable behaviour of someone who'd been on two dates and felt no spark, he did not ask her out again, nor respond to her pleas. "Asking about my feelings during sex didn't extend to caring about them after sex. Consent is not a contract of continuation." Correct. Then there's the *but*.

"But in the days and weeks after, I was left thinking that our culture's current approach to consent is too narrow . . . It should be a culture of making each other feel good, not bad."

This seems like a lot to ask from "consent." It always feels bad to get dumped, whatever the method. I can see why thinking a hot twenty-four-year-old will be cooking you steak and then having to live with the reality that this isn't in the cards would be a letdown, but the twenty-four-year-old also has autonomy. That you don't need another person's permission to break up with them is real Dating 101 territory. It has its own *Seinfeld* episode (a woman George dates refuses to allow him to end things) and, more seriously, is the starting point for a great deal of domestic abuse from the men who will not take "it's over" for an answer and turn to stalking or violence. The only way consent enters into a breakup is if the dumped party refuses to depart, in which case it's the *dumper's* consent that's being violated.

And it's not even clear that this man *did* ghost, at least not in the usual sense. By her own admission, she "texted him a few times in the days that followed, playfully at first, then more pressing." I could well imagine a man who wanted to see a woman again changing his mind once the "more pressing" texts started coming. Yes, a man is in less danger in this situation than women are, but what's appealing about someone who won't take no for an answer? Yet in 2018, during peak #MeToo, Modern Love presented this as a story about a woman who'd been wronged. So entrenched was the idea of male pursuer/female victim that a man's "misconduct" could consist of *insufficient pursuit.*

THE KEEP-IT-IN-YOUR-PANTS BRIGADE

How do you address male skeeziness? Historically, you do so by telling women to keep their legs closed, but no progressive movement was going to do this. It's well and good to celebrate women for going boysober but judgmental to cast doubt on whether women should be out at night drinking with the boys in the first place. #MeToo named a problem but had a block when it came to coming up with actionable ways of dealing with the issue. There was a reluctance, on the part of modern-day progressives, to speak in forthright ways about men and women being fundamentally different, even if this reluctance was at odds with the claim that men are trash. And a feminism rooted in fear of strange men was a poor fit for the 2020–21 racial reckoning. The line between being a woman advocating for her own safety and being a paranoid Karen grew ever fainter. The ordinary suburban white woman convinced that men are going to follow her into the parking lot outside Costco and sex-traffic her is a cliché, not an icon of feminist heroism. Once *defund the police* became the centrepiece of social justice advocacy, it became that much more difficult to articulate how even convicted male offenders should be punished. A good progressive balks at unprosecuted rapes but knows to add caveats about the uselessness and even nefariousness of calling the cops.

The tentativeness of #MeToo, the hand-wringing, the unwillingness on the feminist left to come to any kind of positive vision for what women's personal lives were to look like in this new order, left a void. Happy to fill it were the so-called "reactionary feminists."[24] A group of women authors—most notably Mary Harrington, Christine Emba, and Louise Perry—picked up on the conservative-but-not-calling-itself-that implications of a youth movement against casual sex. They argue that men and women are more different than the liberal, decadent sex-positive sorts would have you believe. They criticize the Sexual Revolution head-on, in a way that #MeToo did not. Rather than aimlessly gesturing at the badness of men, they point to a liberal society that *let* men act, unchecked, the ways they do. Perry, in particular, makes the case that the people who want to have weird sex with a million different people tend to be men, and that post–Sexual Revolution society caters to their preferences.

The sex-positive feminism the reactionary feminists argue against, the sort that treats sexual escapades as a gender-neutral social good, had already gone out of style by the time these writings appeared. In its place was this amorphous idea that the status quo was bad, but so too was all that came before. Rather than classifying relationship dynamics as ever more problematic, they label casual sex itself the culprit. Unlike #MeToo feminists, the neo-traditionalists are not afraid to victim-blame. Don't want to be creeped upon? Find yourself a husband. (This misses that there was plenty of rape and abuse in the good old days. Maybe more of it was happening within wedlock, but it was happening.) They agree with their progressive contemporaries that the modern young woman is miserable, but suggest chastity (or reticence) followed by traditional relationships with men as the solution. The problem isn't predatory men but the libertine culture that encourages these male tendencies. (In the three young men who are having IRL sex, that is.) Perry and Emba both insist that "consent is not enough,"[25] by which they mean that women sometimes leave legal encounters, ones that fall short of rape, feeling used. Change the culture—and the availability of women for casual sex—and the men will exchange their date-rape tablets for briefcases, or something.

The reactionary feminists are right to question the centrality of consent to sex discourse, but the problem with consent-focus is that it makes everything about the sex women don't want to be having, rather than about the sex they do. They miss that one reason women claim to regret casual encounters is for fear of being slut-shamed, of being thought strange or desperate. The time-worn pressures on young women not to sleep around never really went anywhere, despite the arrival of a whole new set of pressures on women to do so. When a married, middle-aged woman refers to her youthful sleeping around in regretful terms, the expression *revisionist history* rather comes to mind.

Emba recounts having had more successful relationships when she waited for a while to have sex. I do not question her lived experience, merely its wider applicability, for other women could say the opposite. It could be that women's own dispositions and libidos—and not just ability to resist patriarchy-imposed, pornography-fuelled external demand—explain differences among women. Emba writes that she's asking people to restrain themselves, which presumes some interest in jumping into bed, but there's this burning-desire element missing from the way she describes female sexuality. While she's straight, her critique of sexual mores reads like what queer theorists have to say about *the straights*, as though women have sex with men primarily because social structures demand this of us.

Reactionary feminism gives the impression of coming from people who find the whole thing distasteful. I can see how this would be affirming for some women. But is it of much use if you don't find sex with men an imposition? As my friend and *Feminine Chaos* podcast co-host Kat Rosenfield put it, when we were chatting about sex-negative sex commentators, "It's the sexual equivalent of, 'never trust a thin chef.'"[26]

THE EQUIPMENT

The most inadvertently amusing posts on the internet come from men who are convinced that no woman *actually* enjoys sex. The female orgasm is a myth, as is the woman who finds sex anything other than a chore. They are, of course, telling on themselves.

That a woman is heterosexual doesn't imply she's *satisfied* with the sex she's having with men, nor can non-enjoyment be chalked up to closeted asexuality. Plenty of women, some of the time or all of it, "prefer a bit of ironing and a round of toast."[27] I'd imagine that most people who are not nineteen have had sexual encounters that did not begin with the frantic tearing-off of each other's clothes, and that the subset of individuals for whom this doesn't resonate are almost entirely men. I also suspect that in times and places where people are/were married off to whomever, the men found it easier to close their eyes and think of England than the women did, even if these women did like men, just not necessarily the man they were with. Women face greater risks than men from sexual encounters—with strangers or with loving partners—simply because of which anatomy is more susceptible to which infections, not to mention in whose bodies unwanted pregnancies occur. Pregnancies, even healthy and wanted ones, lead to childbirth, a process with a well-known disparate impact on moms' versus dads' sexual desires and capacities.

Men are more likely to orgasm during sex, for reasons that cannot entirely be chalked up to the patriarchy. Women perform more oral sex on men than vice versa, which is more on the culture side of things, but even if that gap closed, the disparity would likely remain. The U.S. Republican Party cannot be blamed—or credited!—for the penis being like so. The straight people always down to fuck tend to be men; the ones less keen: women. That heterosexual sex tends to better suit men than women has been observed by everyone from radical feminist Andrea Dworkin to reactionary feminist Louise Perry. It's an asymmetry that's only ever at best mitigated by an individual man's skill and attentiveness. Was it as good for her as it was for him? On a case-by-case basis, it can be, but barring other information, all things equal, probably not.

It could be that young straight men these days are unusually terrible at sex, thanks to some convergence of porn setting strange expectations and Covid lockdowns plus overall online-ness and #MeToo-influenced reticence precluding real-life interactions. But if it's men you're into, any alternative to sex with men simply won't do. Maybe Barbie's happy to abstain, but this is not a viable option for most embodied women, even ones without Ryan Gosling offering himself up.

There was this epic *New York Times* article about the women who "bristle" at their husbands' physical affection, because these women understand an affectionate pat on the shoulder or whatever to be code for *I hope to be sticking my penis in you as soon as this can be arranged*, and the woman is in the middle of loading the dishwasher and that is the only load she's prepared to deal with at that juncture.[28] Epic, that is, because the article framed "bristling" in gender-neutral terms, as though it happened between "partners" and could go any which way. But the commenters knew what was up, and simply proceeded with a discussion of the women who bristle and the men who inspire that response.

I became slightly obsessed with a comment someone left on that article, and you will soon see why:

> As a former heterosexual wife and mother, who is now happily homosexual, I can attest that this dynamics [*sic*] doesn[']t exist in the latter relationship; on the contrary, my wife and I are in physical and emotional contact throughout our waking hours . . . one more reason to switch.

The commenter implies that she might have stuck with heterosexuality, but male selfishness put her off. I'm afraid I call BS, because . . . isn't it likelier that she didn't want to be with men to begin with? Her ex-husband might have been bad at sex, but he's doomed from the start if his wife is closing her eyes and pretending he's Jennifer Lawrence.

I can see how, on a technical level, a woman would be a better lover for another woman. As *Seinfeld* once broached, it helps to have familiarity with the "equipment."[29] It is, alas, irrelevant for anyone who doesn't want to be in bed with a woman to begin with. A modern twist on this came via *Savage Lovecast*, Dan Savage's sex and relationship podcast, wherein a transgender man, one whose genitals remained as nature made them, called in to complain that straight women wouldn't date him. He insisted that trans men make the best lovers and that, really, straight women should *prefer* them to cis men. They know women's anatomy! They aren't putting their penises first![30] Which is all well and good until you consider that for your average straight woman, the fact that a prospective lover is a penis-having man is a plus—a prerequisite, even. A vibrator might get the job done better than any man could, but there is an interpersonal element to sex. At least for women there is. Maybe men would be fine with sex robots—this is for them to sort out, once those become more realistic and affordable.

Let me put it like this: If forced to choose between sex with a cisgender man she found irresistible but who thought the clitoris was located on the elbow, or with a woman or otherwise-identified vagina-haver with an impeccable track record of bringing female-bodied partners to orgasm, who do we imagine a straight woman would pick? I cannot speak for straightwomankind, but my elbow would be getting a *thorough* investigation.

TWO

Soap Dispenser Husbands

A GOOD MAN

Nothing has ever made me question my heterosexuality quite like the 1975–78 British sitcom *The Good Life*. I wish I could say it was because the show stars a feline young Felicity Kendal as Barbara Good, but alas. My wiring may keep me from a deeper appreciation of beautiful women, but it allows me to be repulsed by a terrible man. There are certain men who can make me (fleetingly) wonder what any woman could possibly see in their kind, and topping the list is Barbara's husband Tom, played by the late Richard Briers. His every patronizing gesture—the dismissive way he giggles when his wife attempts to air the occasional all-too-legitimate grievance—reminds me of irritating interactions I've had with men over the years, and of the demeaning way I've witnessed men acting towards other women.

There is one episode that absolutely clinches this, but first, the show's convoluted premise: Tom and wife Barbara are a cookie-cutter suburban London couple, until Tom leaves his advertising job to become a homesteader. Rather than moving to the countryside, the couple decide (or rather, *he* decides) to live off the land they're already on. They turn their modest backyard into a subsistence farm, with goats, farming equipment, things of that nature. It's a wild scenario, in all senses, but also a deeply familiar one. It is the heterosexual male fantasy of not having to bother with *stuff*, with those form-over-function material objects the soft, pathetic womenfolk tend to purchase with your hard-earned money if the leash is too long. The fantasy, more specifically, of having a wife who looks like Felicity Kendal but who loves you *for you*, not your paycheque, to the point that when you unilaterally decide the household will go broke just so you can play farmer, she'll uncomplainingly go along for the hayride.

This brings us to a 1976 episode called "The Last Posh Frock." It opens with Barbara looking at old photos of herself, from before she and Tom went rustic. She used to look *so good*, and misses that. Shortly thereafter, wearing the clothes in which she's just repaired a car because she's now resourceful like that, Barbara gets mistaken for a "boy." She reels from the misgendering. Desperate to reassert her femininity, Barbara goes home and parades around in her last remaining party outfit, a cleavage-baring prairie dress that could easily fetch three figures on the e-commerce sites of the 2020s. She wants to catch Tom's eye, but he's busy, or making a show of indifference. She heads upstairs to change and accidentally rips her dress. She's devastated. To Tom, sworn enemy of bourgeois materialism, such concerns are "suburban rubbish," and they have (he has) rejected them. He suggests she mend the dress and turn any extra fabric into a scarf.

An old friend is in town to visit Barbara. Improbably, given Barbara's status as suburban British everywoman, this friend is a fashion model in Canada. The friend shows up for a casual dinner party at the Goods' house—a dinner Barbara is cooking—wearing a sultry evening gown, as one does. Tom not only shamelessly drools over their guest but also flirts with her by asking her questions about her designer clothing. Turns out he's a sucker for beauty and luxury along with the rest of them. Like so many men before and after, fictional and real, Tom wants a woman to look spectacular, but not be high-maintenance about it.

Anyway, the dinner party is over, and Barbara is livid. Tom says there'd be no point in her wearing gowns because she's "Barbara," as though this were a gender unto itself, and, mid-squabble, spills a glass of red wine on her top. Barbara then goes and grabs the gravy from the table and you think, *Yes, finally, she's going to pour it on Tom*, but no. She's so put-upon that she pours the gravy quasi-seductively on herself. Now not only is her fitted T-shirt drenched but also her breasts are gleaming, the camera lingering. The audience laughter suggests it's all meant to be light and charming. *Bawdy.* By the end of the episode, everything is patched up, and all is forgiven.

As bad men go, Tom Good hardly registers. He's not a rapist or (physical) abuser. Sure, he's a bit rough with Barbara when ordering her to sit, like she were a dog. He's gross, but he's no Josef Fritzl, the Austrian man who imprisoned his daughter and forced her to bear seven of his children. He's no Dominique Pelicot, the French man who subjected his wife Gisèle to years of torment, drugging her and inviting men to come by and assault her. And yet, "The Last Posh Frock" is where my rerun-addled mind goes when I think of the expression *toxic masculinity*. Barbara asks Tom if he loves her and he responds, "Well of course I do, you silly bitch." I'm not a Ban Men feminist, but five minutes in Tom Good's presence and I'm asking why even are men.

THROW OUT THE WHOLE ENTIRE HUSBAND

Ban Men feminism has something for women of all life stages. The message that *to be a woman* means men chase you down the street tends to resonate less the further north you get of, say, twenty-five. By thirty or forty, womanhood's travails lean more towards housework and family responsibilities—or towards the dearth of men to even attempt to form a miserable family with in the first place. In Ban Men feminism for the not-so-nubile set, the nuclear family unit becomes a microcosm of societal sexism. One's own husband, however lovely, becomes a stand-in for the patriarchy. While less titillating a set of concerns than that of the woman who is *so* young and pretty that her boss simply cannot help himself, the audience for "my husband didn't pick up his socks and now he is my EX-HUSBAND" is not niche, to put it mildly.

For younger women, the latest moment of awakening—of sudden comprehension that feminism hadn't won the day—was #MeToo. For older ones, it would have been the Covid pandemic. (I don't necessarily mean *much* older, or even necessarily a different cohort; some of the same women sharing dating woes in 2017 had husbands and kids and that much more laundry by 2021.) Life under lockdowns made clear to many ostensibly empowered careerwomen that if kids needed 24/7 attention and emergency homeschooling, this fell to mom. Hanna Rosin's 2010 *Atlantic* cover story "The End of Men," turned 2012 book, had argued—long before this became a standard talking point—that women had started outpacing men in the professional and academic spheres. Rosin revisited that thesis in February 2020, in light of what lockdown times had revealed: "The recent employment wipeout dates to September 2020, when 865,000 women dropped out of the labor force, compared with 216,000 men. What complex confluence of demographic shifts converged at that critical time? School started."[1] Women who'd had it with keeping it together on the home front had, by 2022 or thereabouts, *really* had it. They could find affirmation in books like Jessica Grose's *Screaming on the Inside: The Unsustainability of American Motherhood*, or Sara Petersen's *Momfluenced*, about the unrealistic portrait of domestic bliss apparently found in corners of Instagram, or in countless online forums or masked conversations at six feet apart.

Unsurprisingly, a couple years stuck in the house with one's loved ones led to a proliferation of women-going-their-own-way content and its tentative cousin, I've-had-it-with-my-wonderful-husband content. It's not that the divorce rate itself has skyrocketed. But there's a sense in which the general public—educated classes especially—was cooped up, fed up, and wanted to contemplate other options.

No, not everyone worked from home during Covid—it only felt that way because white-collar types dominated cultural conversations. Mom staying home while a breadwinner husband goes to work is also more unusual than it once was, as well as increasingly associated with the upper classes. Such women do nevertheless have an outsize role in shaping the culture. The nexus of overeducated and underemployed is fertile ground for the writing of memoirs and personal essays, not to mention Facebook posts from the less literary-minded. Thus the spate of writing from women who know exactly *how it goes for women*, and what they're describing is how it goes for writers whose husbands are also writers, or have nice jobs that kinda-sorta support their freelancing as long as the freelancing doesn't cut into domestic responsibilities.

To call these women *elite* isn't wrong but only gets you so far. It's more specific. They're not high-powered businesswomen *or* working-class ones just scraping by. They're women whose intellectual or artistic goals exceed their earning potential. Who fall into writing because it's a kind of work that can fit around family responsibilities, only to get a bit *too* into the work itself and realize that domesticity puts a cap on where that can lead. These are not the women in the corridors of power, but they are the ones driving discourse about the state of modern marriage. And their consensus is that marriage—heterosexual marriage—brings women down.

A not-unreasonable question to ask about all these bad-marriage memoirs is how it came to pass that these women—modern, educated women, women with options—found themselves stuck with husbands in the first place.

FISH WITHOUT BICYCLES

Writer and tech worker Sophie Vershbow cannot be credited with inventing the humblebrag, but she has provided one of the finest examples I've seen in a social media post about her romantic life: "I haven't decided how to write about this yet but 1 year into making 6-figures and I am consistently smacked in the face by how much earning a decent salary has affected my relationship to men and dating as a cis heterosexual woman." She finished the thought with a nod to relatability. "I cannot be alone in this."[2] Vershbow presented "earning a decent salary" as an unfortunate thing that had happened to her, a violence even ("smacked in the face"), versus the enviable situation it was. Downthread, she explained that she was still hoping to find a male partner, but due to her own financial successes did not require this to lead a comfortable life.

Vershbow's trajectory, as she describes it, is in some sense a proxy for female heterosexuality of the past half-century. It's still around but no longer the only game in town. Women used to need men in ways that, objectively speaking, we no longer do. Women earn more than we used to, get more degrees, and have more professional opportunities. On the whole, if you are not in Iran, and you're a woman, you can kind of just go about your life in a way that wasn't possible a couple generations ago. Compulsory heterosexuality—the requirement of women to get husbands, not (just) to be into men—isn't what it used to be.

And yet there are all these women around, with husbands and boyfriends and such. Why? Historically, at least since society embraced the idea of marrying for love, a woman's social and material need for a husband has been mixed up with her intimate need for a man.[3] Erica Jong has a lot about this in her 1973 classic feminist novel *Fear of Flying*, the way women's lust intermingles with being socialized into husband-seeking. The "zipless fuck"—an anonymous-sex fantasy the protagonist has—is a vision of lust without that baggage. But in the world of actual people, at least actual straight people, decoupling pleasure from responsibility in this way remains elusive.

Much like dieting in recent years (before Ozempic) being referred to euphemistically as *wellness* when women had salads for dinner, man-needing has not disappeared so much as gone underground. It's become gauche to request a *skim* cappuccino in the hopes of going down a dress size. So, too, to be open about wanting a boyfriend or husband.

The receding of compulsory heterosexuality has some positive implications even for straight women. Indeed, its measurable impact is almost certainly greatest on members of the sexual majority. In these enlightened, post–*Sex and the City* times, it's no longer *done* to treat single women as tragic spinsters. The social norm, outside more traditionalist environments, is to assume they're leading the lives they want. Yes, individual women's relatives still nag them to get married, and yes, there are far-right trolls online holding forth about cat ladies, but the tide has shifted towards it not being a big deal if a woman doesn't have a man.

In the days of *you need a husband, lady!*, women were forced to pretend to be sad about not having something they didn't necessarily want in the first place. *The Mary Tyler Moore Show* (1970–77) is remembered—not wrongly—for showcasing the new, pill-liberated single career gal. It still had Rhoda and Mary balancing their happily single reality with these periodic nods to how they were, on some level, waiting for the right man. There's Roz, on *Frasier* (1993–2004), presenting herself as on a quest for a husband, while acting in ways that make clear she has other goals in mind, namely sleeping with Seattle. The 2004–05 British crime drama *Murder in Suburbia* largely consists of two female cops—so refreshing, when the cops on these shows are almost always men!—driving around discussing their need for boyfriends and the eligibility of whichever men cross their path.

You might imagine that *The Golden Girls*, that 1980s-into-1990s icon of women embracing the chosen family, would pass the Bechdel test and be full of women talking about things other than men. Not even a little bit. In a 1991 episode, "Never Yell Fire in a Crowded Retirement Home: Part 2," Blanche has been holding forth about muscular men, as usual, prompting Dorothy to say, "I just cannot *believe* how much you think about *men*." Blanche goes on the defensive. "Men are an important part of my life. Not just *my* life, they're an important part of all our lives." The scene fades out to a flashback of the eighty-something Sophia recalling having put cash in the G-string of a stripper calling himself (in a little prelude to SATC) "Mr. Big." Blanche of course *knows* the gentleman in question and quips that this is merely a "stage name." But it could have just as easily segued to any number of discussions of boyfriends or marriage proposals. The lewd hilarity intermingles with the ever-looming possibility that one of the "girls" will remarry, thereby dismantling their household. Putting female friendship before the prospect of the right male partner is never on the table.

These days, women no longer need to ritualistically claim to be looking for male partners when this isn't what they want. There is the inconvenient fact, however, that most women do in fact want this, even now. Most *people* want sex and companionship. Most adults realize (or should realize) that commitment requires compromise, and deem some of those worth sucking up in exchange for the joys of life with another person. But in an overcorrection for the need-a-husband era, we've reached a point where the only allowable stories of female heterosexuality are ones where the woman is miserable. Where it seems as if a woman is there under duress, or at least, where she has gotten the worse deal.

MEN ARE A CHORE

There's an *I Love Lucy* episode that you might know of even if you're not up on 1950s sitcoms. Lucy and Ethel are working in a chocolate factory, on the assembly line. It keeps moving faster and Lucy, in a struggle to keep up, stuffs her mouth and outfit with absurd amounts of chocolates. The backstory is that husbands Ricky and Fred decide housewives have it easy, spending their husbands' money and offering nothing in return. The women insist it's the other way around, that men are the lazy ones, spared the indignities of housework. They decide to swap roles, not in a gender-subversive 2020s sense, but in the 1950s version, wherein a man preparing rice qualifies as a comedic premise.

"Job Switching" aired in 1952, three years after Simone de Beauvoir's *The Second Sex* was published in French, but a year before its first English translation. Betty Friedan's *The Feminine Mystique*, the canonical feminist critique of housewifery, was just over a decade later. If you imagine that the 1950s was this idyllic time when everyone just accepted traditional gender roles, you don't have to dig to find evidence that some found the role of housewife stifling.

But laundry didn't stop needing folding when Women's Lib came along. Today's straight women are held to the same household-maintenance standards of their 1950s predecessors while expected to contribute at least half the household income. And, oh, also to helicopter-parent their kids, who cannot, as was the case in the 1950s, simply entertain themselves by smoking cigarettes while bicycling (helmetless!) around the neighbourhood. The modern woman enters what she thinks will be an equitable marriage, only to step back from her career because of kids or some other reason, only to wake up and find that she is, despite the best of intentions, a drudge. Lucy Ricardo may have dreamed of being a star, but she didn't ever really *expect* a future other than housewife, so the letdown wouldn't have been as great as it was for the poet Maggie Smith. In her 2023 bestselling divorce memoir, *You Could Make This Place Beautiful*, Smith—not the same Maggie Smith who played the Dowager Countess on *Downton Abbey*—laments how far things have *not* come:

> My life looked surprisingly like my mother's. My mother didn't go to college, married at twenty, and had me at twenty-four. I went to college and graduate school, published my first book and got married at twenty-eight (at which age she already had three children), and had my children in my thirties. Still, *still*, my life looked a lot like hers.[4]

The half-success of feminism thus brought with it its own set of challenges. There's a better life, or a life we're told would be better, but we have no idea because it's always a bit out of reach. Married men are said to be happier than married women. This despite the popular assumption that women are champing at the bit to get married. But it would add up. A married man has someone looking after him and vouching for his not being a complete weirdo. A married woman is just a woman with responsibilities that might interfere with her ability to log eighty-hour workweeks. Thus the counterintuitive—or not—finding that married mothers do more housework than single moms. It seems to suggest that husbands, not children, are the real energy-sappers. It evokes the image of a man, ensconced in his armchair, letting his surface-wiping wife know that she's missed a spot. So, too, the supposedly unexpected fact that women tend to be the initiators of divorce.

Marriage rates are dipping, partly because there are now other options. It may also have something to do with the "sex recession" already underway prior to the Covid pandemic, the one that had its own *Atlantic* magazine cover story in 2018. But there is an additional factor: that men these days are, reputedly, the worst.

In a 2023 *New York Times* op-ed, "Why Aren't More People Marrying? Ask Women What Dating Is Like," Anna Louie Sussman argues that anyone "harping on people to marry from high up in the ivory tower fails to engage with the reality on the ground that heterosexual women from many walks of life confront: the state of men today." The absolute *state* of them, ladies. Men's failings, per Sussman, are a mix of measurable items (substance abuse) and more subjective ones, like being less in touch with their feelings than (some) women would like them to be. She mentions a college friend of hers, a woman who "would like nothing more than to be married," who's "beautiful and successful and not, as far as I can tell, overly picky." Sussman goes on to describe, as though this were evidence that *women* were the normal ones, that this friend "keeps a Post-it note on a bulletin board," tallying how many men she's gone out with until she reaches a hundred, in the hopes of finding a husband and father for her future children. She then, per Sussman, went out with "nearly" fifty men over the course of two years, yet "she's still single." Forgive my cynicism, but someone attempting to quantify romance in the manner of the *It's Always Sunny in Philadelphia*–derived conspiracy-theorist meme, where a man is *drawing connections* between pieces of paper affixed to a wall-mounted board, may be less of a catch than her friend imagines.

The bad-men genre is a standard-issue part of content aimed at women of all ages, in lifestyle content and on social media. A sector that once sold "how to get a man" has pivoted to articles about why men hold women back from leading our best lives. "Why Are Men So Terrible This Summer?" asks a July 2023 *Glamour* headline, in a somewhat forced-seeming journalistic nod to seasonality. The piece itself consists of assembled recaps of celebrity men slut-shaming or cheating on their girlfriends, from a stance less prurient than indignant, decrying "the misogyny and disrespect that still is threaded through many heterosexual relationships."

In October 2022, Emily Gould, a personal essayist associated with what was once called "overshare" and a fixture in the New York media scene, sent out a newsletter post crowdfunding for a divorce from fellow writer Keith Gessen. The post—since taken offline but immortalized in media coverage[5]—read as much like the cry for help of a woman in crisis as like the latest entry in a burgeoning subgenre. Gould hadn't just had it with *her* marriage. She had had it with *marriage* and, perhaps, with men. She would "be taking an infinite hiatus from hetero marriage and monogamy." These she described as "a trap for women, full stop. Sometimes a trap can be cozy. Mine was, until it wasn't." The effect of this document was to suggest that a donation to the Emily Gould divorce fund was effectively feminist philanthropy. This was the cause of the moment, and this one seemingly doomed marriage was but a microcosm. The very same month, *The New York Times* ran an op-ed by Amy Shearn, a feminist case for divorce, with the opening line: "Married heterosexual motherhood in America, especially in the past two years, is a game no one wins."[6]

SOAP DISPENSER DAD, MEET PEACH MOM

On March 22, 2019, Robin Beth Schaer, whose account no longer exists, posted the following anecdote to Twitter, now X: "My friend & her husband lived in an apartment that had a soap dispenser installed on the edge of the kitchen sink. When they moved out after two years, he marveled to her: 'it's amazing how that dispenser never ran out of soap in all this time.' Women's work is truly invisible."[7]

A tiny interaction between two people, out of context, was meant to exemplify how it goes in hetero households. The mood of the moment was to nod along to something like this, in solidarity. But I had some questions. If she hated dealing with soap refills (I'm no fan either!), why didn't she ever say to her husband, *Hey, the soap needs refilling*? Did Soap Dispenser Husband pull his weight generally, and if not, why did Soap Dispenser Wife put up with it? What was in it for her? Was he massively rich (in which case, let the butler refill the soap) or, perhaps, extremely hot? Or was something systemic afoot, such that women really were left doing the household scut work, even though on paper society was past all that?

Schaer pointed readers to Gemma Hartley's massively popular 2017 *Harper's Bazaar* article, "Women Aren't Nags—We're Just Fed Up: Emotional Labor Is the Unpaid Job Men Still Don't Understand." "Emotional labour" was a term initially meant to describe things like service workers having to smile for tips. Was this really the right term to use for when you ask your husband to sort out hiring a maid? (This is the plight Hartley opens her article with.) It hardly matters.

Man-children not picking up after themselves would be a recurring theme in writing about marriage and divorce in the coming years. Writes Lyz Lenz, in 2024's bestselling *This American Ex-Wife*, "I had spent the eleven years of our marriage trying to get him to see that the dishwasher drain didn't clean itself and the socks didn't crawl out of the laundry and find their own mates and put themselves in his drawer. I wanted him to notice. I wanted him to see these small labors."[8]

The events Lenz describes occurred in 2017, but the pandemic brought a greater sense of urgency to these dilemmas. It is here that I must, at last, bring in Peach Mom.

Mary Catherine Starr is a comic artist and illustrator. Her subject matter is, like that of one or two artists before her, her own life. She's the creator of Momlife Comics (@momlife_comics), an Instagram account launched in 2021 and aimed at the Democrat-voting suburban wine mom audience. I don't say "wine mom" as a slur, but to indicate the presence of wine itself in the comics, as well as the overall *live laugh love* aesthetic. It is earnest and milquetoast progressive but tremendously—there is no other word for this, I mean it as a descriptor and not an insult—basic. The cartoons lack facial features—an artistic choice that suggests you are to fill in the blanks with yourself and your family. And the running theme is maternal martyrdom. Things like, Dad has his morning coffee "piping hot" while looking at his phone, but Mom has hers "cold/microwaved" hours later "while wrangling children." The comics don't explore how this came to be for this made-up if semi-autobiographical couple; they just document that it has.

And it was a comic about a disparity in peach consumption that went viral, thus the origin of Starr's designation, among the online hordes who found her via this post, as Peach Mom: "One of the [many] differences between me & my husband," depicting side-by-side images of Mom and Dad, confronted with "the last ripe peach." Mom plans to save it for her children, while Dad will "use it as a special treat in my daily smoothie." He's not even just keeping it for himself, he is pulverizing it out of recognition. Men!

As passé as these complaints may seem, a lot of women . . . do experience them. That you'd think it shouldn't still feel like the 1950s doesn't mean it has ceased feeling that way, even—maybe especially—in the milieus one would expect to be beyond all that. We live in a society where, in theory, no one is forcing a woman to saddle herself to a selfish man-child. But people—not just women—make compromises in exchange for such things as sex, stability, and companionship.

The dissatisfaction is real, if arguably encouraged. The question, then, is what can be done about it. A 2023 *Guardian* advice column ran a letter from a forty-seven-year-old woman whose "initial premarriage ideals of a kind of Scandinavian shared approach to parenting and marriage" gave way, two kids in, to an "expectation . . . that I do everything."[9] The letter-writer has had it with her husband, and with men generally: "I am not interested in being with another man, but sometimes I find myself wondering if I would have a more equal relationship with a woman."

Given that the aspect of a same-sex relationship that appeals seems restricted to the realm of household management, the letter gives little indication of a desire—or even a willingness—to get into another woman's pants. But I well believe she's gone off men. Philippa Perry, *Guardian* advice columnist, suggests this woman's anger at her husband might be perimenopause-related and urges her to seek hormone replacement therapy. Whatever your hormonal state, I could well imagine being repulsed by a man who sat around while you were doing all the housework and childcare. Put off, but also just too tired to even want sex in the first place, with that man or any man, barring a broad-shouldered one who came swooping into the house gamely wielding a Swiffer.

A humour book published in 2007, *Porn for Women*, was just photographs of fully clothed men doing housework. I remember the backlash this got because of what it suggested about female sexuality. Is a woman's biggest turn-on really watching a man in jeans and a button-down do the vacuuming? (This was the book's cover image.) To suggest this, even in jest, offended the sex-positive norms of the time. The premise treated female sexuality as so tame as to effectively not exist. It also seemed to gesture at endorsing the awful view that a man being nice to a woman makes her want to have sex with him. It's not that women crave humiliation (unless they do), but that this alas only works if it's a man she already wanted sex with. Some men fail to make this distinction, thus leading to the phenomenon of the Nice Guy, the man who insists that he's "a good guy" and therefore owed sex. Can I endorse the *Porn for Women* concept as part of my vision for a better version of female heterosexuality? I cannot.

But the point behind *Porn for Women* was—much as it pains me to say it—reasonable. Watching a man fold laundry may not get a woman in the mood, but I suspect that many a woman has been put off sex from knowing that after the act, she's got to return to pairing the household's socks, while he does the man thing of going to sleep. Her lack of enthusiasm gets chalked up to women being less animalistically down to fuck, as though this were purely about men-are-like-so and not even the teensiest bit about entrenched chore-division norms.

Many of the comments to that *New York Times* article about the women who bristle when their husbands touch them, lest the gentle shoulder pat be a request for more, were about variations of that scenario:[10] One recalls a now ex-boyfriend who would grab at her while she was "washing dishes." Another: "I in general love my husband's touches, but boy howdy, do I ever dislike when he comes up behind me while I am cooking or doing food prep and tries to hug me or rub my shoulders. I'm BUSY. This is not a romantic comedy. GTF outta my way!" A pattern emerges, and it has nothing to do with finding it erotic to watch a man wield a dustbuster. To want sex, you need to be awake, which someone doing "everything" is not.

THE GENIUS VERSUS THE LAUNDRY PILE

Culture writer Anne Helen Petersen's Substack essay "Why Are (White) Men So Unambitious?" concludes that the reason is that white men are actually society's real victims, kept down by wokeness and DEI. Just kidding! No, what Petersen argues is that women—particularly women of colour—know that life will be difficult and work extra hard to compensate. "Women begin to internalize the necessity of this infrastructure at a young age. They see it in the media they consume, which is filled with Organizational Queens: Elle Woods, Olivia Pope, Jennifer Lopez in *The Wedding Planner* . . ."[11] The list goes on, eventually climaxing with Taylor Swift and Beyoncé, two women I know I personally find extremely relatable.

I read this and could only think about how one of the onscreen characters I most identify with is Onslow, the layabout brother-in-law on 1990s Britcom *Keeping Up Appearances*. He just wants to sit and watch television, a dog in his lap, eating potato chips.

If men lack ambition, it's because, writes Petersen, they—particularly the white ones, she is careful to note—grow up believing "success is yours to lose." The essay reads as if Petersen took the *Crazy Ex-Girlfriend* song "Let's Generalize About Men" as an instruction manual rather than as the satire it is. But it's the image she presents of *women* I can't get past. It's not just that we're masochistic martyrs but that we are *impressive*. Are we? Aren't most people, of any gender, just sort of getting through the day?

The problem with women being overburdened with housework isn't just that this is uncompensated labour, as well as a buzzkill on the sex front. It's also that for some, time spent scrubbing the bathtub could be going towards producing artistic masterpieces. Think of all the additional women's art we'd have if the laundry let up! Think of the wives and mothers who do the scut work that makes men's adulation-eliciting work possible. Worse yet, there are the women multi-tasking, feeding their husbands and feeding those husbands' brilliant ideas for which they will receive no glory.

For reasons doubtless connected to the nature of who writes things for publication, it's the writing world where one hears about this the most. The woman *thanked for her typing* in a book's acknowledgements probably wrote the thing herself. There's even a 2021 anthology, *Thanks for Typing: Remembering Forgotten Women in History.* The typist-as-author is (apologies for the spoiler) the plot of Meg Wolitzer's 2003 novel (turned 2017 Glenn Close film) *The Wife*, wherein the great genius novelist husband's books were really written by someone else, namely the titular character.

The woman whose typing is authorship appears, no *big reveal* necessary, on Britcom *As Time Goes By* (1992–2005). Lionel Hardcastle, who plays Dame Judi Dench's character's long-lost lover and eventual husband, is a writer, which comes across as more of an affectation than a career. Lionel, played by the late Geoffrey Palmer, reserves hotel rooms in his own city in which to Do His Writing (a memoir and, later, a miniseries) and hires pretty young secretaries to type for him. Dench's character runs a secretarial agency called "Type for You," which is how, in the pilot episode, these one-time sweethearts reconnect decades later. But the secretary scenes, abundant throughout the series, don't involve any dictation. Instead, he asks the women how to put his life story into words. The phrasing itself is theirs. The secretaries are uncredited, poorly compensated ghostwriters. Much as I revile the man—he's up there with Tom Good, without those Ricky Ricardo redeeming physical attributes—my aim here is not to cancel Lionel Hardcastle, a fictional character on a long-cancelled sitcom. Rather, I'm attempting to illustrate the phenomenon of women doing the work and men getting the credit—and even more so, the way that this used to play out *and not even be commented on*. One can squirm at the earnest feminism of pointing out women's invisible labour, but before whichever awareness-raisings about the phenomenon, the Lionels of the world got away with so much.

Men, it is said, fear successful women.They even, I have heard, consider it an achievement to bag a powerful career woman then make her stay home. Some sort of macho flex about earning *so* much that the woman doesn't have to work but also chucking her leverage in the marriage. Men don't want a gold digger, but a woman who brings too much gold to the table (I am picturing a literal pot of gold, like with a leprechaun) is a threat. Too much gold, or, worse, too much ambition without the gold to show for it.

"PEOPLE WHO HAVE EXPERIENCED SIMILAR DYNAMICS"

An excerpt of poet Maggie Smith's divorce memoir appeared on The Cut in March 2023[12] and made a splash not unlike "Cat Person," if for an older demographic. Both tell versions of the same story: that of a woman who is too good for a man, perhaps for men generally. One whose involvement with men consists centrally of being wronged. The gist of *You Could Make This Place Beautiful*, one of two bestsellers Smith has written about her upper-middle-class Midwestern divorce, is that she had a poem, "Good Bones," go viral in 2016. This turned her into a literary celebrity, which turned off her lawyer husband, who laughed at her poet-ing and absconded with an Other Woman.

A writer named Isabel Kaplan responded to Smith's excerpt making the rounds by posting, "Plz send heartwarming stories of straight male partners supporting your creative endeavors. Hungry for a story that isn't 'I achieved unprecedented professional success and my relationship was never the same.'"[13] One gets the sense that this is less prompt tweet than rhetorical question. Kaplan was no disinterested observer to all this. In December 2022, she had broken *that* moment's lady-internet with a *Guardian* personal essay, "My Boyfriend, a Writer, Broke Up with Me Because I'm a Writer."[14] The story told therein is a bit more complicated than that, suggestive less of patriarchy triumphing than of two people, by happenstance a man and a woman, being less than entirely compatible. ("He first broke up with me a few years ago because I wasn't successful and independent *enough*.")

But Kaplan isn't telling just *her* breakup story. This is a how-it-goes-for-women manifesto. Kaplan's goal is for her essay to "resonate with people who have experienced similar dynamics." And she interprets her own experiences with this ex-boyfriend as part of a bigger picture: "The ability to bend an inch at a time while seeming to stand up straight is a useful and gendered skill. Most women I know do it regularly. They bend until they're pretzeled and then blame themselves for the body aches." Do you know who could totally relate to this, I would assume? Maggie Smith, who, elsewhere in her memoir, writes, "When I got good news related to my writing—a publication, a grant, an invitation—I sensed him wince inwardly. So I stopped sharing good news. I made myself small, folded myself up origami tight."[15]

The notion that women everywhere are experiencing the same thing, even if we don't know it yet, is hardly new. During the consciousness-raising sessions associated with second-wave feminism, women would gather—in person and everything, no Reddit in the 1970s—and compare notes. The idea was that individual women were all getting screwed over in similar terms, in households everywhere, and would be able to resist (or at least, vent) if they realized how extremely *not alone* they were. And they had plenty to discuss. American women couldn't get their own credit cards until 1974. It was only in the 1980s and 1990s, respectively, that spousal rape became a crime in Canada and the United States. Sharing overlapping accounts allowed women to see the extent to which they were treated like men's property. Is the plight of a woman writer whose male partner fails to recognize her genius something that should fall into this category? Anne Helen Petersen laments that "a PhD doesn't prevent a date from lecturing on your area of expertise,"[16] so I guess we can call it a *maybe*.

Smith's story is unquestionably about *the straight female experience*, so it's striking that the desiring of men scarcely enters into it. Her ex-husband's shortcomings are clear, but what drew her to him initially? It's understandable she doesn't dwell on this, given that he's now her bad-guy ex, but it's clear from the story that she was not married off to him against her will in a fundamentalist sect. How much can be pinned on compulsory heterosexuality here? She alludes to the existence of a new partner, gender unstated, but is also very clear that her sex life is not up for discussion, stating only that it's been better "in middle age" for her than earlier—a dig at the ex, but a discreet one. The heartbreak she describes is about the loss of the domestic life as she knew it. She lost her children's father, a man she'd lived with for years, and effectively grown up with, given that they were young when they got together.

The spare, polished writing style allows the reader to reach the end of the book and only then think, *Wait a second . . . Did this marriage fall apart because the couple had stopped having sex? And if so, when and at whose instigation?* Yes, some marriages are companionate, but if it's meant to be a mystery why her husband took up with another woman—a mystery about which readers of *a divorce memoir* are invited to speculate—this would seem a pertinent bit of information.[17] If this doesn't come up, I almost think it's less a matter of propriety than of narrative discipline. Of sticking to the script. And the point—the reason you are meant to care, if you are not a member of this woman's inner circle—is that Smith, like so many women, has experience with those *dynamics*. This idea of women's greatness getting stifled by the men in their lives, that we could shine if only the men in our lives didn't keep us down, has an audience. An audience that evidently extends beyond women with MFAS, and who cannot personally relate to Meryl Streep reading one of their poems out loud.

Smith's marriage fell apart because he had an affair, but also because he didn't respect her poetry career. "My husband's lawyer used air quotes when she talked about my work. When you were 'working,' she said." Smith follows this up with a quote from Rebecca Solnit, the writer who popularized the concept of mansplaining, about how writing counts as real work. I want to shout *hear, hear!*, biased as I am towards the position of people who are both women and writers. I am also too aware of what writing pays—and of the amount of it that's done unpaid, especially in poetry—to attribute the scare quotes to sexism. No one is accusing female accountants of "working."

Smith goes on to point out the financial underpinnings of this, that her husband had been "the primary breadwinner." But she asks, "When one person out-earns another in a marriage, is an imbalance of power inevitable? Is the spouse who earns less expected to take on more of the domestic labor?" Smith's implication seems to be that a poet and a lawyer should go fifty-fifty on laundry folding, because feminism. It seems to be coming from the same place, politically, as the supposedly widespread cultural longing for the mommune. (Yes, some women, even straight ones, live happily in these, but nine times out of ten, women who say they wish they did are just expressing the longing for a maid.) But what if the lawyer were the woman? This has been known to happen. Should a male poet feel entitled to his wife's support?

Smith's lament seems less that her ex was insufficiently equitable and more that she didn't get leeway to be an art monster. I say this not in a judgmental way, but because feminism sometimes gets stuck on the idea that 50 per cent is the most any woman could ask. History is littered with examples of women toiling away for boyfriends whose bands are gonna make it big any day now. Also with male poets who forced their wives to work boring jobs that would financially support their lives as underfunded artists. But in these narratives, wanting a husband who pulls his weight gets intertangled with the desire for a husband who will drop everything in service of your Art. Lyz Lenz writes, of her husband suggesting they have a third kid when she was trying to write books, "I could be successful, or I could be married."[18]

A greedier and frankly more compelling take comes from Judy Brady Syfers's 1971 essay "I Want a Wife,"[19] from the launch of Gloria Steinem's *Ms.* magazine. It sounds, from its title, like a lesbian personals ad. What it is, in fact, is a straight woman's lament. It begins with Syfers hearing a divorced male friend say he's on the market again, which gets her contemplating gender roles in marriage: "As I thought about him while I was ironing one evening, it suddenly occurred to me that I, too, would like to have a wife."

The rest is an enumeration of wifely duties she'd rather someone else handle. "I want a wife who will take care of *my* physical needs. I want a wife who will keep my house clean. A wife who will pick up after me." The wife will also deal with childcare and socializing, and will cheerily accept a one-sided non-monogamous *understanding*. One line makes it clear that "I Want a Wife" is not a break from heterosexuality: "I want a wife who assumes the complete responsibility for birth control, because I do not want more children." This is a request to be in the male role in a heterosexual relationship. The one whose ambitions count. The key item for our purposes: "I want a wife who will type my papers for me when I have written them." If Syfers had dreamed bigger, she could have taken this further and gone full Lionel Hardcastle. Many women would gladly be the husbands—breadwinners, art monsters, or dirtbags—if they could. Would ditch the fifty-fifty chore chart in favour of letting someone else deal with all of that so that they can flit between painting and cavorting. None of this has anything to do with being an "Organizational Queen."

WHY EVEN ARE WOMEN?

I have a shameful confession to make: *You Could Make This Place Beautiful* left me less interested in reading Smith's full oeuvre than in hearing her ex-husband's side of the story. Not so as to *take* his side, but out of curiosity about what that side would even be. Is he the villain she presents (while noting she surely made errors in the marriage as well), or is there more to it? How does *he* understand what happened in the marriage?

I started forming theories: Was his dream to be married to a doormat, only to find himself married to a poet-genius? This is roughly Smith's interpretation of events. Or was he a frustrated artist himself, and was that the problem? Did he resent having to work at a law firm to pay the bills? He, like his wife, had studied creative writing, so this is not so far-fetched. Did he, an aspiring playwright, go to law school rather than don a beret and park himself in the local coffee house because of ambient societal pressures on men to be breadwinners, or was something more concrete at play? Does he have, in his drafts folder, an unfinished autobiographical novel whose working title is "Provider's Lament"?

I come to this topic as a male-beauty-appreciation advocate, not a men's rights activist. I am however a reasonably curious person, prone to wondering, when I read an advice column, how the person being complained about views the situation. Those who only know about Soap Dispenser Husband via a popular tweet about his non-refilling of a soap dispenser will never know if he was silently doing chores of his own, and *I demand answers*. At stake here is not just that men are people, too, though Ban Men feminism is admittedly iffy on that point. It's also that many of the complaints about men being the worst can be interpreted as men having been screwed over. Is it that husbands aren't doing the emotional labour of setting up playdates, or that they lack the needed organizational skills? The lack of eligible straight men can be seen either as a problem for marriage-oriented women, or as a sign that men aren't doing so well. Indeed, a meme—"women hardest hit"—emerged from headline after headline that stuffed men's suffering—be it from friendlessness, Covid, or low college enrolment—into a simplistic, women-always-have-it-worse framework.

Men's rights activists, but also intellectuals on the think-of-the-men beat—the latter exemplified by *Of Boys and Men: Why the Modern Male Is Struggling, Why It Matters, and What to Do About It* (2022) author Richard V. Reeves—interpret male suffering as a crisis, not a punchline. They have their own set of somewhat-converging talking points: statistics about overdoses and suicide rates, or (this is the MRA side) anecdotes about ex-husbands screwed over by ex-wives. Per Team Men's less-savoury sorts, marriage itself is a bait-and-switch, with women at first seeming to be carefree twenty-five-year-olds, only later revealing themselves to be scowling fifty-five-year-olds who—it has to be said—have also put on a few pounds. Girlfriends and fiancées claim to be game for anything sexually, but wives are sexually unavailable for months or in some cases years after having a baby. What's *that* about?

Advocates for the menfolk, serious and trollish alike, agree with the Anne Helen Petersens of the world that men are doing worse than women, but the interpretation isn't male entitlement. It's not, to them, about being born on the tenth floor and thinking you hit a home run or whatever. College, per Team Men, has become too feminized, unlike back in the day, when it was mainly about reading *The Odyssey* and jousting. Feminism, they argue, left men aimless, with no positive visions for masculinity. If a woman can do anything a man can, what are the male virtues men should be cultivating? #MeToo, in this lens, created a hostile, confusing climate where men are afraid to make a move, lest they be accused of creepiness. This reminds me, though, of an additional reason it's rarely a father doing the emotional labour of texting another kid's mother to set up a playdate for their kids.

Team Men makes some decent points. There are demographics of men who have it worse than the average woman, and specific forms of suffering that disproportionately impact men. The mere fact that someone's a dude doesn't mean a Fortune 500 CEO-ship awaits him. The man shooting up in a Toronto Public Library stroller-parking section (I, Karen, alerted library staff) has less privilege than Hillary Clinton, no matter how screwed over she was by the 2016 presidential election, or by her own husband.

But I dunno, man. Sexual violence, abortion rights (or the lack thereof) in the U.S., and—yes—chore disparities come to mind among the reasons why, yeah, maybe men do not get to be anointed winners of the Oppression Olympics at this juncture. But *my* aim here isn't to turn straight women into men's rights activists. There is substantial middle ground between thinking men are the real victims in an ascendant matriarchy and wanting them banished.

IF YOU CAN'T SAY ANYTHING NICE

What, then, is the alternative to Ban Men content? Please say it isn't trite appreciations of masculine virtues. As grateful as I am that my husband has the upper-body strength to dislodge the stand mixer bowl from the base that Kitchen-Aid for some reason thinks it needs to be welded to, it's not a compelling anchor anecdote for a personal essay. Nor am I particularly charmed by the periodic admission from straight women that they *like dick*, always voiced as if an edgy trait, versus one that puts them in line with half of humanity. There's not much to say about a marriage that's going well. You can, I suppose, show up in online forums to be the person commenting that you've been married fifty years and still have sex daily. But for the most part, Tolstoy's "happy families are alike" observation holds. No one reads an "I love my husband" story unless it comes with a big, juicy *but*.

Individual cases have a way of falling outside the templates they're squeezed into. It's like what the novelist Taffy Brodesser-Akner wrote, in an essay revisiting *The Rules*: "The problem with dating has always been the power dynamic; that has nothing to do with gender. One person always loves the other more. It's never equal."[20] It's appealing to think you've been jilted because the system is rigged against your kind when the reality is more personal and therefore more painful. Relationships cannot be reduced to a battle of the sexes, or even a more calibrated network of relative systemic advantages. There's a point at which consciousness-raising crosses over into a flattening of human experience.

It is here that I must pick up where I left off in the Emily Gould story. Remember her crowdfunded divorce, the start of her "infinite hiatus from hetero marriage and monogamy"? The hiatus proved finite. In a 2024 essay for The Cut, provocatively titled "The Lure of Divorce" and published on Valentine's Day, Gould tells the story of that time when she contemplated divorcing her perfectly lovely, long-suffering husband, Keith Gessen.[21] Wait, what? The same husband from whom she needed rescuing? Evidently.

Gould offers a larger context for the crowdfunding newsletter. She was going through a mental health breakdown, for which she was institutionalized. But like many people who lose their minds, she did so in ways that at first glance seem like taking a noble stand against a systemic problem. It was 2022. Men were terrible, and none more so than full-of-it successful writer types. This was just known. It *added up* that Keith Gessen, author of *All the Sad Young Literary Men*, was one of the bad not-so-young literary men. This, even though Gould was not—this was clear even at the time—in a stable place, nor the world's most reliable narrator.

What Gould describes is having frustrations in her own life, and assuming they map out neatly onto the stories of other women. Like Emma Bovary, Gould thinks she's the woman in the books she reads, except instead of romances, they're divorce novels and memoirs. Gould reads Nora Ephron's autobiographical divorce novel *Heartburn*, also Lenz's *This American Ex-Wife*, and a host of other texts in which "the husband was the villain and the wife the wronged party, and the inevitable result was splitting up." This writing gives her a framework for understanding the trajectory of her life. After all, she was the one who did the cooking, and the bulk of the childcare. She *had* been a big deal, but for various life-happens reasons—including her choice to marry another ambitious writer—wound up in the same position as so many other lady-writers, dabbling when she could, between household responsibilities. She had every right to be resentful!

Or did she? She assembles the literature about women whose marriages ruined their lives, only to conclude, "This was not quite the way I felt."

If I was stunned by this sentence, it's because Gould describes her marriage in terms that don't fit conventional narratives. The zeitgeist informs you that you, *the wife*, are holding it all together, while your loser of a husband coasts on male entitlement and makes you feel small. You are Taylor Swift and Beyoncé combined. Your husband is dirt.

What complicates matters is that Gould, the woman, was the dirtbag in the relationship. This is the *thesis* of her essay, which is why it was so bizarre to see a bunch of men's-rights types respond to it on social media by pointing out, as if they'd uncovered a hidden truth, that Gould hadn't been very nice to her husband. By her own admission, she's the one who cheated, abused alcohol, and spent recklessly. Gessen, as she presents him, is the responsible one, the one who kept it together when she could not.

I don't know the Gould-Gessens personally. I have no intuitive sense of which one deserves how much blame in their conflicts. A *Slate* reviewer of Gessen's child-rearing book writes that in it, "Gould is relegated to sainthood status," while he's the one haranguing their kid.[22] The reality of their lives is probably more nuanced than these duelling *mea culpas* would suggest. What interests me here is not the black box that is even the most amply documented marriage but rather Gould's willingness to diverge from the expected script in her writing about it. She knows perfectly well how to write a Bad Man personal essay (her divorce-crowdfunding newsletter was one of them!) but decides to transcend a Mad Libs approach to describing one's own subjective predicaments. No faceless sketches here. We're still in the joyless realm of women worn down by daily life, of which husbands are a part. But a recognition that men and women alike are flawed, human, and need one another is a start.

Stories of Peach Moms and Soap Dispenser Husbands can serve as a wake-up call to the partners of good-for-nothing men. They can also have a way of leading people ("people" as in, me) to confuse irritation at having to do the normal chores of adulthood with a righteous cause that could be overcome in a way other than suddenly waking up a gazillionaire. Sometimes, when I'm cooking dinner for my family, I find myself getting into a huff about how I'm the one who does that task most of the time in my household. ("Sometimes.") Then I'll look in the living room and remember that my husband is watching our two young kids while I'm sorting out what will go on our pasta, and that after dinner, he cleans up the resulting sauce-encrusted kitchen. But I've been primed to understand the sentiment "I don't WANT to chop this onion" in gendered terms. *Think of what this chapter would have been if all that onion-dicing time had been devoted to it!* But much as I may want there to be a feminist case for why I shouldn't have to make dinner, I'm not sure there is one.

THREE

"Are Straight Women Okay?"[1]

It's a miserable thing, living as a straight woman, if you aren't one. Never has this been clearer to me than when reading Sara Glass's memoir, *Kissing Girls on Shabbat*. Married off in her late teens, she fled the strictest version of Hasidic Judaism, only to wind up in her early thirties married to her second husband—also religious but less fanatically so. (I don't use "fanatically" lightly; husband number one waited for a rabbi to give the go-ahead so his wife could get meds during childbirth.) So there she is, now with a much kinder husband, but still miserable. What gives? A therapist asks Glass, "Have you *ever* wanted to have sex with a man?"[2] This to-the-point question, plus a fully consummated same-sex liaison, announces to Glass what the reader has already put together, namely that she is approximately 500 per cent lesbian. (Remember this when we get to Chapter 4 regarding the theory that women are inherently sexually fluid.) No sexual fluidity to speak of. Not even a little bit bi. Not, in other words, someone who could sort of wing it as a straight woman while having other urges.

But for complicated reasons relating to custody issues and her own religious upbringing, at that point in the story, Glass sees men as her only option: "Jewish law mandated that I be straight. I was straight."[3]

The mere fact that a woman this definitively not-straight could type the sentence "I was straight" gets at something profound about the multi-faceted nature of heterosexuality. "Straightness" is the term used to describe husband-and-wife pairings, prom-king-and-queen, and things of that nature. The observable, enforced (rigidly or covertly) result of heteronormativity, or the expectation that everyone is/should be heterosexual. In everyday-language usage, you see a girlfriend and boyfriend and say, *That's a straight couple.* Straightness is *also* the name we've got—the only one—for passionate and exclusive opposite-sex desire. There is a heterosexuality of imposition, *and* one that's sincerely felt. Two real phenomena, sharing a name.

A closeted life is tolerable at best, unbearable at worst. But is the heterosexuality itself similarly miserable for straight people? Might one even describe heterosexuality itself as . . . *tragic?*

STRAIGHTNESS STUDIES

Paradoxically, Straightness Studies[4]—what I call the academic or quasi-academic analysis of heterosexuality—has exceedingly few heterosexual practitioners. Straight people of course give plenty of airtime to straight-people concerns (the straightness usually taken for granted), but the majority of analyses of straightness as such, where someone is like, *now, we will be talking about the heterosexuals*, comes from outside observers. This might seem counterintuitive but makes perfect sense. If you're straight, you're probably not giving straightness itself much thought.

The scholars and intellectuals whose beat is heterosexuality don't just happen to be LGBTQ themselves, but come to the topic from

Queer Studies or thereabouts. Before writing *The Invention of Heterosexuality*, Jonathan Ned Katz, a gay man, edited *Homosexuality: Lesbians and Gay Men in Society, History, and Literature: Documents of the Homosexual Rights Movement in Germany, 1836–1927*. Prior to writing *Straight: A Surprisingly Short History of Heterosexuality*, Hanne Blank—straight-passing but, at least at the time of her writing, with an intersex partner—edited an anthology called *Best Transgender Erotica*. Asa Seresin, author of 2019's "On Heteropessimism," the go-to essay on straight women hating this fact about themselves, has more recently co-written an academic article about trans-exclusionary lesbians. He is a transgender man who was lesbian-identified when he coined "heteropessimism." Before *The Tragedy of Heterosexuality*, Jane Ward, queer and "dyke" identified, wrote the (superior) 2015 book *Not Gay: Sex Between Straight White Men*, which is about straight-*identified* people but, as the title suggests, only just. I point this out not because I make it a habit of documenting the sexual orientation and gender trajectory of every author I read, but because it's helpful in understanding where current scholarly and highbrow conceptions of heterosexuality are coming from, namely from people studying it from within a gender studies context, one that privileges marginalized sexualities and edge cases. These are scholars for whom heterosexuality is not just something possible to study from a cool distance, but whose *disciplinary* inclination is to examine straightness in terms of queerness. This is by no means the only conceivable way to do so, nor is it always the most informative.

Credit where credit's due to Queer Studies for inventing a subfield. But Straightness Studies, as it currently exists, is preoccupied with the imposition of heterosexuality. The "key lines of inquiry" in the academic compendium *Routledge International Handbook of Heterosexualities Studies* spell this out. Questions mentioned in the abstract include: "How are individuals socialized to view themselves and others as straight, even when many people are sexually fluid? How do institutions like government bodies, the educational system, and the family reinforce heterosexuality?"[5] This tells you to anticipate a focus on how people who *aren't* straight are coerced into lives they don't want, and shamed out of leading the ones they do. Valid topics all, but none of them addressing how it goes for straight people who face whichever relationship-related obstacles (rigid gender roles, domestic violence, pressures to settle down / not settle down at various ages, everyday squabbling) but whose opposite-sex attractions are simply facts of who they are. People, that is, who may be thorough supporters of gay rights, and who doubtless benefit in some respects from broader redefinitions of what marriage looks like, but who would in no *individual* way benefit from being more readily able to find a same-sex partner. As is typical of human beings, I have no shortage of personal grievances. But if someone said, *Here, Phoebe, you now live in a world free of homophobia, you can now hold hands with a woman in any locale on Earth*, I'd say that's fantastic news for the people to whom it applies but useless to me personally.

PITY THE FOOLS

The anchor text of Straightness Studies, the one that best articulates the Queer Studies answer to Ban Men feminism, is Jane Ward's academic but polemical and lively *The Tragedy of Heterosexuality*. In it, Ward puts "straight culture" under the microscope, and what she finds is troubling. Straight men and women hate one another. Out in search of unhappiness, it is unhappiness she finds. She writes of what she calls "the heterosexual-repair industry"—marriage manuals, self-help books, and dating coaches, all aimed at the despondent straight person, and finds a marked absence of happy straight people.

At the beginning of *Tragedy*, where the author states her positionality ("queerness, femmeness, whiteness, able-bodiedness . . .") and possible blind spots, it almost seems as if Ward is going to get at this.[6] I thought, OK, along with the usual identity-acknowledgement checklist, she is noting that her "queerness" might lead her to miss things about straightness knowable only to straight people.

Not so. *Very* not so.

Ward argues that straight people cannot be authorities on "straight culture," and have no place questioning outside criticisms thereof.[7] Any correctives actual straight people would give—any pushback to her arguments—would amount to defensiveness from those who "feel implicated or threatened by new and/or critical ideas."[8] The time has come for the tragic straights to shut up and take notes. If we suggest we've been misunderstood, this is only evidence she has our number.

The particularly tragic, per *Tragedy*, are straight women. "Straight women's lives," writes Ward, "are very, very hard."[9] That the book's ostensible aim is saving straight women is clear from the book's dedication: "For straight women. May you find a way to have your sexual needs met without suffering so much." One section bears the title "Are Straight Women Okay?" I think by this point you could hazard a guess at Ward's answer.

In a noble effort to push back against the belief that only heterosexuality is natural, Straightness Studies leaves the impression that straightness itself is imposed, unnatural, at least where women are concerned. Where men are concerned, everyone knows the dick gets hard for women, men, or occasionally both. Women are more of a mystery. And in a Straightness Studies interpretation, the girl who thinks she likes boys, and only boys, has simply been subjected to too many princess fairy tales. Consider Ward, praising lesbian writers who "documented the ways that girls and women were groomed by straight culture to desire relationships with men despite the overwhelming evidence that heterosexual relationships were unequal."[10] It's certainly true that *lesbians* have been shoved into heterosexual relationships they didn't want, and that bisexual women's options were and are curtailed. But the idea that a woman's sexual orientation could be chalked up to "grooming," or that a woman could un-straight herself if she simply read up on gender inequity, is so far off it's hard to know where to begin. I get that there's subversive fun in throwing "groomer" accusations back at the straights, but if the aim is to understand where straight people are coming from, it doesn't enlighten.

The grooming theory of sexual orientation, whichever ideology it's in service of, always reminds me of the way teens are lectured against succumbing to peer pressure to use drugs, as if the only reason someone would take a pleasurable or disinhibiting mind-altering substance is to fit in. Sometimes you just have to accept that people mean it when they say they're seeking out whatever it is they're seeking out because it's what they enjoy. Straight women have our share of gripes about men, but you will not find a heterosexual who finds *heterosexuality itself* an artificial imposition. We know this because of the grating tendency of straight women to announce they wish they were otherwise wired.

"GREAT, BIG, LARGE, PENDULOUS BREASTS"

In the *Absolutely Fabulous* episode "Fat," middle-aged London fashion-obsessive Edina, a chain-smoking, champagne-swilling layabout who ostensibly runs a public relations firm, goes on a diet. She tries to slim down from her unremarkable middle-aged-lady proportions to whatever was desirable in 1992, failing miserably. An attempted jog around the block has her winded. Her icons may be Twiggy and Kate Moss, but this look is not in store for a pre-Ozempic-era Edina Monsoon.

Edina's waifish young personal assistant Bubble has a different perspective on body image. Bubble complains—*to her boss*, as though expecting sympathy—about being unable to gain weight. Specifically Bubble envies Edina's "great, big, large, pendulous breasts." Edina angrily responds that Bubble doesn't know her own mind: "You think, just because you feel better with a couple of oranges stuffed down your cups, you know what it feels like. Well, you don't. It's hell."[11]

In one sense, Edina is correct. Would Bubble, an inept pseudo-secretary whose sole qualification is looking fashionable, trade bodies with a chubby woman twice her age? Clearly not, and it's insulting for her to even say she would! No one is hiring Edina for anything based on *her* looks.

And yet one gets the sense that Bubble is speaking her truth. Just as there is a multi-gazillion-dollar diet industry, breast implants do a brisk business. The latest entertainment-industry news cycle, as I write this, revolves around the idea that *breasts are back*, as indicated by the well-endowed actress Sydney Sweeney having showcased her cleavage during a *Saturday Night Live* hosting stint. Given that Sweeney looks roughly how Bubble would if she suddenly had Edina's bosoms but was otherwise unchanged, it's not so far-fetched to imagine that Bubble's chest-coveting is sincere.

An analogous dynamic exists between straight women and their lesbian friends. It's not about breasts (not directly, that is). Rather, heterosexual women regularly barrage lesbians with the question: *Why can't I be gay like you?* Rendered miserable by their dealings with straight men, these ladies nevertheless lack the backbone (one hesitates to say "balls") to give up men entirely.

How widespread is the phenomenon itself? Formal polling neglects such questions, so if you're the sort who'd only be satisfied with info like *83 per cent of straight women have thusly microaggressed a lesbian*, you're out of luck. My sense is that most are not straight-splaining about how great lesbians have it. If nothing else, alienating your lesbian confidantes requires having some to begin with, and most straight women aren't going to.

It would not shock me, however, if most lesbians *have* had dealings along these lines. Accounts from queer women who've encountered envious straight ones abound, and reliably elicit nods of recognition. Reddit has forums such as "Lesbians what do you think about straight women saying they wish they were lesbians?"[12] TikTok has its very own "Woman Who Wishes She Was a Lesbian" corner.[13] Queer women plead to us in think pieces with titles like "Dear Straight Women: Please Stop Saying You Wish You Were Gay" (*Study Breaks Magazine*, 2020) and "Straight Women, Please Stop Saying That You Wish to Be Gay" (Living by the Word, on Medium, 2023). British gender-critical feminist Julie Bindel, co-founder and co-director of The Lesbian Project, writes, "Over the years, a fair number of heterosexual women have told me, 'If only I could fancy women, my life would be much easier,' as though nothing bad ever happens to us because we don't have to scrub dirty boxers and put up with mediocre sex."[14] A 2017 *Reductress* post headline satirizes the phenomenon: "I Wish I Could Just Be a Lesbian So I Could Ruin that Relationship Too."

The overarching theme of all this commentary is that the straight woman who announces she wishes she were gay is exhibiting unchecked privilege. Have these women speaking so blithely about the advantages of a partner who knows what it's like to be a woman, and might even want to share clothes, considered . . . homophobia? *Have they?* In the moment, at least, it's clear that they have not. They're like Bubble wishing she were more top-heavy. They don't know what it's *like*.

A more sophisticated refutation may get at the fact that life amongst lesbians isn't 24/7 sisterhood—that women are human and thus irritating to live with, so even if you spared yourself some male-specific annoyances, life wouldn't all be clothes-sharing, chore-dividing bliss.

The Straightness Studies approach takes lesbian-envying straight women at face value. Maybe they've simply picked up on the fact that it is, even given homophobia, *better to be queer*? Maybe straight women want out? Per Ward, "queers are braced for the inevitable moment when a straight woman proclaims, offhandedly, 'I wish I could just be a lesbian.' Sigh. Why don't you be one, then? some of us wonder. It's not *that* hard."[15] Ward recalls having been "a young dyke who would occasionally date boring straight men, especially after a difficult queer breakup,"[16] as though if she could give up men for political reasons, what's stopping any other woman?

"Like most lesbians," writes Asa Seresin, "I have found myself on the receiving end of approximately 100,000 drunk straight women bemoaning their orientation and insisting that it would be 'so much easier' to be gay. Sure, it probably would be! That 'men are trash' is not something I am personally invested in disputing." The question Seresin asks is what's holding these women back: "In announcing her wish to be gay, the speaker carelessly glosses over the fact that she has *chosen* to stay attached to heterosexuality—to remain among the (slightly more than 2 or 3) women who are, despite everything, still straight."[17] Seresin would certainly seem to be implying that sexual orientation is a choice. Seresin now uses he/him pronouns, so his time as a harangued lesbian has come to an end. Maybe there are now women drunkenly telling him they wish they could be men.

APPLES AND ORANGES

In "Political Lesbianism: The Case Against Heterosexuality," a 1979 pamphlet version of a 1977 talk, the Leeds Revolutionary Feminist Group engaged in a spot of what would today be called *feminist gate-keeping.*[18] Their verdict was, if you want to call yourself a feminist, you'd best be a lesbian. But not just any kind of lesbian. A *political* lesbian. A what now? A political lesbian is a lesbian (or, possibly, a non-lesbian) whose lesbianism is motivated not by a lust for labia but by political objections to sleeping with men. Some lesbians, they explain, are merely women into women, and therefore not *political* lesbians. Conversely, political lesbianism "does not mean compulsory sexual activity with women." The compendium their pamphlet appears in includes some counterarguments, and one detractor gently suggests that if you're abstaining from men but not sleeping with women, a feminist you may be, but a lesbian, not so much.[19]

But as attuned as the feminist revolutionaries of Leeds were to the social and economic pressures on women to be and stay with male partners, as insightful as they were on that aspect of things, they missed a piece of the puzzle. A section addresses the counter-argument "But I like fucking," allowing that there are women who at least claim to enjoy sexual intercourse with men. Their advice to such women? Get over it.

> Giving up fucking for a feminist is about taking your politics seriously. Women who are socialists are prepared to give up many things which they might enjoy because they see how these things tie into and support the whole system of economic class oppression which they are fighting. They will resist buying Cape apples because the profits go to South Africa.[20]

A woman named Penny Cloutte is not convinced. In a response in the compendium *Love Your Enemy?*, she writes, "The Leeds sisters don't seem to have much respect for sexual pleasure as such—or why do they . . . compare it to Cape apples?"[21] In the Leeds revolutionaries' defence, the sentence that follows the apples one is this: "Obviously it is more difficult for some feminists to give up penetration which is so fundamental to the system of oppression which we are fighting." Obviously, some women's sexual urges exceed anyone's need for a specific type of apple. Or one might think it would be obvious. An additional response, from one Jean Clitheroe, who acknowledges that "lots of women have experienced, do experience 'heterosexual desire,'" but then analogizes their love of men to her own plight as a meat-loving vegetarian. It's a funny piece of writing, including, as it does, the line "I bet it's the first time lesbians have been compared to a kidney bean stew."[22] I suppose vegetarianism (if you like meat) is a bigger sacrifice than eschewing one apple variety. But we are still in apples-to-oranges territory. There's wanting a sausage and there's wanting a *sausage.*

I don't know what it was about the late 1970s and early 1980s—the chest hair poking out of unbuttoned polyester?—but this was a heyday for the woman who'd gone off men. Cue Adrienne Rich's 1980 essay "Compulsory Heterosexuality and Lesbian Existence."[23] While the title implies the existence of non-compulsory heterosexuality—voluntary, inherent, whatever—this essay is a key source of the idea that "heterosexuality" should be used as shorthand for heteronormativity. For Rich, heterosexuality is "an institution." It is the name she uses for what other feminists call "patriarchy." She faults her feminist contemporaries for critiquing the oppression of women but not suggesting lesbianism as a way out. And—here's the crucial bit—she argues that the existence of anti-lesbian oppression is evidence that given their druthers, most women would rather be with women than with men, suggesting that "for women heterosexuality may not be a 'preference' at all but something that has had to be imposed, managed, organized, propagandized, and maintained by force."

And so Straightness Studies was born.

From this point on, the various mechanisms keeping women from leading full lives have gotten conflated with the ones keeping women from having all the sex we're apparently all desperate to be having with other women. The problem: All the restraints historically placed on women's sexuality—ones hardly limited to prohibitions on same-sex involvements—in no way demonstrate that most women want sex with other women. If anything, the focus has been on curtailing what's possible for us to do *with men*. This imagined society, where what's demanded of women is finding men sexually attractive and where any woman who's down to fuck dudes is in the clear, has never existed. Women by and large *are* sexually attracted to men. What's at stake for the female population generally is the types of relationships it's possible for us to have with them. The prioritization of male desire. The threat of male violence.

The blind spot at the core of Straightness Studies is about exactly how compulsory most women find heterosexuality to be. Even if you allow that a certain number of "straight" women are closeted something-elses, there are seemingly *some* women whose straightness just . . . is. Where are they left in this understanding? Consider Romeo and Juliet, who faced one or two obstacles, but none of those barriers was the absence of legal same-sex marriage. Or take a more everyday situation where a girl or woman is in love with a guy whose cultural or religious background is in conflict with her own. Even extremely homophobic, super-conservative subcultures—or rather, *especially* those subcultures—are not particularly welcoming to opposite-sex partners who fall outside their parameters.

Is a woman who resists marriage to a specific man, who refuses to have twelve of his children, pushing back against *heterosexuality* or patriarchy? Does anything change if her reason for not wanting to marry Dude A is her all-encompassing lust for Dude B? Would there be any point in offering such a woman, frustrated though she is with patriarchal demands, a loving relationship with a woman, or a chance to be a celibate "political lesbian"?

Another of the replies to the Leeds revolutionaries comes from Justine Jones, a woman who went from having masochistic fantasies about men to identifying as bisexual and then, at the urging of her feminist sisters, as lesbian. She blames the patriarchy for having "put up with faking orgasms and feigning headaches for 2 years of monogamous heterosexuality," which doesn't come across as a ringing endorsement.[24] But it can't just be that *she* is a lesbian-leaning bisexual. This is about womankind being brainwashed into thinking they like men. "I think women are influenced to be masochists, from a very young age, so that we'll become heterosexual and 'enjoy' it."[25] It's not about this one lady preferring women, but that all the world's women who imagine a preference for men simply don't know their own minds.

This is a big theme in the compendium, that sexual orientation is a choice, and women's liberation demands making the right one. A woman signing "Marlene Packwood, Radical Feminist" also insists that there is a lesbian inside every woman just screaming to get out. "In understanding that lesbians are not different from other women, heterosexual women begin to see that potentially any woman can be a lesbian—it is conceivably possible."[26] Another, Alexandra Stone, "demand[s] of heterosexual feminists that they acknowledge *their* choice, that they are and have chosen to be heterosexual . . ."[27] It's almost as if none of these women had heard the 2011 Lady Gaga song "Born This Way."

All of this might seem like mists-of-time material, and very well might have gone that way, had it not been for a Ban Men feminism–spurred revival. Contemporary understandings of gender are a particularly convenient fit for a revamped version of lesbian separatism. But the new theorists aren't banishing penis-havers from music festivals. Rather, they're dividing the world into cishets (unenlightened bigots with bad taste) and queers (next phase of humanity). They're not advocating for political lesbianism, but rather against what might be deemed political heterosexuality. That is, a heterosexuality rooted not in heartfelt or crotch-felt desires but in reason and principles. They define heterosexuality in exclusively ideological or aesthetic terms, as though straightness is something people only ever go in for because they lack the courage or edginess for a different path. A straight woman, in this understanding, isn't a woman into dudes. She's a woman who has decided that life would be easier as some dude's plus-one.

BACK TO BASICS

The first thing that struck me about Tranna Wintour's *The Walrus* essay "Why I Can't Stop Watching *Say Yes to the Dress*"[28] was its year of publication: 2023. I remembered the reality series where women shop for wedding gowns at a famous, or maybe just famous-from-the-show, New York wedding-gown store, but as a relic from 2008 or thereabouts. But it's apparently one of those shows that stuck around, and Wintour—the name a tongue-in-cheek homage of sorts to iconic former *Vogue* editor Anna Wintour—is a fan. Or more like an anti-fan. The reason this is a big-ideas essay in *The Walrus* and not a gushing post on some forum is that Wintour, who's transgender, uses viewing *Say Yes to the Dress* as an opportunity to gawk at the basic cishets.

The show, she writes, offers a "terrifying glimpse into the cult of heteronormativity." Her interpretation of the brides themselves, and their motivations, suggests she and I were watching different programs. She comes away from it concerned not (as I half-was) that these women are heading towards wedding-related debt, but that they are fooling themselves by getting married to begin with. "The women on the show have so much invested in their marital hopes, but is the safety they think they've found real?" To imagine a guilty-pleasure reality show has anything whatsoever to do with *marriage*, even the marriages of the women who appear on it, is a fundamental misunderstanding. It is about shopping, and more specifically, shopping for what you've decided will be the most flattering and expensive garment you will ever own. High-pressure, but the stakes have zilch to do with finding the right husband, and everything to do with choosing the right dress. I mean it's right there in the show's name: *Say Yes to the Dress*. These women are not sheep—or no more or less than the next person. They know about divorce and disappointments as possible outcomes, arriving on the show with varied life experiences. They're into pageantry and dress-up and—evidently—appearing on television. I can't say I get it. I once spent $260 (Canadian, before tax) on a pair of black-and-white loafers at upscale department store Holt Renfrew, and if a TV crew had captured this, I'd never live it down. But to each her own.

Given that there is no one forcing Tranna Wintour to watch saleswomen with New York accents cinch ordinary women into princess dresses, one might wonder why she tortures herself so. It is about feeling smug about *not* being the lady in the dress. "Ultimately, the feeling I have when I watch SYTTD is relief . . . Thank god I didn't say yes to patriarchy. Thank god I didn't say yes to heteronormativity."

Tranna Wintour is herself a reality TV performer, but not, it would seem, a *Say Yes to the Dress* completist. I had this faint memory of at least one two-bride couple back when I was tuning in, so I looked it up and sure enough . . . A 2022 *Autostraddle* article by

Sa'iyda Shabazz—a Black woman with a wife, writing on a progressive lesbian website—combs the show's many seasons for all its queer moments, and finds rather a lot. Shabazz tracks how the show is a product of its time, yet always a bit ahead of the mainstream curve, introducing first some lesbian couples, then trans brides, and then—here's the bit I was not expecting—a polyamorous throuple. One groom: two brides. A missed opportunity, though: How much better if they had gone with *three* brides and therefore three gowns?

I can understand, to a point, why a trans woman would hate-watch a wedding-industrial-complex reality show. There's subversive joy in caricaturing one's oppressors. Where it gets tricky is if, as Straightness Studies does, you claim you're doing so in order to save straight people, straight women in particular. When the criticism is at the level of *your world seems awful and I'm* GLAD *I've escaped it*, fair enough. Straightness Studies claims to be about understanding in order to help, which calling straight people mega-basic does not accomplish.

The subreddit "Are the Straights OK," and the meme of the same name, get at this dynamic. It's this complicated version of mockery dressed up as concern. The poor straights, they live such limited lives! But also not *the poor straights*, because if this punch didn't understand itself to be upward, it would not be presenting itself as self-righteousness, as *resistance*.

What is it about straightland that's cause for concern? Much of it would appear to come down to the existence of heteronormative knick-knacks, like keychains and whatnot with references to *the old ball and chain*, to husbands as needy babies, wives as nags—the stuff of tourist kiosks. It doubtless points to something in the culture that these tropes are entrenched enough that some factory in China is making them, but the centrality of an I'm-with-stupid T-shirt to anyone's lived experience of heterosexuality is very possibly being overstated.

Some of the examples do not have any clear connection to man-woman relationships. A baby outfit that reads "Made of 100% recycled genetic material" (a May 2023 item on the "Are the Straights OK?" forum on Reddit) is cheesy, but the science it references is true of human beings generally, even a baby born to gay men who've used a surrogate. Another from the same month, a greeting card bearing the message "Marriage is like a walk in the park. Jurassic Park," is only hetero-specific if you consider complaining about wedded life to be a uniquely heterosexual phenomenon. If I'm skeptical, I'm not alone. The forum participants themselves aren't always persuaded that the things they're being prompted to look at as examples of hetero shenanigans qualify as such. A meme about a husband not listening and asking his wife to repeat a story gets the following much-endorsed reply: "This could be a totally innocent interaction too, even between LGBT folks," with further replies offering that the behaviour relates more to "neurodivergence" than sexual orientation.[29]

Jane Ward's deep dive into the basicness of the straights comes primarily from the part of *Tragedy* where she surveys a bunch of not-cishet individuals to get the only accurate look at straightness possible, namely one from the outside. She writes that "it is time to spill the tea—to reveal what queer people say about straight people behind closed doors so that we may help save straight people from themselves."[30] The best she can do is that we're stuffy and dull.

Why is this so predictable? Relationship advice to straight people marketed as *from a gay person* is the conceit behind advice books and columns and podcasts and television shows, from the hit *Queer Eye for the Straight Guy* to the 1988 "Norm, Is That You?" episode of *Cheers* that had normie hetero Norm posing as a gay man in order to sell his interior decorating services. Even people who'd like to think themselves above clichés have been known to use the preponderance of rainbow flags in a neighbourhood as a clue that there might be good cafés around.

Anyway, let it be known that "queer commentators like to point out just how *basic* straight culture is." Ward provides, "for older readers," a definition: "to be 'basic' means to be a follower, to lack any special and unpredictable characteristics." We apparently have an "addiction to mainstream media and mass-marketed tchotchkes" such as "Live, Love, Laugh [*sic*] posters."[31] This might seem to be conflating being straight with being what Hyacinth Bucket in *Keeping Up Appearances* would call *lower-middle class*, at least where cultural capital is concerned. The distinction up for discussion starts to seem less like a divide between queers and cishets, and more like one between a town's business-tourist district and its understated, independent-boutique-having, unaffordable-to-buy-property-in residential neighbourhoods.

Ward writes, incredibly, that "straight people's attachments to mainstream culture and the status quo are sometimes accompanied by apathy about social justice projects, and *this* is what makes heterosexuals the worst people to get stuck next to at a dinner party."[32] I'd rather plaster my house with Live, Laugh, Love posters than hear about a tablemate's "social justice projects." One is meant to nod along to the idea that "straight men suck the energy out of the room,"[33] but . . . while I will grant her that there is a certain type of bore who is almost invariably a straight man—the sort who goes to a lecture and has *more of a comment than a question* and could use some help trimming his ear hair—the presence of *certain* straight men does the opposite of what she says.

Ward's innovation is to offer straight men advice on loving women, from the perspective of a woman-loving woman. Lesbians, per Ward, love women without expecting them to adhere to beauty standards or behave submissively. Why can't straight men be more like that? It's a timely argument, given all the Ban Men feminism about, but a bit toothless. As delighted as people of all stripes may be to take decorating advice from gay male designers, straight men are not about to take instruction from lesbian theorists—even ones who found just the right Audre Lorde passage to cite—about which women to find attractive. It also—again, the blind spots—misses the large-scale extent to which straight men are *already doing the thing she asks*, namely enjoying sex with ordinary-looking women. Not because they're such good feminists but because their tastes vary or because they prefer sex with the women actually in their lives to staying celibate until Zendaya returns their call.

WHY MEN THOUGH?

Insofar as Straightness Studies remembers that there are genuine heterosexuals in the world, alongside the people shunted against their will into heterosexual lifestyles, the go-to thing is to ask straight people—or rather, straight women—*why*. Straight women, why are you so committed to directing your energies towards men? This is the question. And it's a fair thing to ask, to a point. It's good to know that various sexualities exist, and not to fall passively into opposite-sex relationships simply because that's what's generally done. But if you conclude, *as most women will*, that you are in fact into men, what's left to interrogate?

As an alternative to heteropessimism, Asa Seresin suggests a navel-excavating dig into the *why* of it all. A woman might think she likes men, but has she interrogated this? Has she done her homework? He recommends "the writer Harron Walker's podcast *why do i like men*."[34] When Seresin turns to "articulations of women's desire," it's striking that the voices he emphasizes are mainly those of trans women and that in his estimation none of the women *doing straightness right* are cisgender heterosexuals. While some trans women are straight, Walker, at least, does not identify as such. And the people for whom man-liking is fraught *in the ways pertinent to heteropessimism* are cisgender heterosexual women. Cisgender bisexual women are—in principle—not penned in by heterosexuality. Their man-liking may strike some lesbians as curious, but they cannot be accused of unwillingness to contemplate other options. And no one's accusing trans women, as a class, of basicness.

You will at this point in the chapter be stunned to learn that Ward also encourages straight women to interrogate their alleged desires: "When I ask straight feminist women such questions—including 'Why are you straight?' and 'What do you like about men?'—I am struck by how often they look like deer caught in headlights."[35] She treats these women's inability to articulate *that which cannot be articulated* as a gotcha. If you can't explain *why* you like men, and conversely why women and non-binary people aren't your jam, then you've lost the argument.

Why do *I* like men? Because I do. Same as the reason why Man A does it for me and Man B does not. Any attempt at an answer would diminish clarity. If I named individual anatomical traits, one could counter that many of these—all of them, in a trans-inclusive understanding—could be found in women as well. If I tried to rationalize or justify the parameters of my attractions, I'd be setting things up for a debate. It also wouldn't be accurate, because the majority of my *he seems interesting* thoughts have been about men I've only ever seen clothed, men whose bits I could only infer.

If I were to attempt to interrogate my way out of heterosexuality, I'd be engaging in something no less futile or faith-based in its own way than what Sara Glass was doing when trying to make herself straight to appease some rabbis. I'm sure there are straight women who could, because their understanding of feminism demands it, give up men, just as there are lesbians whose investment in being a member of a strict religious community is higher than their commitment to building a life with someone they love, as in someone they are happy to see naked. Lots of things are *possible*. Advisable is another matter.

FREE TAYLOR

At the time of my writing this sentence, the biggest celebrity in America is a tall, thin, symmetrical thirty-four-year-old blonde singer-songwriter named Taylor Swift. Swift is not just incidentally straight—the assumption still made of almost everyone, famous or not—but arguably the voice of female heterosexuality these days. All those songs about crushes and exes, all those crushes, all those exes. This is a woman who has found a way to make adolescent female boy-craziness lucrative (she's a billionaire!). Yes, it's catchy music, but the thematics don't hurt. Swift inhabits—well into adulthood—the role of the gawky teen who wishes the popular boy knew she was alive. Except that she now has a (hot) professional football player fiance, whose literal job is called "tight end."

I am not, I confess, a Swiftie. For me the last name "Swift" summons Clive Swift, the late actor who played Hyacinth Bucket's henpecked husband Richard on *Keeping Up Appearances*. But I accept that some people find Taylor Swift infinitely compelling. One such person is Anna Marks, an Opinion editor at *The New York Times*. Marks's 2024 essay "Look What We Made Taylor Swift Do" conveys the extent to which every move Swift makes gets dissected by her fan base.[36] What colour leotard did she have on when performing in Omaha and what did it *mean*? That's the level of attention to detail we're talking. Marks is both reporting on obsessive fandom and a part of the fandom itself.

Branches of Taylor Swift's fan army evidently do have strong feelings about her sexual orientation. There are "gaylors" who think/want her to be gay and "hetlors" invested in her heterosexuality, though perhaps less invested in having a name without unfortunate Nazi resonances. The hetlors do have, in their favour, the fact that their celebrity obsession does seem rather committed to exclusively dating men. The gaylors have . . . well, they have straws at which they grasp.

And Marks, in the staid pages of the *New York Times* Opinion section, makes the case for gaylordom. It's not Marks willing Swift to be queer (I mean it *is* that), but rather Marks projecting closetedness onto Swift. Swift, *as Marks understands her*, is a straight woman whose liberated state would be one of queerness-type-unspecified. Marks is going to *free Taylor Swift* from the shackles of . . . being a massively rich and successful musician who dates one beautiful man after the next.

Marks never spells out exactly *which* form of queer Swift is meant to be. She suggests "homophobia" may have prevented Swift from an "I'm gay" announcement. (So, too, might Swift's not being gay to begin with. It's significant, apparently, that Swift released a song on Lesbian Visibility Day, which is definitely a real thing that actual human lesbians have in their calendars.)

Marks's skepticism regarding "Ms. Swift's extracurricular activities involving a certain football star" suggests this is a theory about Swift being gay.

Or is Swift bi? Here, the coded messages abound: "The aesthetic of what would be known as the 'Lover Era' emerged as rainbows, butterflies, and pastel shades of blue, purple and pink, colors that subtly evoke the bisexual pride flag." Further evidence: "In early August, Ms. Swift posted a rainbow-glazed photo of a series of friendship bracelets, one of which says 'Proud' with beads in the color of the bisexual pride flag." There was a time when she had "hair the colors of the bisexual pride flag." Much like Lesbian Visibility Day, the bisexual pride flag is one of those things wherein you could live a full life as a member of the group in question and it would never come up.

Marks understands Swift's career as follows: There is a real Taylor Swift, who is "queer" in some unspecified capacity, one that seemingly precludes having authentic romantic relationships with men. (How this squares with the "dropped hairpins" pertaining to bisexuality is unclear. If she's secretly bisexual, this wouldn't mean she's *not* dating men!) But *the culture* can't handle anything so risqué, even in 2024, so she allows (encourages?) her fans to think she "desire[s] men," when this is outside the bounds of her interests.

The evidence Marks presents is shaky. She successfully roots out the fact that Swift presents herself as a friend of the LGBTQ community, which would if anything seem to diminish (but no, not eliminate) the case that she's a tortured self-hater in denial. The most generous interpretation I can come up with is this: If the idea is that society would only allow a straight Taylor Swift, if lower-tier celebrities can come out but a megastar who needs to appeal to *everybody* cannot be gay or bi, then we know less about Swift's true sexual orientation than we do about that of Sharon from sales, who had no vested interest in hurling herself at Dennis from the mailroom at the holiday party.

All this to say, I am neither a gaylor nor a hetlor. Given the level of fame we're talking about, and the nature of pop-music stardom, I have no idea if Swift-the-persona, a creation for public consumption, aligns with Swift-the-person. It could be that in her private life, Taylor Swift sheds the blonde bangs and lives a hermetically closeted existence where, behind several well-guarded gates, she goes by they/them and lives in post-gender communal polyamory. Or maybe she has a secret husband and ten kids. The extremely rich and famous are mysterious like that.

Now, would I be stunned if, by the time you're reading this, a book called *The Last Straight Woman*, Swift has openly joined the ranks of the man-dating female bisexuals? I most certainly would not. That sort of announcement has long since lost the capacity to shock.

To me, it does not seem momentous if it turns out that a straight woman is in fact a mostly-straight woman. To Marks, the line between queerness and not-queerness is of cosmic importance:

> We can consider the album's [*Lover*, 2019] aesthetics and activism as performative allyship, as they were largely considered to be at the time. Or we can ask a question, knowing full well that we may never learn the answer: What if the "Lover Era" was merely Ms. Swift's attempt to douse her work—and herself—in rainbows, as so many baby queers feel compelled to do as they come out to the world?[37]

A line, then, divides the sort of woman who wishes LGBTQ people well and feels some sort of affinity, and women who are, themselves, *actually queer*. But this actual queerness need not consist of having same-sex relationships. The minute one allows that Swift—or any woman—so much as *might* be queer herself, what looked like interloping was in fact membership in good standing. What's interesting is how this is about something much bigger than the right to go to Pride as a *part of the community*. It transcends anything to do with gender or sexuality at all.

A Reddit forum post from a self-identified "new-ish swiftie and an even newer gaylor"—who is, additionally, "a queer person with ADHD," though the relevance of the diagnosis remains elusive—gets at what it means to read Swift as queer:

> Before I really got into Taylor Swift, I kinda just thought of her as someone who serial dated men and then wrote songs about them, so her stuff never really resonated. When she started re-recording her music, I gained more respect for her, but now it's like even just the speculation of her being gay/bi/queer has given her depth, and almost humanized her in a way (to me at least).[38]

Some of this is a simple desire for a famous person to share one's own identity, because representation is nice. Another piece, though, is this idea that queerness functions as a proxy for complexity. A basic white lady has no inner life, but a *queer woman*, well! This is someone whose femininity is intentional and a *performance*, who is capable of sending coded messages with her lyrics and imagery. This is an *artist*, conveying profound things about the human condition. Absent the queerness angle, you're looking at some ditz who has boyfriends and is incapable of forming thoughts beyond *when will he propose?* and, when a bit older, *but is the house in a good school district?*

Examined through a Straightness Studies lens, Taylor Swift is therefore either an airhead or a serious artist worthy of attention. And this hinges not on the quality of her output but on the unknowable and arguably irrelevant fact of whether her sex thoughts include any women. Queer desire is subversive, complex, *conveyed via bat signal*. The hetero variety, at least as expressed by women, is boy-craziness and evidence (I cannot handle how absurd *in this case*) that a woman doesn't take her career too seriously. In any event, once I realized about *the line*, it started making sense to me how there could be this great big article about whether Swift is queer that does not spell out which sort, specifically, Swift is meant to be. She just needs to be *something* other than cishet, even a millimetre across the line. Like that *Seinfeld* episode ("The Note," 1991) where George Costanza gets a massage from a man and thinks this caused his penis to *move*. Something along those lines would, if Swift embraced it, be enough.

Marks faults Swift for coming across, initially at least, as a woman who *feels she needs a man*: "Despite the expansive storytelling in Ms. Swift's early records, her public image often cast a man's interest as her greatest ambition." This is a strange way to look at the phenomenon of pop-music love songs. Does anyone imagine that a male rock star with groupies lacks professional ambition? For straight male musicians, the art and the girl-getting are implicitly entwined. Why, then, is it aspiring tradwifery when Taylor Swift does it? In Marks's view: "All of the sexist undertones with which Ms. Swift's work can be discussed (often, even, by fans) flow from compulsory heterosexuality, or the way patriarchy draws power from the presumption that women naturally desire men. She must write about men she surely loves or be unbankable."[39]

To me, this interpretation completely misses the gender dynamics involved. Swift's work is seemingly *about* men but not in service of "male power." That these things are different gets at the crux of where heterosexuality differs from heteronormativity. What she's doing is not queer, but it is subversive. That gender-swapped nature of Swift's very *brand* gets why this utterly conventional-presenting woman, a blonde who goes to professional football games to cheer on her fiance, aggravates the right. She is the protagonist, the alpha, the star. It is *her* perspective one is inundated with, not those of the men she's involved with. She's putting men into the love-interest role, in songs and in her public-facing life. None of this is unprecedented—was Queen Elizabeth II not more famous and powerful than Prince Philip?—but it's enough to rile the sort of men who type, from mom's proverbial basement, that women belong in the kitchen. Many a Swift song is a story of straight womanhood from the woman's perspective. Turning a love of men (even the ones clearly "trouble" from the moment they "walked in"[40]) into art and becoming massively successful is not appeasing the patriarchy. It is—and I say this without any portal to Taylor Swift's inner life—heterosexual feminism in action.

TRAGIC OR JUST BASIC?

The basicness accusation is the conceptual problem with *The Tragedy of Heterosexuality*, "On Heteropessimism," the "Are the Straights OK" subreddit, the Tranna Wintour article about *Say Yes to the Dress*, and the broader Straightness Studies project. Are straight women victims in need of rescue, or squares to be mocked? You do sort of have to pick. As Twitter user @reegnkay once aptly put it, "Saying 'are the straights ok' when women talk about literal domestic abuse at the hands of male partners is very WEIRD."[41] It *is* weird, and yet this is what's done! But Straightness Studies rests on the conviction that heterosexuality itself is a relic. It's something embraced only by the memo-missers of the world, the basic bitches and the ardent reactionaries. Seresin insists he's not asking straight women to be anything other than straight but doesn't seem to think we've got much of a future. "Yes, universal queerness and the abolition of gender may be the horizon toward which we are eventually moving—but what happens in the meantime?"[42] Straight women are relegated to "the meantime." The future is queer, so straight women can be treated with a mix of pity and disdain.

HETEROSEXUAL FEMINISM, JUMBO SHRIMP?

The political lesbianism compendium I mentioned earlier, the one with the women in Leeds who equated giving up men with buying a different apple variety at the grocery store, includes some pushback from feminists who don't see their doing of dudes as in contradiction with their principles, but also some tough words for heterosexual so-called feminists. Paula Jennings writes that there has been "no theory of heterosexual feminism which describes how emotional/sexual relationships with men contribute to feminist revolution."[43] Marlene Packwood concludes her entry by noting that she has "never yet read or heard anywhere, heterosexual feminists . . . justifying in feminist terms, their relationships with men."[44]

Well, ladies, your time has come.

If feminism is about not being pushed around by any *man*, then lesbians sure have an edge. So, too, if the idea is for a household not to default to gender roles. Whoever is earning more or cleaning up less, this is a woman. If feminism is women going their own way, husbands and boyfriends are a drag. And if you wish to enrage religious conservatives, you *could* be active in the non-marital-sex department, but you could save a bunch of time and lead an uneventful life by simply having a spouse the same sex as yourself.

But it doesn't take long to come up with a feminist defence of heterosexuality, not that sexual orientations should need defending. And it goes like this:

Opposite-sex relationships allow for greater role reversals. In a two-woman relationship, whoever is doing more of the mindless chores will be *a* woman; there's just no predetermined script for which one it must be. In a gender-role-subverting straight relationship, a woman can have, as the Judy Brady Syfer essay puts it, "a wife," without any actual woman needing to demean herself in order to be that person. Now I make no claims of personally living that life—I'm in one of those, shall we say, high-cultural-capital-only marriages where we're both working full-time and continuously folding laundry—but maybe a third of the couples I know arrange things in this manner. And in practical terms, a fine way to guarantee that a woman isn't stuck with the *woman* tasks is to hand that role off to a man.

But this to me is the crucial bit, the one applicable across different economic arrangements and life circumstances: Straight women *objectify men*. We look at those self-serious deep-voiced individuals in their suits or cargo shorts, the ones society views as the *doers*, and think about what fun it would be to do *them*. We look at the people generally running the show and reduce them to a simple *hot or not*. We do this not because we're out to get even with men for objectifying us, but because *we cannot help it*. That is what female heterosexuality *is*: it's liking some men and not others, which means that determinations are being made *constantly*. Show me any man on Earth and I can give you a *would*-or-*wouldn't* assessment. Show me any woman and you'll get the same non-judgmental answer: n/a.

What straight women see, when we look at men, is what society associates with a woman-directed gaze. All that human complexity reduced to the mindless question of whether this is or is not a person who you would, under the right circumstances, plausibly want to have sex with. Lesbians have (roughly) the same sexual interest objects as do straight men and therefore share those of mainstream society. Looking at women, sizing them up, is integral, even if—as Ward claims, and as fits everyone's commonsense assessment of how the world works—queer women tend to be less conventional-beauty-standards-focused than are straight men. This is not a criticism of lesbians or for that matter of bisexuals, but merely a definitional fact about people with a sexual interest in women. They are judging women partly on sex appeal.

Straight women also size up other women's looks all the time, but the difference is, we have the option of not doing that. We *could* turn it off, or greatly de-emphasize its importance. We might even find life more enjoyable if we stopped assessing other women to sort out if they're younger or thinner or prettier than we are, and therefore of more interest to men, and just look directly at the men themselves. Do it for feminism, or better yet, do it for fun.

FOUR

Are Straight Women Real?

ARE STRAIGHT MEN REAL?

"'Like being chained to a lunatic.' That's how a man feels in relation to his libido."[1] So wrote theatre critic Lloyd Evans in the U.K. *Spectator*, by way of explaining how attending a Cambridge history lecture had him fantasizing about the historian herself: He didn't pay attention to the content of her talk, focusing instead on her pretty blonde hair. He understood, however, that this woman was unattainable to him. Needing an outlet for his frustrations, he made his way to a middle-aged Chinese sex worker—not his first-choice partner, he spells out, but a man has needs. Insult to injury if you're the sex worker, though one imagines she has bigger concerns. Of interest here is not Evans's sexual arousal pattern, nor even why anyone saw fit to print them (let alone to include the name of the historian, who was neither amused nor charmed). Rather, it's the way any individual man's story of irrational lust gets interpreted—by men and women alike—as something inherent to their kind. There's even an expression for it in British English: *You know what men are.*

Male sexuality is by no means universally celebrated. It is, however, *believed*. There aren't languid musings about what men want. Straight men's desire is widely assumed to be something they genuinely experience, and not the product of heteronormative socialization. There is the hard evidence, from which flows, among other things, a degree of respect. Men want inappropriate people at inconvenient times. It's just how they are. Thus the *Seinfeld* episode ("The Shoes," 1993) where Jerry and George ogle a fifteen-year-old's cleavage. The show is not congratulating men for such activities but rather having a self-deprecating laugh at the fact that men are like so.

Nobody doubts that straight men are real. The occasional wishful-thinking gay man, perhaps—there are some hot straight men out there—but otherwise? Male sexuality is recognized as a force, one that even good men struggle to control. I think of Canadian writer Stephen Marche's *New York Times* op-ed "The Unexamined Brutality of the Male Libido,"[2] which faults the feminism of the moment for failing to take men's nature into account when looking for answers to sexual misconduct. A strange criticism, given that men's dangerous nature was the assumption behind all those essays about how women dare not leave the house at night lest a man jump out from behind a hedge, overcome with lust. But in Marche's defence, he published this in November 2017, as the #MeToo movement was just getting started. "There remains no cure for human desire," writes Marche. By human desire, in this context, he means male. The implication being: half of humanity has tepid urges in no need of a remedy.

Shortly after seeing the Evans article, I was waiting to enter the post office. It was 9 a.m., opening time, but doors were still closed, so an antsy crowd gathered. I stood outside, waiting with the empty stroller (this was after daycare drop-off), watching a worker at the pharmacy that shared the space rearrange a display of *The Golden Girls*–themed socks and beach towels. Among the crowd out front, I clocked a very cute dog, a cute baby having a good scream, and . . . and no, it did not escape my attention that among those waiting was a tall, symmetrical, catalogue-model of a man.

When the post office finally did open, the worker behind the counter giggled and smiled as the man, who was ahead of me, asked her where he should park the very *large* box he was mailing. (It was comically enormous.) She kept talking to him beyond the point needed for the transaction, not wanting the moment to end. She was entirely professional when it was my turn, but ringing me up for a prepaid envelope was not, I am quite certain, the high point of her day. Neither this mailwoman nor I responded to the presence of the handsome man by propositioning him, nor did we drop what we were doing to sublimate matters with the nearest gigolo. She went about her workday and I did the same. Presumably there are also straight, unattached men capable of seeing a pretty lecturer or box-mailer and not hightailing it to an adult-services purveyor, but the demographics of who offers such services points to a gender disparity in demand.

But we notice. We notice! The woman who reacts to a historian's lecture the way Evans did (without the brothel postscript) will stand accused not of lecherousness but unseriousness. When women respond to credentialed speakers with a *he's cute*—something women have said during newscasts since newscasts existed—it's assumed this is because our tiny brains cannot make sense of the material. It doesn't come across as threatening or demeaning to the ogled men. When women comment on which world leaders are hot, when women fanfic Emmanuel Macron with Justin Trudeau, it's seen as frivolity, but also just a bit odd. After all, men are the doers, not the done-to. They aren't sex objects. It's not *how dare you make light of British politics*, but more like, *what a weird thing to think about John Major of all people*. (Hear me out.)

A JOKE QUESTION?

Considering that most of the global population is women, and that most people are heterosexual, it might seem a given that straight women exist—and yet doubts persist. The social phenomenon of heterosexuality is real enough, and not up for discussion. Nobody questions whether any women have husbands and boyfriends, or tick "straight" on forms. No, what's questioned is whether heterosexuality exists among women in the way it does among men. Everyone gets that most men want, *need*, women. If anything, men's sexual requirements are sometimes exaggerated, in ways that make the lukewarm man feel bad about his indifference. A straight man is one whose urges point him, member-first, in the direction of good-looking women; and if none are available, at OK-looking women; and if none are available, at penetrable foodstuffs that they can pretend are women. But do straight women feel anything equivalent?

The current thinking—popular, scientific, and mishmash of the two—is no. Straight women merely put up with men's advances because we don't want them to murder us, or because we rely on them for a roof over our heads, or maybe because they seem nice and this is our way of saying thank you. Women don't spontaneously crave sex but, rather, find that they get in the mood after their partners initiate. Women are turned on not by looking at their partners but by imagining their partners looking at them and finding them beautiful. Women are less visual than men, so we don't care what men look like, except the status-fixated sorts who make shallow demands about height and hair. Women prefer to contemplate female beauty. Oh, and women don't fall in love with the sex or gender but with *the person*. Even having a sexual orientation is a man thing, like wearing your underwear until it disintegrates.

The impetus to examine female heterosexuality came long before I thought of it as a book, well before #MeToo or contemporary gender identity discourse. And it was prompted by a nagging sense I had that society didn't see straightness, in women, as a real phenomenon. I kept getting the message that something I experienced on the regular—immediate, unambiguous, unambivalent attraction to men—didn't exist. This wasn't what women were like, apparently, yet there I was. What I understood female heterosexuality to be, from the culture, looked so little like what was taking up huge parts of my brain and my life that I found myself wondering whether I was unusual—not merely the last straight woman but the *only* straight woman—or whether, perhaps, there was something fishy about the messaging itself.

This chapter is in a sense an attempt at excavating where I was getting these messages from. What I found is that there really are several different but converging angles on why straight womanhood is fake. It's right there in highly publicized sex research and viral short stories and romantic comedies and the wedding announcements that think they're romantic comedies. I wasn't imagining things, nor was I—contrary to what the more Britcom-centric bits of this book may have you thinking—overinterpreting on the basis of niche sources.

I'm not here to say that male and female sexuality are identical, or would manifest themselves as such in a sexism-free Utopia. Depending how you measure, Team *Women are like so* has observable facts on its side. Women are on average smaller and physically weaker than men, and we're the ones who get pregnant and have babies. Even a trans-inclusive definition isn't going to throw off those averages. Men will swipe *yes I will sleep with that woman* pretty much indiscriminately on apps. There have always been rather more men prepared to pay to have sex with women than vice versa. People who have taken testosterone—cis and trans alike—report sexual desires of an intensity that my dainty lady-brain could not fathom.

But is female desire really that different from male? If women aren't sexual, what can explain all the efforts, across different societies, to curtail female sexuality? Why execute adulteresses or excise clitorises if not to keep us in check? (The existence of *slut-shaming* presupposes the existence of *slut*.) If sex is something women at most tolerate, what can explain the immense popularity of romance novels, which women read not as marital instruction manuals but as porn? If sex is just about placating husbands, why are some women the higher-libido partner in a libido-mismatched straight relationship? And if female sexuality is inherently fluid, how do we explain all the lesbians who have tried and failed at straightness, not to mention the ranks of straight women who have attempted in vain to expand their horizons?

Nobody's saying straight women aren't real, Phoebe, stop making things up. Except they are! When Emily Ratajkowski told *Harper's Bazaar*, "I don't really believe in straight people,"[3] this read not as some bizarre off-the-cuff utterance of an avant-garde eccentric, but as a celebrity aligning herself with the zeitgeist.

There are several separate theories that amount to a belief in the falseness of straight womanhood. I present each—along with my doubts—below.

STRAIGHT MEN LIKE WOMEN.
STRAIGHT WOMEN LIKE WEDDINGS.

During antiquity (2006ish), when I was a recent college grad living in Brooklyn, I remember comparing notes with female friends about a strange pattern we'd noticed in male behaviour. A woman would start seeing a new guy, would be happy with things but not overthinking it, and all of a sudden, the gentleman in question would panic about how she wanted to settle down ASAP—and do so with him—and he just wasn't ready for that kind of commitment. He needed his freedom, he was going to see the world. He liked seeing her but wasn't about to be saddled with responsibilities. He didn't want her getting notions.

The woman would be confused. Had she said she wanted to marry this man? She had not. But it was just assumed. She was *the woman* and of course this is what the woman wants, in all contexts. She had doubtless already picked an elementary school for their future children. Except she had done no such thing. So she'd be like, *Fine, go have your adventures*, and break up with him, and lo and behold, guess which of the two was demanding a commitment?

It was in this context that I began thinking about female heterosexuality as such, writing about it for *The New Republic* and on a blog I had at the time. It started to become clear to me the extent to which straightness, in women, isn't even understood as a sexual orientation in the usual sense, but as a desire to lead a conventional life. Or not even a desire—that suggests agency—but a lack of imagination about other possible paths. I was in my early twenties and kept hearing that a straight woman wants marriage and kids. I wasn't opposed to those things eventually, insofar as I thought about them at all, but this was not, shall we say, how my interest in the opposite sex manifested itself.

The straight woman, in the culture, wants the status of girlfriend, fiancée, or wife. There are rare exceptions, is the thinking—the nymphomaniacal exceptions proving the rule. But I wasn't out there Samantha-ing it up a storm, nor trying to do so. I wasn't unusually sexually voracious (though I may have been above-average afraid of pregnancy and STDs), but it was *men* I wanted, not a wedding registry. I was clear on this. Why, then, was everyone else so confused about what man-needing entailed? If the whole point of being a straight woman was doing the approved-of thing then why did I have high school crushes—crushes *on male classmates*—that I considered too embarrassing to reveal to my friends?

And yet, here I am, a married forty-year-old with two young children. Didn't I just claim to be above such preoccupations? I did not claim anything of the kind. I am, to borrow a phrase, like the other girls. Most *people* want human connection. Most, khaki-clad or not, have fairly conventional desires for love and stability, and want these things in different ways at different moments of their lives. The big difference in boringness levels isn't gender but age. By their thirties or forties, lots of people stop going out as much and start forming strong opinions about kitchen backsplashes.

The baseline confusion about female heterosexuality is this idea that *no matter her age or life stage*, a woman wants a man with second-order goals in mind. The myth is that women's interest in men—the thing we call straightness—is about status or affirmation or protection or really just about anything other than a desire to be close to a particular man or men because of that being exciting in its own right.

FEMALE DESIRE IS RESPONSIVE

"Women's desire, sexology research suggests, is more 'responsive' than men's, more likely to be sparked by methods of seduction than the always-already horny male."[4] So writes Magdalene J. Taylor in 2023 on The Cut, by way of explaining the appeal of "negging" as a pickup strategy. Alas, the 2018 article she links to as evidence, also from The Cut, makes the opposite point. It's about how research on responsive sexual desire found that this is not a uniquely female phenomenon, and that "a lot of men are out there having sex without lusting after it." Dr. Rosemary Basson, the sex researcher, "points out that the male libido is typically viewed as an innate, automatic, animal drive always ready to be aroused. Admitting that that isn't always true might feel threatening to our concept of masculinity."[5] Katherine Angel's book, *Tomorrow Sex Will Be Good Again*, which Taylor mentions, also addresses the notion of female "responsive" desire, but to complicate it, not to endorse the idea that this is women's nature. "Seeing women's desire as responsive without interrogating gendered power dynamics can quickly turn into a nightmarish coercive fantasy."[6]

There's a formula for heterosexual romance. A script. And it goes like this: A man is smitten with a female friend. She says she doesn't see him like that, but he persists. He's a nice guy—much nicer than the bad boys she's allowed to distract her—so, in the end, the woman rewards him with reciprocation. Men know who they want and pursue those people. Women haven't the foggiest and thus require guidance.

But "script" is vague. What I mean, concretely, is not just literal rom-com or sitcom scripts (such as Niles spending the first ten trillion seasons of *Frasier* pining for an oblivious Daphne) but the *New York Times* Vows column. The wedding pages offer meet-cute narratives, wherein the messy ways people actually get together are tidied up for public consumption. Tidied up, or, perhaps, selected on the basis of tidiness. It can't just be, here are two people who met, had sex, hit it off, and now they're getting married. There needs to be a story, and it must be one that readers recognize as romantic. Often, this means he noticed her from across a crowded room (or on an app), whereas she took more convincing.

The phrase "out of my league" appears incessantly in the Vows column, and with the exception of the occasional usage in a same-sex announcement, it's the bride who's out of the groom's. *She's Out of My League*, not just the title of a 2010 rom-com. One groom after the next would like *Times* readers to know that he punched above his weight. And this is not an authorial flourish but something that comes up no matter the Vows byline.

One groom, Mr. McMahon, thirty-two, had the following reaction to his betrothed: "We had never talked, but I remember seeing her across the room and thinking, 'That girl is really cute, but she's really out of my league.'"[7] An unscientific recent-years search I did yielded at least five more examples of men describing their brides in terms of league mismatch, where he got the better end of the deal. The stories all end in the same happy way: with the man learning his league is higher than he'd thought. The league assessment reinforces the idea that men are making snap judgments, while women are more malleable.

The league script is such a perfect example of how straight people are socialized to understand romance because it combines man-initiates with the quantitative rating of women. It's implied that all men would agree about which women fall where, league-wise. Never is this more explicit than in a 2014 column: "'I thought Kiki was out of my league, but she also had a down-to-earth quality and some nerdiness,' said Mr. Sirpal."[8] As this is the announcement of his marriage to Kiki, things clearly resolved. How, you might wonder? "In July 2011, Ms. Perez and Mr. Sirpal, along with some of his friends, took a trip to Nashville. It was an opportunity, he said, for his friends to see he actually was dating a '10.' 'The guys couldn't believe she was dating me,' he said with a laugh."

It's leagues, it's *sports-adjacent*. It's objective, all this rating out of ten. So in one sense it's a way to masculinize romance. But it's more fundamentally about the script according to which a man will only get married when he meets a woman he believes is more beautiful than the likes of him could get. He wouldn't curtail his freedom for just anyone!

To which one might say, isn't that just human? Who would want to be considered anything less than ravishing by their own life partner? Women, apparently. We're imagined to find it sexier, or more romantic at least, if there isn't an immediate attraction on our end. Here the epic example is a Vows where the now-bride literally *didn't know they were an item* well into the relationship: "When Robert Hall and Amy Cheng, who bonded over Chinese art, first started dating, only Mr. Hall was aware of the change in their relationship status. Months later, Ms. Cheng finally caught on."[9] This is presented—in 2023!—as charming, and not as evidence that the man was making what were, at the time, unwarranted assumptions. As presented in these *New York Times* wedding announcements—from recent years and liberal, educated environments—straight womanhood isn't a woman liking men. It's a woman awakening something in a man by her mere presence, and then not definitively turning that man down.

In *Tomorrow Sex Will Be Good Again*, Katherine Angel writes about the myth that women's sexuality isn't quite a sexuality to begin with. She points out that mental health practitioners view an absence of sexual desire as a problem that can only exist in men. In women it's considered normal, default. Women, per modern psychiatry, only ever view sex with men as a means to some non-sexual end. Angel flags a disparity in the fifth *Diagnostic and Statistical Manual of Mental Disorders*, according to which disorders of sexual desire are listed as possible only in men. This is significant, she writes, because "a woman, in the DSM, does not seem to have any sexual desire that is capable of being disordered."[10]

Angel, to be clear, is *criticizing* this disparity, not saying that it accurately describes an inherent difference in male and female sexuality. She goes on:

> In the manual, men have desire while women have incentives and motivation; men have desire disorders while women have disorders of interest and arousal. These semantic differences speak volumes: women's investment in sex is seen as more cognitive, while men's is more libidinal. Women consider sex, while men want it. Women's interest in sex is less, well, sexual.[11]

Yet this is what the popular interpretation of the supposed science of female sexual responsiveness amounts to: the supposedly incontrovertible fact that women are sexual only when someone else is sexual in our direction. Women as passive seems like the stuff of social conservatism, but one finds this on the end of the ideological spectrum as well. The transgender critic Andrea Long Chu, whose 2019 book, *Females*, defines femaleness as submissiveness, has probably done the most to perpetuate this idea in recent years. "To be female is to let someone else do your desiring for you, at your own expense."[12] While Chu is a theorist making ever so sophisticated arguments (femaleness as an abstract quality not restricted to biological women), one nevertheless arrives at the same place.

The penis visits, the vagina receives visitors, fair enough. It doesn't work to project, from this anatomical reality, a grand theory of women-are-like-so. Spend three minutes in the world of actual people, and whatever notions you may have had about a *man active, woman passive* division crumble. They don't have to hold true during sex and they make no sense whatsoever in clothed settings. Any notion that women are only aroused when prompted flies in the face of women's unprompted arousal. All it tells you is that there are some women out there having sex they weren't super up for but getting into it once it starts. Nothing about this says that same woman couldn't be having other sex, of a different kind or with someone else, that wouldn't require her coming around. Nor, for that matter, that there aren't men doing the exact same thing. There's nothing hardwired about women seeming to like whatever it is that's offered us. It's a coping strategy and no more.

WOMEN FIND NAKED MEN A TURNOFF

Given her nod to straight women's "sexual needs" in the dedication to *The Tragedy of Heterosexuality*, you might imagine Jane Ward accepts that these are a factor to reckon with, but in the book itself, she considers the possibility that straight men and women do not in fact want to have sex with one another. (She does what now? I will explain.) As evidence, she points to the straight men who insist they'll only date women who look like supermodels. (Such men are out there, but it's #notallstraightmen, and thank goodness.) More relevant, for our purposes, is her flagging of what she presents as scientific evidence that even straight women find naked men ick: "Studies show that many straight-identified women find penises 'unattractive,' are 'turned off' by images of nude men, and prefer to gaze at naked women when given the option."[13]

That's certainly the premise of the classic scene from *Seinfeld* ("The Apology," 1997) where Elaine Benes advises Jerry against being nude in front of his girlfriend, explaining that even to straight women, men's bodies are unappealing, whereas "the female body is a work of art." I've known people to bring this scene up as though it points to something true about female sexuality, but I've never been convinced it did. So I had to find out: Do studies really show that straight women would rather look at nude women than nude men?

I looked up the 2003 paper Ward cites on this point, an article interviewing "23 men and 22 women," which suggests certain limitations.[14] But however definitive this is or isn't, the paper's analysis is the opposite of Ward's conclusion. Beth Eck, the author, first explains the differences between the prevalence in our society of male versus female nudes intended as erotic or beautiful. Eck does indeed say that women look at images of one another naked, but suggests this is primarily done "as a comparison for the self." [15] The way I interpret this is, yes, we flip through magazines with scantily clad models, but this is because we enjoy(?) the way it makes us feel bad about ourselves, setting forth a process by which we buy whatever product is being sold to us, lest we be one spritz of the right perfume away from looking like the lady in the ad. A lady whose opportunities—with men, and in general—doubtless exceed our own, because I mean look at her. This is, at least, the principle behind why advertising shows a sea of mostly straight women images of stunning women and not men. It's not about all women, deep down, finding women sexier than men. (Sorry to disappoint, gentlemen.)

What Ward writes about women being supposedly put off by penises seemingly comes from "a couple in their late 20s" Eck discusses: when looking at *Playgirl* with her male partner—while being observed by the researcher—and discussing it with him, the woman claims she'd rather not see the unclothed bottom half.[16] I do not understand how you could interpret that information as women not liking to look at naked men. It is not how Eck interprets it, either. It's the story of a woman *unwilling, with her boyfriend present, to cop to appreciating another man's naked body*. Indeed, Eck finds that straight women claim an aversion to the male nude *that they don't feel* because—paradoxically—they think admitting to it would make them . . . less straight! "For women, the fear is that the active subject who captures the nude male in her gaze is not a properly heterosexual, 'feminine' subject."[17]

Yes, in the very paper Ward cites as evidence that straight women aren't into male nudes, the following sentence is found: "It appears that these women have been socialized to find the naked male body unattractive"[18] This socialization is, if anything, evidence that female heterosexuality is more robust than imagined. Yes, the women who aren't straight are asked to put on an act, to claim crushes on football quarterbacks that they do not in fact harbour. But for the women who are enthusiastically into men, the expectation is that we tone it down.

WOMEN GET OFF ON BEING THOUGHT BEAUTIFUL

To say that Kristen Roupenian's December 4, 2017, *New Yorker* short story "Cat Person" received critical acclaim for relatability would be to understate matters.[19] It's the story of a twenty-year-old college student named Margot, who has terrible sex with Robert, a man in his thirties, a Nice Guy who won't take no for an answer. It seems at first that he's been gracious about the rejection, but the story ends with his harassing text messages to her, calling her a "whore." Because "Cat Person" appeared amidst the Harvey Weinstein exposés (and in literally the same publication as some of them), it took a place in the culture alongside #MeToo-themed personal essays and reporting, rather than works of literature. Such skilful fiction that it read as a story about real people, "Cat Person" took on the cultural status of this meta-narrative of what "every woman" deals with.

I put "every woman" in quotes—not scare quotes—because this was the gist of the coverage. *The Telegraph* had the headline "The Universal Truths Every Woman Felt After Reading Cat Person." From *Nylon*: "With vivid detail, Roupenian describes the constant heightened self-awareness that every woman feels around a man they don't know very well, and even men they do."[20]

The New Yorker itself was only slightly more measured. In a companion piece, photographer Amanda Petrusich, responsible for the bad-kiss accompanying image, wrote, "Nearly every woman I spoke with about it found Roupenian's detailed articulation of a strange and terrible sexual bargaining—is it easier (or safer) for me to just let this happen, rather than to try and stop it?—queasily familiar."[21]

I almost wish I could locate Petrusich's dissenter, the lone lady on whose behalf *The New Yorker*'s famous fact-checkers demanded the inclusion of "nearly," and ask what about the story didn't speak to her experience. Was "nearly" just to cover for the existence of virgins and lesbians?

Because I, too, would need to be included under that "nearly" umbrella. A *Vox* reviewer notes that "Where 'Cat Person' is acclaimed, it's mostly for the eerie accuracy in depicting what dating is like for a 20-year-old woman," but adds a caveat. One might hope the caveat is that twenty-year-old women actually enjoy the sex they're having with men. But no, it is the requisite disclaimer about how the relatability extends only to "middle-class, thin, white" women.[22] I'm a middle-class thin white woman, a year younger than Roupenian. There is no identity-based reason for me to have found the story anything but accurate. I found it compelling and well-crafted as fiction, but did not have the OMG *been there* reaction. To me this is not a criticism. Why must art speak to your own experiences to be any good? But I can't imagine getting involved with a man who makes you feel beautiful, only to wind up in bed, consensually, with someone who *you* find repulsive. This, specifically, is a bullet I have dodged, and not by chance.

Behold, *the sex scene*, the part that sent shudders of recognition through "nearly every" female reader. First, there's Margot, eroticizing what she pictures he thinks when he's with her: "She's so perfect, her body is perfect, everything about her is perfect, she's only twenty years old, her skin is flawless, I want her so badly . . . The more she imagined his arousal, the more turned-on she got . . ."[23]

It's a kind of dissociation. Margot's desire centres on putting herself in the position of the man who desires her. Hot sex, for her, is sex that affirms her own hotness. Even so, it goes poorly. The sex with Robert is bad—this much is clear—not just because of his technique. It's bad because *she doesn't find him attractive*. "When Robert was naked, rolling a condom onto a dick that was only half visible beneath the hairy shelf of his belly, she felt a wave of revulsion that she thought might actually break through her sense of pinned stasis."

This "revulsion" at not just male shittiness but the ordinary, unwaxed, unchiselled male form is what womankind was meant to find a relatable experience. (Would anyone imagine this of gay men? OK, bad example, some probably would imagine gay men think this way, but they don't, and nor do straight women.) Having sex with a man apparently involves finding his body tolerable at best, but getting turned on by the knowledge that you made his dick hard. Close your eyes and think not of England but yourself.

For what it's worth, Alexis Nowicki, whose real-life relationship apparently inspired many of the contours of "Cat Person," wrote in *Slate* about her story diverging from the fictional treatment, and a key area was that the real-life Robert was good in bed.

There's a school of thought that female sexuality is, at its core, about wanting to be wanted. In this interpretation, female sexuality is best categorized not in terms of sexual orientation but as autogynephilia. Autogynephilia is the name for when people get off on the thought of themselves as women. The concept typically comes up in the context of transgender women. Some view it transphobic, as conflating gender identity with fetish. Then again, some transgender women are like, *yup, that's me*, and who am I to say otherwise? One of them even wrote a book on this with the intriguing title *Autohetero-sexual: Attracted to Being the Other Sex*. Let others hash out the precise relationship between autogynephilia and transness because—apologies to the British feminists—the possibility that there are men turned on by seeing themselves in the mirror in lingerie does not keep me up at night.

What's relevant, for our purposes, is the extent to which eroticizing one's own feminine allure is imagined to be the way women in general function sexually. A 2009 article by Charles Moser in the peer-reviewed *Journal of Homosexuality* found that cisgender (of whom 90 per cent were straight) and transgender women share an erotic interest in their own womanhood: "If genetic women and MTFS both endorse the same statements and exhibit the same behaviors, then autogynephilia may not be an unusual sex interest of men, but a sex interest shared by both groups; it could be a characteristic of female sexuality."[24] This is by no means a fringe view of women's desires. In a 2017 interview with Goop, the Gwyneth Paltrow–led lifestyle website, high-profile psychotherapist Esther Perel explained, "You rarely hear a woman say: *What turns me on the most is to see him really into it*. What turns her on the most, is to *be* the turn on. The secret of female sexuality is how narcissistic it is."[25] Perel frames this in feminist terms, that sex is a way for women to escape a caregiving role. I suppose you could look at it that way. But where does this leave the woman who craves a respite from being judged (favourably or otherwise) on the basis of her attractiveness? Or in simpler terms, a woman who gets off on being in bed with a man she thinks is hot?

In 2013's ubiquitous *What Do Women Want?*, the book version of a 2009 *New York Times* article of the same name, journalist Daniel Bergner tells the story of a lawyer named Isabel, whose sex with an ex-boyfriend who objectified her was much hotter than with her new one, a nice guy who doesn't mind if she wears a loose dress. Bergner then goes to a strip club with Marta Meana, a sex therapist, who informs him, "To be desired was at the heart of women's desiring."[26] This, you see, explains Isabel's deal. Women are aroused by feeling attractive, or just being in the presence of ogled women. According to Meana, for women, "'Being desired is the orgasm.'" Which leaves actual orgasms where? "Narcissism, [Meana] stressed—and she used the word not in damning judgment but in plain description—was at the core of women's sexual psyches." Hashtag not all, but Bergner goes on, explaining Meana's assessment: "The females in the audience gazed, erotically excited, at the women onstage, imagining that their own bodies were as searingly wanted as those in front of them."[27] Fascinating and extremely scientific how it's possible to read these women's minds.

In Toronto, there's a strip club I walk by frequently as it's next to H Mart. It would be impossible to overstate my interest in shopping for East Asian ingredients. But I've somehow managed to restrain myself where the naked ladies are concerned. I have no doubt that there are women who'd be "erotically excited" in such a context, who would find boobs more exciting than all varieties of dried seaweed, each with its own culinary function, but I would not assume it was because they were "imagining that their own bodies were as searingly wanted as those in front of them."

Is narcissistic eroticism just how female sexuality operates? Per the experts, yes. But not in my personal experience. Nor, more importantly, per the sitcom canon. The Cloris Leachman character on the later seasons of *The Facts of Life*, wherein she is and isn't her "Phyllis" character from *The Mary Tyler Moore Show* and *Phyllis*, plays a sassily sexy middle-aged woman, whose exact quasi-maternal relationship to the girls (now young women) on the boarding school sitcom is I'm sure explained but immaterial for our purposes. There's a 1987 episode ("A Rose by Any Other Age") where a younger man is into her, and she's telling her castmates (younger women, one of whom had hoped to date this man) that she isn't sure if what she feels for him is being flattered at his attentions or a genuine attraction. To her, these are two distinct experiences. They can be difficult to separate, but you've got to try.

The distinction is best articulated, however, by Blanche, a.k.a. the "slutty" one, in a 1986 *The Golden Girls* episode. Her twenty-year-old niece is visiting Miami, sleeping through the bulk of its men within the course of a few days. Blanche objects, and the niece says she's one to talk. The show part-celebrates, part-mocks Blanche's promiscuity, but however that shakes out, the fact of the matter is, this is Blanche's central trait. So why the double standard?

Blanche clarifies that there's a difference between what she does and what the niece is up to, and it's not about age. She admits that she "enjoy[s] the company of gentlemen" and "always" has done. There's no coyness, no self-censorship for the benefit of a younger relation. Twenty was a grown-up in those days. And Blanche articulates why she sleeps around, in a way that makes clear this is something she's considered: "When I'm with a man, it's 'cause I like him, not 'cause I want him to like me."[28]

All I could think when I heard Blanche deliver this line was, *that's it*, that's the whole entire point of this book, and she just blurted it out, before I'd even started preschool.

Blanche is no bra-burning feminist. She's intensely concerned with her own looks, vain in the old-school sense of hoping others think she's gorgeous while also convinced that they do. This is a character who contemplates extensive cosmetic surgery and goes around announcing that she's an attractive woman in her forties, which she doubtless once was. But this preoccupation is utilitarian. Someone with her insatiable needs requires men who reciprocate. Her end goal is pleasure-seeking, not people-pleasing. She's not out to cheerlead for men generally, and when cads or sexual harassers bother her or her friends, she's the first to shut that down. She likes the men she likes; there just happen to be a lot of them. And it's Blanche's genuine, uncomplicated enjoyment of men that distinguishes her from other sitcom nymphomaniacs, the ones presented as having loose morals or as trying to find love in all the wrong places. She isn't trying to compensate for something or to fill a metaphorical void. For Blanche, there is no doubt: orgasms are the orgasm.

Lest you think what I'm describing is some quirk of the 1980s that I share in, like pastel floral drop-waist dresses (of which I own several and would never speak ill), think again: In 2024, on the culture website Dirt, Daisy Alioto asked a bunch of largely female writers and creative types to answer the question "Is it better to desire, or be desired?"[29] And "to desire" was the clear winner. Some of the responses get at the way women are expected to want to be desired, only to be like, nope, not what does it for me. As writer Sari Botton puts it, "Well, I was raised to believe the latter was better. I'm learning to prioritize the former." Katy Kelleher's response also gets at the way such sentiments evolve: "I used to think it was better to be desired but now I know it's better to desire. There are more possibilities in desiring/yearning."

I don't have any interest in climbing into anyone's brain and telling them what they should be thinking about during sex. If what does it for you is thinking what a beautiful woman you are, then knock yourself out, whether or not "beautiful" (or "woman") accurately describes what others see when they look at you. What I have a problem with is the myth that this is how women are wired, when it is so abundantly clear that it's what we're pointed towards doing, so that we keep up (and keep spending money on) our own looks, or so that we don't objectify men.

STRAIGHT WOMEN—AND LESBIANS—ARE BISEXUAL

"Are All Women Turned on by Other Women?" A *Men's Journal* headline, doubtless typed with one hand, answers this non-question exactly as you know it will. Sure enough, according to science (something to do with pupil dilation), the hot barista you've been eyeing, man-who-is-reading-this, not only wants you but also has an even hotter friend she'll be bringing over later.

By 2022, when that headline appeared, the supposed scientific fact of women's potential for infinite arousal was already old news. The big one came from a scientist named Meredith Chivers, who real-time monitored the vaginas of a bunch of women in a lab in Toronto.[30] Straight women and lesbians claimed to be aroused by what one would expect, but their anatomy reacted to nearly all stimuli, including randy bonobos. Gay and straight men, meanwhile, were found to like what they liked, per this same method. As Daniel Bergner memorably (at least, I remember it) reported for *The New York Times* in 2009, "The genitals of the volunteers were connected to plethysmographs—for the men, an apparatus that fits over the penis and gauges its swelling; for the women, a little plastic probe that sits in the vagina and, by bouncing light off the vaginal walls, measures genital blood flow."[31]

While this is easily the most interesting thing to have ever happened in Toronto—I live here, I can say this—I've heard about this study for years but never found it entirely persuasive. Can female anatomical arousal really be used as a proxy for desire? How can this be, when women have been known to get wet and even orgasm during rape, which is to say, during sexual activity they did not want?[32]

What if physiological arousal, in women, can mean different things, one of them being, effectively, *this seems sexual and will involve me whether I want it or not, so I'd rather it not hurt*?

The thing is, researchers themselves aren't claiming that this sort of research scientifically disproves that women have sexual orientations. *They* know that physiological responses are interesting and all, but not definitive. They do not suggest women leave their husbands or wives for bonobos. Women do seem to have evolved to prepare our bodies for whatever may come on the sex front as injury prevention.[33] The more careful interpreters of the data, like Katherine Angel, urge listening to what women say they want over taking the plethysmograph for some sort of genitally based lie-detector test.

Given that measurable physiological sexual response in women is not analogous to the hard-on, you'd think we could quickly dispense with the idea that According To Science, women are lying when they claim exclusive attraction to men or women. But there's stronger research, albeit with issues of its own, that involves studying women's lives, not our anatomy.

If you've heard murmurings about women being sexually fluid, whether you're aware of it or not, you're under the intellectual influence of another Bergner interviewee: Lisa M. Diamond, the University of Utah psychology professor whose 2008 book, *Sexual Fluidity: Understanding Women's Love and Desire*, set the whole thing forth. I'd been hearing about women's supposed fluidity for ages, wondering what to make of it as a sexual solid. So imagine my surprise when I actually read the book and learned that this truism about women's wiring comes from a decade-long study of one hundred women, of whom precisely eleven identified as heterosexual. Diamond hadn't even intended to include straight women at all—her focus was on women who were at least somewhat attracted to other women, to see how same-sex attractions varied over time—but recruited some (from a gender studies class) to serve as a control group. I'm no statistician, but it seems possible that a random eleven straight-identifying gender studies students might prove heteroflexible (not that they all did; getting to that part) without this telling you much about straight womanhood more generally. Because what she found was that all the straight women in her study "reported having a current or past pattern of emotionally intense bonds to female friends."[34] Some might look at this and say, alert the presses, eleven straight women have not experienced lifelong friendlessness. Diamond presents it otherwise:

> Fluidity appears to manifest itself similarly in both heterosexual and sexual-minority respondents, the primary difference being that heterosexual women take the gap between their physical and emotional attractions more seriously than do sexual-minority women: in their estimation, if their attractions to women are exclusively emotional, then they are probably not gay.[35]

Beneath the academic language, what's happening here is, Diamond uses the fact that straight women have female friends—friends they *don't want to sleep with*—as evidence for women's inherent sexual fluidity. The "probably" is incredible, allowing as it does for the possibility that a woman with zero physical attraction to other women might be gay.

Understandably, Diamond—who thanks her wife in the acknowledgements and so has skin in the game—pays careful attention to the ways anti-gay activists could (and have) used her research to further their cause. If sexuality is fluid, they'd argue, why can't gay people be conversion-therapied into heterosexuality? Diamond tries to address this, explaining that fluidity doesn't mean people can choose their attractions, nor that women lack sexual orientations. That said, she also argues that "the existence of sexual fluidity would mean that all women are sensitive to interpersonal and situational influences on their sexuality, albeit to different degrees."[36] Also that "we may never accurately predict the future course of a woman's sexuality on the basis of her current or prior experiences."[37] The use of absolutes—"all women," "never"—makes for a strongly argued book. But it winds up being its own way of erasing human complexity, and cannot help but give credence to the idea that women categorically lack fixed, non-negotiable sexual orientations in the sense usually meant by this.

Indeed, Diamond argues that what we think of as sexual orientation is specific to men. Women, who remain under-researched in human sexuality as in other fields, are not merely men with different bits (remember that 2008 was a different universe on the trans-awareness front), but have our own ways of being. And it's an appealing argument in the abstract. In a world where people are always trying to claim that you're on a path towards becoming your true self, it's exciting to see someone insisting that you're equally *you* throughout your life. The person you are at fifteen is just as authentic as the one you are at fifty-five. There's no such thing as "going through a phase," except insofar as life is made up of phases. Diamond points to famous and ordinary women who've had male and female partners at different points. Rather than insisting that these are straight or gay women in denial, why not accept that they've been genuinely interested in both?

To which one might counter: OK, yes, bisexuality exists, and these women are bi, mystery solved. More women than men identify as bisexual and therefore may have male and female partners. While there are more gay men than lesbians, if you add up the number of same-sex-attracted men versus women, women are reliably—and increasingly, with younger generations—in the lead.

There are some who argue that the world is headed towards universal bisexuality. "In this future, the vast majority of people will be open to the possibility of both opposite-sex and same-sex desires, regardless of whether they act upon them," writes activist Peter Tatchell,[38] to which *I* would ask, what does that openness entail? It seems odd to me that one would conflate an absence of personal or ethical objections to same-sex attractions with the actual *having* of those attractions. These are two different categories: *straight person who isn't a raging homophobe* and *bisexual*. I consider myself "open to the possibility" of any number of things that seem massively unlikely given past experience. This is nevertheless what it means to say that a straight woman with no principled objections to others' lesbianism or bisexuality is exhibiting sexual fluidity.

But fluidity, as Diamond defines it, is not bisexuality. She points out that the women themselves often ascribe other labels—or none at all—to their sexuality, or different ones depending on their partner at the time. To apply a blanket *they're just bi* approach would be to force their sexually fluid, infinite-capacity-having selves into a box, all in the name of artificially creating a sense of lifelong consistency where none exists. Nor is fluidity a characteristic specific to the women who date men and women at different times. Rather, it is *the fundamental truth about female sexuality*. If you're a woman, your sexuality is fluid. If your sexuality is not fluid, you are either a man or, I suppose, chopped liver.

The fluidity framework strikes me as misapplied where straight women are concerned. It is somewhat more useful in making sense of the lesbian-identified women who make life choices one would more commonly associate with straight or bisexual women. The highest-profile example of the latter would have to be Chirlane McCray, wife of former New York City mayor Bill de Blasio. *The New*

York Times profiled the couple about the ultimate demise of their union, with de Blasio admitting, "'For the guy who took the chance on a woman who was an out lesbian and wrote an article called I Am a Lesbian,' he wasn't sure the marriage would stick.[39] And yet the two were married for decades and had two children. They're a candid pair, and theirs was by all accounts not a companionate marriage. Fluidity theory allows someone like this to call herself lesbian rather than bisexual or queer, without needing to address the tall-husband-sized elephant in the room.

Or consider the case of a then-sixty-six-year-old comparative literature professor suspended for sexually harassing her thirty-four-year-old male grad student. The Avital Ronell story broke in 2018, as part of a mini-wave of women getting #MeToo downfalls. (The other one was Asia Argento.) But here, there was a twist. As an epic *Advocate* headline announced: "Investigation Finds Lesbian Professor Sexually Harassed Gay Student." How this lesbianism squared with her alleged actions towards Nimrod Reitman, I cannot say: "Mr. Reitman . . . says that Professor Ronell kissed and touched him repeatedly, slept in his bed with him, required him to lie in her bed, held his hand, texted, emailed and called him constantly, and refused to work with him if he did not reciprocate." Sounds extremely lesbian. But again, if women are sexually fluid, there's nothing remarkable about a woman who calls herself a lesbian getting quasi-cancelled (she went back to teaching and everyone other than me—and presumably Reitman—forgot about the whole thing) for an inability/unwillingness to keep her mitts off a handsome man.

But Ronell's authenticity as a lesbian is not what interests me here. It's that if any woman is relatively free from the clutches of compulsory heterosexuality, it would be a lesbian-identified New York University humanities professor. This is not someone who'd be invested in having the people around them think they're straight. I cannot claim to know Ronell's mind, but it seems unlikely that she saw in Reitman, who among other things is (actually) gay, a sensible life partner who would become Mr. Ronell and confer some hetero respectability she'd always secretly wanted. More likely, she did as men have done since time immemorial and exploited her position of power over someone she found attractive and who would never in a million years have paid her any mind were it not for a professional relationship.

Diamond's concept of sexual fluidity sheds light on what might seem, on its surface, a re-closeting. Rather than thinking of a Chirlane McCray or an Avital Ronell as a fake lesbian, "fluidity" rejects the very notion of consistency. The lesbian who seeks sex with men is therefore not a curiosity or a failed lesbian but merely expressing female sexuality in its normal state. I see why Diamond's thesis would be appealing to women who see themselves reflected in that narrative. I also get why—for all the book's 2008ish gender essentialism, painstakingly discussed on Goodreads—fluidity theory might reassure cisgender women whose partners transition and who (unlike cisgender men, as a rule, in this circumstance) opt to stay in the relationship. There's a sense in which fluidity just means your sexual orientation doesn't have to be carved in stone, and that much seems potentially liberating, albeit with an air of *it's a woman's prerogative to change her mind*. There is also, of course, the less upbeat interpretation, which is that fluidity theory could make women feel as though they *must* stay with a partner who transitions, because what sort of woman other than a bigot would have such body-specific requirements in a partner?

While reading *Sexual Fluidity*, I kept thinking of a scene from a *Sex and the City* episode where Charlotte tries to join a lesbian clique, only to learn that lesbianism is about more than girl power.[40] She's about to go on a trip with her new girl gang, when one of them asks her, bluntly, "Are you gay?" Charlotte demurs:

> "No, no I'm not, but I do so enjoy the company of all these women. Everyone's so smart and funny, and after spending way too much time and attention on men, it feels like such a safe, warm environment. And while sexually, I feel that I am straight, there's a very powerful part of me that connects to the female spirit."

Charlotte's answer is exactly the sort of thing Diamond would classify as evidence of even straight women's sexual fluidity. But in context, going by the way Kristin Davis as Charlotte delivers the lines, the viewer understands that this is not a woman expressing heretofore unknown capacities, but rather a straight-lady interloper who's mixed up the idea of girlfriends with *girlfriends*. One of Charlotte's new pals says it best: "Sweetheart, that's all very nice, but if you're not going to eat pussy, you're not a dyke."

There, in so few words, is as definitive a test for sexual orientation as you're going to get.

That said, what's at stake isn't merely willingness to sleep with a woman—something no shortage of straight women and gay men have expressed—but rather a burning desire to do so. The stories of women who gave the ladies a go, not out of lust but because they felt (for a variety of reasons) they should, shed light on why.

"THE COLLEGE TRY"

Can a straight woman opt to tap into this inherent fluidity flowing within us all? Jane Ward, author of *The Tragedy of Heterosexuality*, makes this case. In her earlier book, *Not Gay*, she recalls hookups with "boring straight men," sprinkled amidst her queer relationships. She abandoned these hetero liaisons for political reasons.[41] If straight women are so miserable, they could just . . . not be straight. After all, it worked for her. If fluidity theory is correct then we could all do the same. That we cannot is why I have my doubts.

There's a 2015 song about just this phenomenon by the comedy act Garfunkel and Oates. "The College Try"[42] is sung from the perspective of a woman who has come to the enlightened conclusion that "people are just people," only to sleep with a woman and feel "repelled like negatively charged ions in a magnetic field." There are many unflattering yet hilarious sensory descriptors of what female anatomy is like up close. But what's more pertinent here is the way the song protagonist's sense of self is shattered once she realizes that a belief in the idea of transcending sexual orientation does not amount to . . . transcending sexual orientation: "I mourn the cool new life I'd envisioned / Where love renders gender preference obsolete / 'Cause when I looked a vagina in the eye / I made a hasty, ungraceful retreat."

The song is told from the perspective of a straight woman, as in a first-person-singular persona of the two women singing it. But it could just as easily be interpreted as a satire of straight women aimed at gay or bi women who've been *on the receiving end* of a look of horror along those lines from an experimenting straight woman, something the favourable YouTube comments on it, from self-identified lesbian and bisexual women, would support.

For some straight women, it does not take being nose-to-vulva to realize women are not for you. Conversely, there are others who give sex with women a go and don't recoil in horror. Surely these women are what fluidity is all about? Not so much.

In her memoir *Bad Sex,* Nona Willis Aronowitz recounts an attempt at extricating herself from heterosexuality. Prompted by a substantial feminism-past-and-present reading list, a disappointing marriage, and #MeToo-inspired disgust at patriarchy, Aronowitz undergoes a kind of self-administered conversion therapy, albeit in the progressive direction. She decides to "truly contemplate what it would mean for me to select my sexual orientation."[43]

So she decides to give lesbianism—or, rather, queerness—a shot. She knows that in her social environment, "being queer seemed far more modern than clinging to heterosexuality." Straightness was a quality she found embarrassing and so she decided she would dispense with it. But after some dues-paying encounters, she concluded that "when it came to sex, I preferred the bodies and energy of cis men."[44]

My initial thought was how insensitive this quest must seem to queer people from traditionalist families, who face actual consequences for living their truths, consequences more dire than feeling a bit basic. But maybe some people really do live in milieus where it's shameful to be cishet, and she's one of them. She also didn't believe in being a straight woman given the current state of gender relations. "I continued to doubt that someone with my values and interest in sexual exploration would fail to tap into their queer side, especially because things between men and women were so plainly bad."[45] Alas, the same rigidity that prevents gay people in homophobic environments from opting into straightness makes it impossible for a straight person to will a "queer side" into existence where there is none.

Aronowitz explains that women didn't repulse her but also didn't turn her on, which seems maybe a bit sad from the perspective of the women she was sleeping with. She has read *The Tragedy of Heterosexuality*, and at Jane Ward's prompting, she interrogates what it is about cis men she's so fond of. She offers an artful ode to the erect member but concludes that her reasons for man-loving cannot be put into words. "Ultimately, I didn't owe anyone an explanation—another lesson I've gleaned from queer friends who refuse to back up the authenticity of their sexual identity with data points." And yet the "queer friends" evoked serve as "data points," because without their implied support, she's just some straight lady. Aronowitz quotes a trans woman who had delved into her own sexual attractions, only to establish: "Who cares? I like men, and that's that."[46] After a lot of hand-wringing and time-wasting, and only once granted permission by an off-screen cast of queer arbiters, Aronowitz lands at the only reasonable place on this topic: We like who we like. All attempts to articulate *why* we have the sexual orientations we do are just awkward attempts at retrofitting rational explanations where none exist.

On paper, Aronowitz is the kind of woman Diamond cites as an example of sexual fluidity. After all, here's a straight woman who has had sex with women without fully hating it! But sleeping with women leads her to a distinctly non-fluid conclusion about her sexual identity. She's living proof that you can be surrounded by queer friends and deeply read on the topic of political lesbianism, that you can do your gender-studies homework and despise Donald Trump, and still need your intimate relationships to be with men.

But I'm glad Aronowitz did her college-try experiment, because it addresses, at last, whether *everyone is queer* is any more liberating than *everyone is straight*. Setting aside the inevitable leading-on of queer women involved, is it being fair to *yourself*, as a straight woman, to have sex you're not excited about from the get-go out of some abstract belief that you should?

Though also set in a liberal Brooklyn enclave in the 2010s, the world of Molly Roden Winter's hit 2024 polyamory memoir *More: A Memoir of Open Marriage* is thoroughly—unselfconsciously—heterosexual. Gay people barely register. She suspects her therapist is gay upon meeting him, but this is never established, and is seemingly only relevant insofar as he's a rare man mentioned who is never a love interest. Trans people were (I can attest) out and about in the borough and decade in question, but none of them figure in this story. I say this not to fault the book—although I guess one could harangue the author with *doesn't she know that queer people* INVENTED *polyamory*, if one were so inclined—but because this indicates something about the persistence of heterosexuality as a way of life, even among people living within walking distance of bars offering a plethora of options.

It is only over halfway through *More* that Winter first broaches the topic of including other women in her escapades. "In college, and immediately after, I'd had a few crushes on female friends, though I was never sure if my attraction to women was truly sexual."[47] But her husband had an ex-girlfriend who presented herself for such an encounter, and Winter was—as she so often is, in the book—happy to oblige. She even found a way to describe this as something she was doing for herself. "Maybe an FFM threesome would be a safe way to test the depths of my bisexuality."[48] I read this sentence a bunch of times because . . . "my bisexuality"? Her what now? This is a woman whose zeal for sex with different men has been well-established. In context, it does not appear she was genuinely confused about her sexual orientation, but rather that this is part of what being *modern* about sex consists of.

You will be stunned to learn that the extent of this "bisexuality" is nil. Recalling how this three-way played out, she writes, "I expected sex with a woman to be soft and gentle . . . But it never occurred to me that a woman's touch would be a turn*off*."[49]

Again, Garfunkel and Oates: "I thought it'd be smooth and non-threatening / Or nonexistent like Barbie's / Instead it looks like a half-eaten Beef and Cheddar / In the garbage can at Arby's."

Fluidity discourse gives straight women the impression that sex with a woman is something they'd at least find a little bit nice. But as gay men can attest, it's not for everyone.

Nevertheless, Winter decides she must say yes to a different two-women-one-man threesome, many years later, with her (extramarital) boyfriend and his girlfriend, for reasons she herself can't quite articulate. None appears to have anything to do with wanting to have sex with a woman generally or that one in particular. Unfortunately, this new lover's girlfriend is the genuine article and considers straight women not a category inherently unattainable to her, but a challenge.

Aronowitz and Winter arrive at kissing-a-girl-and-not-liking-it under different circumstances. Winter isn't trying to will herself into lesbianism, and Aronowitz isn't trying women at the behest of any men. But what the stories have in common—apart from geography, and adventures very possibly undertaken with literary content in mind—is this idea that sexual adventurousness, for a woman, inherently includes giving women a go.

I was going to say that the same is not assumed of men, that a man gets to be sexually adventurous just by doing interesting things with impressive numbers of women, or wishing he were. But that's not even it, because "sexually adventurous" is such a gendered term to begin with. People tend not to refer to men in this way, because it is what's presumed of men generally.[50] Women are the ones thought to come in various degrees of adventurousness. And adventurousness isn't the same as desire.

The unsuccessfully sexually fluid straight woman is not a 2020s-specific phenomenon. Meghan Daum's 2014 essay "Honorary Dyke"[51] is a tongue-in-cheek exploration of the author as straight woman trapped in a lesbian's coveralls. Daum describes being drawn to lesbian culture and indeed to many lesbians themselves. Fluidity theory might seem a perfect fit for Daum, who describes a childhood with intense albeit non-sexual feelings towards other girls, and even has one romantic relationship with another woman . . . which leads her to realize she is not even the slightest bit gay. She's drawn to the *trappings* of lesbianism, to an aesthetic or attitude stereotypically associated with lesbians, and this just feels like a natural next step. There's only one problem: women don't do it for her.

Things do get more confusing when she writes about a consistent platonic attraction to actual lesbians. Is that not, at last, female sexual fluidity in action? But this is more about how she enjoys . . . not so much sexually attracting lesbians as *passing as one* herself. She associates lesbians with being chic and interesting—the same as she regards Jews in her 2001 essay "American Shiksa." (I am neither chic nor interesting, but I'll take the compliment.)

"Honorary Dyke" is less about lesbianism than about the limitations on female heterosexual identity. Daum feels alienated from conventional femininity—"long lair, long fingernails, a skilled and thought-out approach to cosmetics"—which convinces her that she must in some way be into women. She reflects on how her preferred self-presentation made it harder to attract men, noting that she could have—but didn't—treat the fact that women looked her over more than men did as the "constructive feedback" it was.[52] (She has since, she writes, adopted a less "butch" look.) She's put off by media representations of women as "not only . . . a special interest group" but one "whose primary interest is themselves."[53] She's not excited by dieting and clothes shopping, nor having her eyelashes extended. She is, however, interested in men, and lives in a society that expects these inclinations to match up.

What Daum, Winter, and Aronowitz all demonstrate is that consenting to same-sex encounters is not the same as having same-sex desires. Motivation is complicated, and people are game for experiences for all kinds of reasons. The test, as it were, is not whether you'd vomit if faced with another woman's vagina—straight female gynecologists seem capable of keeping down their lunch—but whether that's a situation you could imagine being devastated *not* to experience. Yes, we all get to pick our own labels. But if words are going to mean anything, I'm not sure you can say that a woman is sexually fluid or bisexual if she has never been in agony over *not* being able to get into another woman's pants. Along the same lines, I'd have trouble calling a woman "straight" if she exclusively dated men but found this a chore and was only doing so because she saw no other option. Desire is about curiosity, but also the pain of not getting, the preoccupation of wondering if you stand a chance. That female heterosexuality persists even where bisexuality or lesbianism would be welcomed seems like the strongest evidence there is that straight women are real.

THINK OF THE LESBIANS

In high school, circa 2000, a friend taught me the phrase "bi now, gay later." This was almost certainly in reference to some ill-fated crush I had at the time. But it refers to how young gay men will often do a waters-testing pitstop where they're out as bisexual. The sentiment behind this expression is understandably irritating to bisexual men, whose orientation is its own end point. You don't see this as often in reference to women. It's not that bisexual women are universally believed, but that skepticism so often goes in the other direction, namely that she's straight but thinks she's more interesting than the husband-having plebs.

But the queer-lady-with-husband phenomenon can be evidence that the social pressure on women to have husbands is so great—still—that even women meh about men wind up marrying them. For some women, it's easier to say who they are than to live it.

Kimberly Zapata's 2020 personal essay "I'm a Queer Woman and I'm Married to a Man"describes the heartache of realizing she was (effectively) a lesbian once married to a man.[54] She started by coming out to her husband as bi, but he was *into it* and this alerted her to her truth: "I wasn't bisexual. That was a cop-out. That was a lie. I was a woman who *really* loved women. Today, I identify as queer." But the world sees one of those straight ladies who calls herself "queer" for no particular reason: "I still live very much 'in the closet,' i.e. I present as a heterosexual woman, living a 'normal' heterosexual life." She's in that boat because she loves her husband in a non-sexual way, because they have kids, and possibly because of religion (she mentions "my pastor"). The reason she's exclusively attracted to women but married to a man has zilch to do with fluidity and everything to do with a closing-off of options.

Paradoxically, the insistence that women are sexually fluid can make it *harder* for lesbians to come out. I think of a *Savage Lovecast* caller, a twenty-five-year-old "bisexual" who spent "90 per cent" of her intimate moments with her boyfriend thinking about other women. Dan Savage suggested she and the boyfriend consider an open relationship that allowed her to see women on the side. As I see it, this woman should at least consider *gay* as a possibility. A man who fantasizes about other men 90 per cent of the time while in bed with his girlfriend *could* be bi, but he—and goodness knows his girlfriend, if he told her—would allow that he might be a gay man. But once it's established that bi-curiosity is effectively a part of female heterosexuality, it becomes more difficult to make the leap towards realizing there are women whose same-sex attractions are anything but peripheral.

The myth that women, as a class, aren't physically attracted to men can be confusing for . . . the women who are not, in fact, physically attracted to men. One such woman posted on Reddit that she considered herself straight, even though she was attracted to women and put off by men. Sure, she found the idea of man-woman sex revolting and only watched lesbian porn, but that's just, she figured, how women are. So she asked fellow forum participants: "Do straight women actually enjoy men? Are they actually attracted to men? I know this sounds stupid, but I always just assumed women weren't seriously attracted to men."[55] It doesn't sound stupid. It sounds like this is a woman who has internalized a widespread myth.

She's not the only Redditor confused along these lines. A different post—"Are straight girls actually physically attracted to guys?"—delves further into these matters. One of the replies clarifies: "Imagine how you think a gay man might feel about guys. Then imagine that a woman felt that way. Boom, you now understand straight girls." A part of me can't get over that this needs to be *explained*. But . . . it does! It's *not* self-evident that women want sex with men. Not with all that one hears about women as sexual gatekeepers. Not with a cultural conversation stuck on the sex men demand of women and that women, at most, put up with.

Another commenter spells out how the myth that all women are grossed out by men made it an uphill battle for her to realize she was a lesbian. She explains that "like 99% of the time" she saw the woman in a straight couple as "way out of his league." (Leagues!) Eventually she realized this was not a comment on women's objective superiority but rather on which people caught her eye. "This is a genuine reason I kept dating guys for a while, 'cause I thought secretly most women felt this way."[56] How would she *not* have thought this? It is a part of mainstream culture to say that women are too good for the men they're with. It's in best-man speeches and feminist think pieces alike.

STRAIGHT WOMEN ARE REAL

Men and women are different, so it stands to reason that there are population-level differences in how heterosexuality operates in each. Innate differences, such as the small matter of where babies come from, play a role, as do biological but malleable factors like hormones, as do cultural factors. I have never once heard of a woman reacting to a history lecture by visiting a lady (or gentleman) of the night, and don't expect I will. But going by my own experiences and some of what I've observed beyond my own perhaps-unrepresentative example, human sexuality is a whole lot closer to the thing experts call "male sexuality," but for largely cultural reasons, women are not allowed access to it. Women are socialized out of going after what we want, especially but not exclusively in the sexual arena. We're expected to be agreeable, receptive, open to suggestions. To wait for the man to make the first move.

The theories about straight women not existing are all just a little too convenient. Straight men rather famously enjoy looking at beautiful women, and if two or more of those women get together, all the better. The fluidity hypothesis is not the liberation it may seem. Willingness to sleep with someone of any gender or anatomy is not so much a "fundamental" element of female sexuality, but what happens when women do not feel empowered to bluntly state what they do and don't want. It is of a piece with a culture that expects women not to care what the men they're involved with look like. If women see sex as fundamentally about our own bodies and what those look like—the narcissism hypothesis—then we're not looking too closely at the bodies of the men we're sleeping with. Women don't care about the physical traits of their lovers, according to science, so why should a straight man need to bathe or work out or eat a vegetable? And if female sexuality is responsive, what even is a *no*, anyway? Fluidity, responsive desire, all these fancy ways of trying to reclaim amenability as our superpower. I'm not convinced.

FIVE

Are Straight Women Gay Men?

SYLVIA FINE: She thought that you could meet the man of her dreams hanging around gay bars.

FRAN FINE: Ma, I said Zabar's.

—*The Nanny*[1]

"I FEEL IT IN HER VOICE"

There are many *Savage Lovecast* calls that have stuck with me over the years. But one from 2017 stands out even in that field, crowded as it is with centaur fetishists and husbands asking Dan Savage permission to step out on wives who've just given birth to *their kids*. The call I'm talking about is tamer than most, less sex question than riddle.[2] It begins, "As you can hear, probably, a lot of people think I'm a female, but I actually identify as a trans man." The "probably" is a stretch. But voice-depth or lack thereof is the least of it. The caller explains that he "present[s] as a female," and has no immediate plans to medically transition, *and* that this is not because of material obstacles. He just doesn't feel he owes this to his "community." Principle of the thing. He reserves the right to be a gay man, no matter his physical presence. Or even his attire, which includes "feminine clothes" as well as other clothes, a description that would also cover just about every cisgender woman's wardrobe.

We thus have someone who looks and sounds like a woman, who reads as female in virtually all situations *due to his own self-presentation choices*, and who is taking no steps beyond the linguistic to disabuse anyone of the notion that he's a she.

Now for his dilemma: "I can't get anyone in the gay community to date me or take me seriously as a gay man."

As riddles go, it's a good one: How do you find a willing lover among the people whose defining trait is not wanting to sleep with you? Complex as the question sounds, the answer is disappointingly simple: You don't. As far as fantasies are concerned, he'd have had better luck with a centaur.

Savage invites guest Buck Angel, a female-to-male transsexual (Angel's own preferred term), to help answer the question. Angel is male-presenting, certainly more male-sounding than the caller, but has not had all the procedures on offer. He is evidently making a go of it in the vagina-scarce professional realm of gay porn actor, and more power to him. His mere presence is a data point in favour of the notion that there are, in this world, *some* gay men who will sleep with *some* vagina-havers. A reminder that the issue with the caller is not that he is a trans gay man, but rather that he is an adamantly non-passing one.

Something jumps out in Angel's response. "I feel for this person. I feel it in her voice, I feel how much they really want to be taken seriously as a person who identifies as a trans man."

"Her." "They." Whoops.

If it is difficult even for Angel to say "he"—not out of malice, but rather the automatic response to a caller with *that voice*—what hope does anyone have who's less versed in the issues? Savage's own diagnosis is a blunt-but-fair assessment that "this person would rather complain than get laid." Indeed, the caller's insistence on not sleeping with the straight-identified men available to him tells us that this is voluntary celibacy. A bisexual man, Savage suggests, might be drawn to both the caller's female-presenting reality and masculine self-perception. The caller, though, is dead set on finding *gay* men who would look at him, a person with the complete physicality of a woman, and see a fellow man.

There's a saying, "a gay man trapped in a woman's body." This was used, in less *aware* eras, as a lighthearted way to describe women who related to a gay male sensibility, or whose unabashed enthusiasm for sex with men strayed from the gendered-female expectation to only have sex as a means to an end. Today, a cis woman who refers to herself "trapped" in this way would offend, or give the impression that she is stuck in the early 2000s. (Same thing, really. To be passé is to offend.) An earnest 2017 *Huffington Post* essay, "No Dear, You're Not a Gay Man Trapped in a Woman's Body," alerts the straight women that the utterance dismisses the plight of trans and cis gay men, marginalized populations whose culture should not be our costume. But here, in this podcast call, we have the genuine article. A person who's 100 per cent woman on the outside, 100 per cent gay man inside, trapped by his own stubbornness. How would someone end up in that doubtless frustrating state?

Maybe the caller's problem is that he's simply taken gender self-identification to its logical conclusion. One hears that *there's no such thing as "looking like a man."* Also that *you can't always tell a person's gender just by looking at them*. Both are true in the abstract. But it doesn't work, as a practical matter, to present entirely one way and expect to be received—particularly in a sexual context—in another.

I have an alternate theory. It violates *thou shalt not question people's stated identities*, but given that this person is an anonymous caller to a sex advice podcast now several years old, I think I'm in the clear. My hypothesis, then, is that the caller is *not* best understood as a gay man trapped in a woman's body. I have no qualms about using he / him pronouns for someone who requests this. His experience, if not identity, is nevertheless that of . . . a straight woman with an unrealizable fantasy.

I know what you're thinking. Or rather, I know the two possibilities. Some of you are going to stop reading right here and label me an irredeemable TERF, this despite being quite clear that I absolutely think trans gay men exist, just that this particular caller is . . . complicated. Others, however, including some members of the LGB-without-the-T community, will read the above advice-call summary and be more like, *Of course she's a straight woman, what else* would *she be?*

"A CLASSIC MILLENNIAL SEX PICKLE"

In January 2020—pre-pandemic, Trump administration, so same general universe as the 2017 one—an advice-column letter appeared entitled "I'm a Heterosexual Woman Who's Politically Opposed to Heterosexuality. Who Do I Date?"[3] The letter-writer describes herself to *Slate* sex advice columnist Rich Juzwiak as "a cis woman in kind of a classic millennial sex pickle: I'm really repelled by heterosexuality politically and personally, but I'm also really into dick." Juzwiak disputes that this is a "classic millennial sex pickle," but it kind of is. She has been consuming the millennial-oriented Ban Men content of the #MeToo era and knows that she is meant to find her own heterosexuality repugnant. You might imagine her options would be male feminists or—someone has to say it—penis-havers who don't identify as men. It is, after all, "dick" she wants. She has another idea, which she runs by Juzwiak. She could seek out "bi dudes/bicurious gay dudes," if only she knew where to find them. "Rich," she asks, "what would you think of a woman being on Grindr or Scruff?" The place she thinks she, a woman, should seek out sex partners is on apps where men look for other men.

While the tone and identity categories are different, we are somehow back in the headspace of the *Savage Lovecast* caller. Here, once again, is a female-bodied individual who wants to be with men but, to borrow a phrase, *no hetero*. She likes men, but in a way that is somehow different from what those *straight women* experience. She's queer . . . in the manner of her liking of men.

Working in the *Slate* letter-writer's favour is that she understands herself to be a woman, and therefore anyone who'd have her would be someone whose sexual orientation points them womenward. What she wants—men who like men *and* women—has the benefit of being plausible. She seems somewhat plugged into the world as it exists, and the perceptions of those around her. She even knows to do the hand-wringing when addressing Juzwiak, who is a gay man himself: "I do want to be respectful of gay men's spaces and not horn in where I'm not welcome."

Juzwiak addresses the essential: namely, the futility of her trying to fish in this pond. He gives his OK to her seeking out bisexual men in arenas that are not gay apps, though he points out that she'd probably have to identify as bi herself in order to join bisexuals' websites, and per the question's title, she is not. He casts doubt on the letter-writer's conflation of heterosexuality with sexism, pointing out, not inaccurately, "At least straight guys will pretend to be civilized for the sake of getting laid."

Taken at face value—and coloured by Juzwiak's read on her—the letter-writer is a feminist disillusioned with the hetero dating scene, who has invented a way to make her life more difficult than it needs to be. But what if that's not it? Consider what it is she's actually saying. She wants to enter the gay male dating pool. Why?

Another possibility, not as far-fetched as it may seem, is that this is a woman who gets off on having the sex life of a gay man. Maybe what she wants isn't a more "civilized" man than she finds amongst the straights, but rather a series of hot encounters with men who don't assume their hookups are looking to settle down.

GRINDR AND THE SINGLE GIRL

The existence of gay male hookup apps might seem the hardest evidence that male sexuality is more fervent than female, or else straight and lesbian apps would be similarly to-the-point. Proof that men are like so. And on a population level, there is undoubtedly something to this. At the same time, it is precisely the sex-only nature of these apps that has some women intrigued, and popping up on these apps, to the confusion or annoyance of the men attempting to virtually cruise.

What does a woman imagine she'll *get* on Grindr? It's one thing to want a sleazy tryst of the sort open to gay men. It's another to plop your woman-self onto an app for man-seekers and expect to be barking up remotely the right tree. Is it all just voyeurism? Per the copious reporting on this topic in Buzzfeed, *Vice*, and more, some women are on these apps seeking bisexual men or man-man-woman threesomes. Others have no intention of meeting up with anyone, but something about a gay male space—the transgressiveness of being in it, the blunt scheduling of sex, or just this great big sea of *men*—gets them off.

Anxieties about women on gay male apps tend to centre on the idea that women are using Grindr to find a shopping buddy—that they are, in other words, oblivious and homophobic. This does not appear to be the only or even primary thing happening. Indeed, a 2012 Buzzfeed article, "18 Girls Looking for Gay Friends on Grindr," includes screenshots of profiles of women, some in search of a gay bestie, but others seeking "dates," a "gay lover," and, in one case, men to "wrestle."[4] Also on Buzzfeed, but in a very different 2022 reported article,[5] Hallie Lieberman asks whether straight women on Grindr are "the digital equivalent of drunken bachelorettes stumbling into gay bars." One gay man tells her he imagines the women are on the app in search of gay best friends like the ones they've seen on television. She also quotes a woman who arrived there, at the suggestion of a gay male friend from her off-app life, because she wanted to find men who were "into butt stuff." One presumes there'd be more efficient ways of going about that.

My hunch is that the *Slate* advice-seeker knows *exactly* what Grindr is, in terms of the types of relationships sought, and that this for her is a feature, not a bug. I don't think it's incidental that she wants to be wanted by men who want men. Is that its own special kind of gender dysphoria? If so, is this "heterosexual woman," without yet realizing it herself . . . a gay man?

But barring any such pronouncement from her, she's a problematic straight lady, one whose unequivocal understanding of herself as a cishet woman winds up being her downfall. The *Savage Lovecast* caller can at least point to a queer identity, and must thus be treated with sensitivity. *She* is owed no such reticence. As she anticipates, Juzwiak calls her out for not knowing her place. He doesn't say she *can't* use these apps, but if she insists upon doing so, she'd best watch her etiquette. "The world is not your bachelorette party."

BACHELORETTES AT THE GAY BAR

Of all the faux pas, the most faux of them all is deciding to celebrate your last big girls' night as a single straight woman, prior to your wedding, at a club that caters to gay men. There is a long history of women hosting bachelorette gatherings at gay bars, and a seemingly equally long one of gay men objecting to their doing so. Sometimes this converges with the murkier should-straight-women-be-in-gay-bars discourse. You can't know if a woman is straight just by looking at her. Nor, from a glance at a crowd, can you tell if a woman is hanging out with a gay male friend and this was where *he* wanted to go. Or indeed if the "woman" is someone who identifies as male or non-binary.

But bachelorettes, they are unmistakable. They lend themselves to a certain sort of unflattering media coverage, even when they're not specifically bothering gay men. They represent unproblematized heteronormativity, unapologetic consumerism, and a kind of tackiness one can feel righteous about while mocking. It feels a bit misogynist to bash women for going out in a group and getting trashed. But a bachelorette is like a Karen: fair game.

The bachelorette at the gay bar is the straight woman as uninvited guest. In times and places where gay marriage wasn't legal, this seemed, to the men who worked in and frequented these establishments, like the flaunting of heterosexual privilege, perhaps because *it was*. And even with greater marriage equality, there's the lingering issue of these women sometimes behaving in disrespectful ways, understanding themselves to be in male strip clubs when surrounded by scantily clad gay men doing their own thing. They think they're on safari. They ruin the vibe. Or so I've read. Tragically, no one has invited me to an event of this kind.

The classic romp through gay-bar bachelorette parties, which Juzwiak links to, is from an April 2016 edition of *Out* magazine. It follows roving groups of Boston-area straight ladies who bring heterosexuality and, more concerningly, basicness to Provincetown, the famous Massachusetts gay enclave.[6] The journalist interviews the bartender at a sex-centric bar for gay men, who has had it with the gate-crashing females. "'This has been the worst year yet, and it has been worse every year,' he says. Earlier in the season, a bunch of women came in, took out their phones, and began recording men in heavy cruise mode and the porn on the TVs. 'I told them, "Ladies, there's no recording in here," and they said, "Fuck you."'"

This is obviously out of line, but it's not about straight women viewing gay men as handbags. It's straight women doing exactly what (#notall) straight men would do if "hardcore-porn, red-light, sex-pig bars" for lesbians were a thing. I could go further down the road of explaining-not-excusing the bachelorettes, but this would be to miss the most telling part. The byline, Chadwick Moore, sounded familiar, and I soon saw why: Less than a year after his 2016 bachelorettes article, he was cancelled for profiling right-wing provocateur Milo Yiannopoulos, also for *Out*, as opposed to, I guess, writing repeatedly on a blackboard, *Milo is a fascist, Milo is a fascist.*

Moore has since pivoted to right-wing punditry, with a favourable biography of conservative U.S. pundit Tucker Carlson as well as a book arguing against DEI. A headline for an excerpt from the latter that ran on a gay Republican website: "What the Heck Is a 'Queer' Anyway?"[7] In some cases, Moore writes, "It's the culturally appropriating heterosexual virtue-signaler."

But it's the women of this type he has it in for.

"The straight female Queer is thoroughly basic. She likes Taylor Swift and the TV show *Friends* . . . While there's nothing wrong with being basic, she's convinced there is . . . [S]he wishes she had unconventional impulses but just doesn't."

Now wait for it:

"She's always loved the gays—they're nonthreatening, 'fabulous,' and she doesn't feel competitive with them."

Between 2016 and 2022, Moore may have taken on new political labels for himself and updated the label he ascribes to the women he's objecting to (first bachelorettes, then faux-queers), but this is, unmistakably, the same grudge, against the same kind of woman. What comes across in both articles is a degree of resentment at women who get to play at being sexual renegades, while at the end of the day getting to settle down with men and face no stigma for doing so. His point is, in effect, that gay men don't have the privilege of playing tourist in gayland. At the risk of psychoanalyzing a stranger, he sounds a bit resentful. Which is sort of the point. Where straight women and gay men are concerned, grass-is-greener flows in both directions.

HAVING SEX LIKE A (GAY) MAN

Who's to blame for straight women seeing gay nightlife as entertainment for our benefit? It's clear enough what brought this sort of thinking into the mainstream: *Sex and the City*. The very first episode, in 1998, asked the question of whether a woman could have sex like a man, and the subsequent episodes sought to find out.

The gay men in the *Sex and the City* universe itself would plant the idea in the heads of the future bachelorettes of America, and beyond, that *the gays* were a good time. A 2010 *Salon* article by Thomas Rogers[8] rightly describes "the two main gay characters, Carrie's chubby pal Stanford (Willie Garson) and Charlotte's sassy BFF Anthony Marantino (played by Mario Cantone) [as] tragically asexual helpmates." Rogers also takes issue with the choice the franchise eventually makes to couple off Stanford and Anthony, calling it "the clichéd, condescending hetero fantasy, the one in which you introduce the only two gay men you know, and magically, the sparks fly." *Sex and the City*, in other words, popularized the my-gays phenomenon. It did not invent the idea of gay male characters as straight-girl-protagonist sidekicks. One thinks of the 1997 Julia Roberts rom-com *My Best Friend's Wedding* or Rickie (Wilson Cruz) on the 1994 teen series *My So-Called Life*. But a sidekick is one thing. An accessory is another.

Rogers points out what would be a central paradox about the show: that the straight women characters read more like gay men than do the gay male ones. The gay-mannishness of the female protagonists would come to be the standard reaction to the show. As evidence, in his 2002 *New Republic* pan,[9] critic Lee Siegel pointed to creator Darren Star and writer-director Michael Patrick King, gay men both. That much Siegel was fine with, writing that it put the show in line with "a long imaginative streak in popular art [by] gay figures whose portrayals of heterosexual life brilliantly subverted heterosexual conventions even as they were providing models for (unwitting) straight boys and girls." What he objected to was a "subtext" he interpreted as endorsing "raw, rough, promiscuous, anonymous gay male sex," but for straight women, and going so far as to suggest women were biologically capable of being into that sort of thing. Siegel went as far as writing, "The picture of heterosexual life projected by *Sex and the City* . . . is the biggest hoax perpetrated on straight single women in the history of entertainment."

If *Sex and the City* represented a kind of gender-neutral sex positivity, it's no great surprise it has detractors today. The "homosexualization of heterosexuality"—a phrase perhaps first uttered in a 1999 article[10]—remains, in the 2020s, a critique of the show.[11] And I do kind of see this. A type of sexuality that works for many-not-all gay men has indeed been suggested, in gender-neutral terms, to all. This type of advice, ostensibly liberatory, doesn't take into account that men and women are different, or that relationships are different where reproductive potential is in the mix. What it misses is the profound degree to which women *fantasize* about a world in which we could live as gay men can seem to, adventures awaiting us for all our remaining days, no sell-by dates or biological clocks holding us back.

That the show was based on Candace Bushnell's *New York Observer* dating column casts doubt on the *these are just gay men* hypothesis. But what matters here isn't whether *Sex and the City* was realistic or a good influence but that it was received as wish fulfillment. Women from all over the world travel on show-themed tour buses to line up for cupcakes at Magnolia. The cupcakes are good but not *that* good. I think of my late grandmother, who grew up in Montreal in the 1920s, giggling in her un-hip Brooklyn apartment about Samantha. The series is firm evidence that a whole bunch of women thought it would be fun to live like a gay man. This was not merely imposed on us by gay writers who were not yet free to write overtly gay stories, but something straight women sought out.

Gender non-conformity is not commonly discussed these days in the context of cisgender heterosexual women. Certainly not the ones who sip pink cocktails in designer stilettos. Such women are thought to epitomize gender conformity, and therefore to be *comfortable in their femininity*.

Not so!

Indeed, if you stop and think about it for a moment, straight women have been chafing at gender norms since forever. We even have this extra context in which to do so: our intimate relationships with men, relationships we require, but that always risk falling into scripts we may not want. It stands to reason that the women who want men, as in who *really* want them, interpret this desire as somehow unfeminine. Odd as it may seem, lusting after men is *not*, in a woman (or in a man, albeit for other reasons), gender-conforming behaviour. And this is, at its core, *the relationship between straight women and gay men*, at least from the straight woman's perspective. What if you could like men but also be a person?

The very act of ogling a man is gay-male-coded. Images of attractive men—boyish or big and hairy—are classified as *homoerotic*. "An adult male who remains slim and lovely and keeps the hair on his head rather than growing it on his face and body may play a boy's role for as long as it is congenial," writes Germaine Greer[12] in her strange erudite coffee table book, *The Beautiful Boy*. I read this and immediately thought, *OK, she means twinks*. It's no coincidence that there is no heteroland way to explain it. Per Greer, "Discussions of visual pleasure as it relates to the depiction of human beings almost invariably assume that the viewer is male; histories of the male nude are all histories of homosexuality in the visual arts."[13]

It's almost as though drooling over men is something straight women stand accused of having appropriated from gay men. The woman who *admires the male form* comes across as performative, as though she's trying to make a protest-too-much point, or maybe even looking to get back at men for their objectification of women. It reads less as authentic thirst and more as argument.

WHO'S LOOKING?

When I was thirteen, circa 1996, there was this twenty-something art teacher at my all-girls school. I assumed he was gay—the young male teachers at this school tended to be—but this was immaterial. He was not a romantic prospect. (Nor was anyone my own age.) All I knew was that he was the best-looking person I'd ever laid eyes on. A female colleague of his must have picked up on my crush—I can think of no other explanation—and had me assist in his class, which I did, barely able to speak to him, my face beet-red.

When I look back on this as an adult, with daughters of my own, I'm struck by how weird this was. Weird, but harmless. I did not harass this man, nor was I ever alone with him. That I remember my time as art helper as well as I do owes something to "The Art Teacher," a Rufus Wainwright song.[14] It's sung from the perspective of a former New York City girls' school pupil, now a boring old rich married lady, looking back on her "work of art"–level gorgeous instructor from back in the day.

A proper interpretation of "The Art Teacher" would point to the layers, queerness-wise, in the lyrics and in who's singing them. It would emphasize the (lightly) coded subversiveness of a gay man signing in a kind of drag, in the role of the straight woman. And yet—echoes of *Sex and the City*—the proceedings feel so extremely true to how some straight women (one, at least) experience desire for men. Eerily so, in this case, to the point that I can only assume that Wainwright wrote this song by time-travelling to my eighth-grade brain.

This is more plausible than it sounds: "The Art Teacher" is from 2004 and evidently inspired by stories a schoolteacher told Wainwright at the gym, about female students falling for him. How many stunning male art teachers could there have been in New York City at this time, and how many girls as ridiculous? The idea that I could have served as the inspiration for this song—that the song could, in fact, be about me—is a little bit neat, a lot bit embarrassing . . . and utterly uninteresting compared with the image now in my head of the very beautiful Rufus Wainwright and this not-un-Rufus-like art teacher, *together, at the gym*.

VERY GOOD FRIENDS

The expected relationship between straight women and gay men—sometimes heteronormatively referred to as, between *women* and gay men, the "straight" part implied—is that of platonic friends. Levels of tokenization may vary—sometimes people are just friends, and it is not a whole thing—but when they're present, they can (unlike binary-orientation-havers themselves) go both ways. (The straight woman who thinks of her gay male friends as accessories; the gay man who enjoys the company of a certain dramatic sort of straight woman for entertainment value.) But the idea is that there is an affinity based on shared interests (men, most obviously, but also, per cliché, the arts or interior design; I know that not all gay men are aesthetically minded, and that some straight men are, and thank goodness for that). They're meant to be *easy* friendships, devoid of the competitiveness that can exist between female friends, but also of sexual tension.

A 2007 anthology, *Girls Who Like Boys Who Like Boys: True Tales of Love, Lust, and Friendship Between Straight Women and Gay Men*—reissued the following year with the more staid subtitle *True Tales of Friendship Between Straight Women and Gay Men*, chucking the "love" and "lust"—explores these friendships from both sides.[15] Edited by Melissa de la Cruz and Tom Dolby, the book presents a range of perspectives, but hovers around the glamorous world of New York nightlife, Hollywood mingling, and Harvard dormitories. The authors are novelists and television writers, one—Cindy Chupack—from *Sex and the City*. This is not, like Robert H. Hopcke and Laura Rafaty's 1999 *Straight Women, Gay Men: Absolutely Fabulous Friendships*, a pop-sociological explanation for a burgeoning mainstream phenomenon, but rather a portrait of an aspirational milieu.

Due to some mix of Y2K revival and the fact that it was objectively not that long ago, 2007 seems aesthetically like the present day, but on gender matters, it was not. Imagine being so binary as to only discuss *straight women* and *gay men*, and without any qualification about these people being cisgender. Imagine doing this even when some of the women are not straight, and when one of the gay men goes on a possibly artful, possibly serious out-of-nowhere digression about how he might have considered getting a sex change operation but has come around to being a man.

For all the book's emphasis on friendship, there are rather a lot of contributions from straight women about falling in love with gay men. The subtitle, with its sneaky mention of "lust," hints at the non-platonic angle. The pretense that a straight woman–gay man friendship is non-sexual only works if you assume that straight women aren't sexual, or that we are but only in response to someone desiring us.

Anna David's essay "Love in Other Lifetimes" is about her pattern of "falling for gay guys."[16] David writes of finding gay crushes (as in, crushes on gay men) transgressive and so exciting they ruined straight crushing. "The notion of a date with a regular old straight guy, who wouldn't have to sacrifice or defy anything to go out with me, seemed downright dull in comparison."[17]

Women have yearned for gay men since the actual dawn of time.

My favourite onscreen representation of this is in "The Matchmaker," a 1994 *Frasier* episode. Frasier thinks he's setting Daphne up with the dashing new boss at his work, but the boss is thrilled to believe Frasier wants him for himself. Frasier instructs Daphne to dress up to meet the man, which she does, putting on a dress that, she explains, requires an uncomfortable but flattering bra. She's all in. When it's revealed at the end of the episode that the man is gay and into Frasier, there's this *perfect* moment where Daphne, who was entering the room, turns around and leaves it, unclasping the painful bra in midstride. Onward and upward.

The gayness itself is not the appeal here, although male homosexuality serves as a stand-in for a man being eligible in all other ways. He's gorgeous, sophisticated, at ease with women. The woman doesn't know the man is gay but once she does, everything suddenly makes sense. *All the good ones are gay.* And because of differing understandings of male and female sexuality, fluidity or bisexuality is never considered a possibility.

Other times, a woman will marry a man she believes to be straight, only to learn, decades on, that he is not. This lends itself less to sitcom fodder but was nevertheless the premise of *Grace and Frankie* (2015–22), about the friendship of two elderly women whose husbands have run off with each other. Also the 2011–13 *Happily Divorced*, where Fran Drescher of *The Nanny* plays a fictionalized version of her real-life self, amicably split from a husband who came out following their marriage.

Falling somewhere between the *oh oops* and *oh no* models is the backstory to *Will & Grace*. The protagonists dated in college until Will came out, which broke Grace's heart. Evidently she got over it, given that this is a show about a straight woman and her gay bestie, not about a straight woman hung up on a gay ex.

These are all examples of women whose attraction is to *straight* men, but who lacked the requisite mind-reading abilities (or gaydar) to avoid falling for gay ones. Most people are straight, so they figure the men they like are into women. Mistakes happen.

Then there are the women who fall in love or lust with men they know to be gay, which gets dicier. One way involves a straight woman wishing such a man were into women, and hoping she can somehow make that happen. It's Elaine on *Seinfeld* trying to get a man to change teams. It's the 1998 Jennifer Aniston–Paul Rudd movie, *The Object of My Affection*. These are women who want straight men. They're just willfully—disrespectfully—ignoring that the men they're into are not that.

Finally, there are the women for whom a man's gayness is the draw. Something about gay men does it for her. Maybe her type is something other than slovenly men in cargo shorts, and she has yet to realize that some straight men bathe and go to museums or whatever. Or she's intrigued by the potential for a MMF three-way, in which case it's technically bi men she's after . . . or is it?

Why would a woman who understands how sexual orientation works nevertheless go for a man she knows is gay? It's not a wise thing to do, but it's not pure foolishness. Crushing on a gay man is a way to avoid being turned down for a failure to measure up as a woman. He won't like you back, but you can't take it personally. There's a convoluted sense in which the crush on a gay man is the purest form of female heterosexuality, focused as it is on man-wanting and not man-attracting. There is also, however, a straightforward sense in which an inherently unrealizable crush is very much not that, given that sex itself is not in the cards. Or rather, women *should* understand that gay men won't have sex with them. But people are complicated and sometimes knowingly impractical in their desires.

There are women out there, cisgender women, who see their sexual selves as men. Another *Slate* advice column letter-writer—same column, but (seemingly) a different letter-writer—describes this state of affairs. She's bisexual (or so she says when identifying herself; nothing in the letter indicates an interest in women) but, since adolescence, only aroused by gay men.[18] And it's not just that she likes them. She's turned on by thinking of herself as one: "Even when I'm being penetrated vaginally, I like to think that I'm a guy being fucked by another guy. (I'm definitely not trans—besides this,

I love being a woman and have never had any kind of dysphoric thought or desire to transition.)" She's not trying to convert gay men to heterosexuality or bisexuality for her convenience. She is, and isn't, wishing *she* were someone else.

In a 2018 study, also called *Girls Who Like Boys Who Like Boys*, British university lecturer Lucy Neville investigates the women who—like herself—enjoy and produce man-on-man content. As its subtitle, *Women and Gay Male Pornography and Erotica*, suggests, we are worlds away from the women who think of gay men as handbag chihuahuas to bring on shopping expeditions. And Neville finds that women don't just like contemplating (or watching) two men having sex. Some get off on imagining themselves as gay men. She quotes a subject who wonders whether her desires, though male-oriented, merit embracing a different identity, but which?

> If I imagine myself to be a man having sex with another man while I'm getting off, what am I? A straight woman (after all, I'm imagining having sex with a man)? A gay man (because I'm also a man in this scenario)? A heterosexual woman engaged in a homosexual act (because I'm engaged in an act of self-love)? Trans-identified (because I'm a woman imagining I'm a man)? Queer (because this is an act that is hard to explain through conventional sexual scripts)?[19]

This doesn't fall within the usual identity boxes. If you say that you're a trans gay man or non-binary, then the right-thinking progressive stance is that you should be welcomed into the queer male dating pool. But! If you say nothing of the kind, if you refer to yourself as a (cisgender) woman, then you're not only deluded but are thinking about gay men in a sexual capacity without their consent.

A ROM-COM WITH A TWIST

I stumbled across the 2010 movie *Violet Tendencies*[20] in 2024 via a scrolling sinkhole. I'd been streaming 1980s U.S. boarding school sitcom *The Facts of Life*, leading me to the Instagram of Mindy Cohn, the actress who played Natalie Green. Having been something of a Natalie to a Blair in middle school in the 1990s (if you know you know; if you don't, Natalie's the frumpy Jewish one, Blair the popular blonde), I got sort of sucked in, and not even for what I imagined were professional purposes. I found myself captivated by her apparently off-the-wall vibrant social life, a kind of who's-who of a certain sort of celebrity, many of them gay men. Isaac Mizrahi! Harvey Fierstein! *Ricky Martin!* So very different from my own life, passing out on an IKEA couch in Toronto after little kids go to bed. And I suppose I guessed Cohn was gay or bi as well, inasmuch as I'd given it thought, which is to say, I hadn't. But when I arrived at a post where she referred to herself as an "ally," I thought, *huh*. The straight woman with a lot of gay male friends: one of those once-ubiquitous things, like frozen yogurt, you don't see so much of these days.

In the name of research, I learned that Cohn not only identifies—or did, in old interviews—as a "fag hag" but also was the star of a whole entire movie about the exploits of one such woman. When the film first appeared, a journalist from *The Advocate* asked her whether she could "relate" to "the unhealthy potential of a straight woman's friendships with gay men," as depicted therein. She could not: "While there are times I am very enmeshed and comfortable in the gay community, I don't live there like Violet, who doesn't have anything other than this family of gay friends. I'm such a different 'fag hag' than Violet. I've never wanted to be a gay man, and I don't want to have sex like a gay man."[21] Whoever this "Violet" was, this was even more relevant for my purposes than the actress portraying her. I had to watch this movie.

Violet of *Violet Tendencies* is *the last fag hag standing*. "The last" as in, the film opens with the penultimate one getting married and therefore parting ways, making Violet the last one left in their friend group, but also as in, 2010 was end times for the phenomenon itself. The very concept of the fag hag was starting to seem dated and stale, *irrelevant*, at just the same moment that Violet is forty and on the cusp of aging out of a hard-partying lifestyle.

What was different in 2010? Everything and nothing. Same-sex marriage was legal in Canada, but not too many other places. It was not yet—not in the mainstream, even in circles with many gay men and lesbians—the world of gender-innovative self-identified queers. But it was already a bit late for a straight woman to be hanging around with a group of gay men. It would all seem a bit tokenistic, cringe, "I'm a Carrie." Unless, that is, the woman was gay or bi herself, in which case she was simply one more member of a queer friend circle.

Violet is heterosexual, this much is obvious. A lesbian colleague hits on her, which she gently rebuffs in a way that makes it clear it's an orientation-alignment thing. And she loves *her gays*—or is she *their straight*?—and prefers their company to that of straight men. But she'd like to find a man for herself. The movie follows her quest for a mythical being called a "fag stag," a straight man who lives amongst gay men. Violet dates various men but is always a bit *too much*. Accustomed to the frankness of her gay male crew, she speaks bluntly about topics like anal sex, sending even open-minded straight men running for the hills.

Watching the movie out of context, on my laptop, I had trouble making sense of its intended purpose or audience. Roughly half the movie is a hetero romantic comedy. The rest—interspersed throughout—is a vaguely porny series of scenes of interchangeable-looking beautiful young men making out and having sex parties and whatnot, all strung together by the flimsiest of side plots. I am not complaining. I am merely noting. What's the relationship between these moving parts? This is not as it first seems.

Violet's quest for a gay-seeming hetero man—*not* a metrosexual, this is specified—seems sincere, and you think you know where you are, rom-com-wise, when she meets a column-fixated (*get it?*) architect. He's cute, he likes her, what could go wrong? Echoing certain *The Facts of Life* plotlines—particularly the episode where Natalie is the first in the group to lose her virginity, at the tender age of twenty-one, at which point all the "girls" on the show seem about thirty-five—it is the man who wants the white picket fence, and the woman whose second-wave-feminist impulses have her resisting that kind of fairy-tale ending.

Violet likes the architect but isn't sold on moving to Idaho with him. The tension in the movie is over whether Violet should *change for a man*. Violet nods along to a female friend's advice about putting up with mediocre sex. But then the friend asks if she would rather be loved or "entertained," and Violet gives the wrong answer.

Her gay-guy clique is *not having it*. They stage an intervention, telling her, "your heterosexuality is hurting us," and expressing their sense of betrayal. But is it her new attempts at squareness they object to or do they—selfishly—not want to lose their sidekick to coupledom?

Violet's happy ending—happy, too, for her friends—comes from not changing for a man, on a level more profound than has perhaps ever been represented in cinema. It's not just that she is a forty-year-old woman of size not trying to look otherwise. It's that she gets to *be* the gay man she always was, without needing to transition. It turns out that one of the members of her friend group—among the more chiselled, even—is actually straight, but for reasons (he's an HIV-positive go-go dancer), he has wound up passing as gay. Straight and—how convenient!—he has a thing for Violet.

Freshly out of her relationship with the architect, Violet hooks up with her new guy *at a gay sex party*, which he is attending with the express purpose of meeting up with her. Two men in their underpants run screaming from the backroom where Violet and her new boyfriend are consummating things. "They got breeders back there," one complains to the organizer, Violet's roommate Luke. "Guys, I'm just bringing queers together," Luke reassures them. The three men then hear Violet, mid-activities, yell "Split me like a wishbone!"—to which her erstwhile detractor replies, "Okay, that's . . . that's pretty queer." And just like that, she's in. The inclusivity here is based not on categories but on human complexity. It's not that everyone female-bodied who identifies as male would get let in. This is never tested—no trans men in this cinematic universe—but guests have their bits approved at the door and are required to measure up. An exception is made for *this* woman—who is, there is no ambiguity, a woman.

How would all this play out today, in this landscape with ostensibly so many more opportunities for gender expansiveness? Would Violet be better off, more able to *live her truth*, if she could identify as trans or non-binary? Did 2010 just lack the vocabulary for whatever it is she is, which is *what*, exactly?

While proliferating identity categories are helpful to trans and non-binary people trying to articulate who they are, I don't see how these terms would be of much help to Violet. Her goal, which the movie graciously permits her to meet, is to have the physicality of a heavy-set middle-aged lady, while living the life of a fitter-than-fit young gay man. Given that Violet's brief flirtation with trying to be someone she's not is illustrated by her wearing a tent dress rather than a latex catsuit, it's hard to picture this same movie—rebooted for the 2020s (not that this is imminent)—encouraging her to change her pronouns, let alone trying to morph her own body into that of a toned gay man.

There's no indication that *she* would want anything of the kind. Her gay male friends' acceptance of her is not contingent on her showing interest in other women, or in embracing anything but a feminine self-presentation. She is not an interloper or a bachelorette. She gets to enjoy Mr. Chiselled Torso in a sea of similarly built men without going through the possibly futile bother of trying to physically resemble the sort of person who typically gets to do such things.

Violet, then, lives the life that the non-passing trans man mentioned atop this chapter cannot: a social *and* sexual welcome from gay-man-land. Why does she succeed where the *Savage Lovecast* caller fails? Is it just because Violet is a fictional character in a thoroughly unrealistic movie, whereas the caller is—maybe—a real person?

Violet's authenticity is what saves her. She doesn't ask anyone to see her as other than what she self-evidently is. She has zero expectations that people look at her and *see* a gay man. And—odd as this may seem, given everything I've just said about this movie—*she does not attempt to date gay men*. She's clear that what she's looking for romantically is someone with certain gay-man-coded qualities (likes show tunes, has abs) but who is attracted to women.

And you have to love the almost certainly inadvertent intertextuality with *The Nanny*. Her female friend, in awe of the hunk her friend has landed, asks Violet, "Where did you find him?" Violet answers, in Natalie Green deadpan, "Gay sex club." Gay bars, Ma, not Zabar's, not that Violet would be remotely out-of-place in either locale.

The movie's creators are gay men, not straight women. If you focus on artist(s) rather than the art itself, you'd have to conclude that the wish the film fulfills has nothing to do with *women's* desires at all. Beneath the writhing and rom-com plot arc, it is a movie about friendship. From a gay male perspective, this is about the fantasy that one's straight female bestie never disappears off into straightland but, instead, finds some way to remain forever incorporated into the gang, without morphing into an involuntarily celibate Debbie Downer, nor getting hung up on any actual gay men. All that is well and good, but art is open to interpretation. Watching it as a straight woman, I saw it as a hetero rom-com with a twist, a twist that gets at something profound about female heterosexual desire. This isn't a woman who falls for a man who turns out to be gay, but one whose hot, seemingly gay friend has an unexpectedly delightful surprise: he's into heavy-set middle-aged women! As with *Sex and the City*, what's relevant isn't whether straight women viewers find the proceedings relatable or advisable, but whether what's happening onscreen looks like fun. And it does.

JUST HERE TO LOOK

There is no special name for the sort of man who finds it hot when two women make out. This is not a quirky subsection of male heterosexuality. It is standard-issue. Imagine a man sitting down his girlfriend and confessing that his turn-on is . . . seeing two women together. Would she be shattered? Would she be able to summon a look of even mild surprise? It would be like a straight man admitting that some of his socks have holes in them. *We know*.

Lucy Neville has the data on how prevalent her predilection is in the population at large. The answer is: very. It's not just that women found *Brokeback Mountain* sexy and have looked for such scenarios elsewhere. Over a third of the viewers of gay male Pornhub content are women.[22] That may not seem like much, but if you'd imagined only gay and bi men were watching, how wrong you'd be! There are women consuming and creating stories where two men (real or fictional) get together, and no, not all of them are quaint little tales where two fully clothed men hold hands. Indeed, there's nothing niche or obscure about straight women wanting in, in one way or another, on gay masculinity. Women and girls form the audience for, and are creators of, all manner of homoerotic content, from slashfic (written erotica imagining two male characters getting it on) to 2023's *Red, White, and Royal Blue*, a mainstream movie (with Uma Thurman and everything) about a fictional U.S. first son and British prince engaged in various activities.

Neville surveyed "over 500 (self-identified) women who engage with [man-man] sexually explicit media [SEM] as to what they enjoy about it."[23] It seems perhaps more relevant that women have these desires than how exactly they explain them when prompted by a scholar, but some of what she found is the obvious. I cannot say I was shocked that "women are turned on by seeing or thinking about two attractive men together" wound up being the reason most gave for their predilection.[24]

One question Neville seeks to address is whether women enjoying gay male erotica is best classified as straight or queer.[25] To me the answer seems obvious the minute you swap the genders and consider the absurdity of asking whether it's queer for a man to watch "lesbian" porn: no, it is not a "queer" thing for a woman who likes men to like men in any which permutation. Women aren't imagined watching porn at all, so it's subversive for them to do so. Objectifying men is transgressive. *Queer*, though?

Neville makes the case that queerness does enter into it. She points out that most of the women she's surveyed who are into gay male porn are not heterosexual themselves. Indeed, only 45 per cent of the women she surveyed are heterosexual. But how you interpret that depends on what you make of the remaining 55 per cent. Lesbians make up an unimpressive (though higher than I'd have guessed!) 4 per cent of those into man-on-man content. The rest are "bisexual," "pansexual," "asexual," "questioning sexuality," "queer," "demisexual," and "prefer not to say." Looked at in this way, a whopping 96 *per cent* of those surveyed (91 if you exclude the asexuals) might be in, or contemplating, relationships with men. As it happens, of the partnered, "87 per cent are involved with a man, 9 per cent with a woman, 2 per cent with a person who identifies as trans/genderqueer/gender fluid and 2 per cent with both a man and a woman."[26] While the women who are available for surveys about their porn usage may be disproportionately queer-identified relative to the population at large (Mormon tradwives ain't signing up), the women who spend their spare time contemplating men getting it on are women who, by and large, like having sex with men. They may not be straight, but they are somewhere in that ballpark.

Neville may be politically invested in describing women's most hetero of fantasies in other terms. Her acknowledgements section includes a thank you to those who "called me out on any lingering vestiges of heteronormative indoctrination."[27] But is it "heteronormative" to think there's something rather straight about women getting off on two-men content? A bisexual woman might enjoy seeing men together, but when that's the case, it's *her bisexuality* that places her under the queer umbrella. Indeed, per Neville herself, her findings affirm "the seemingly unradical notion that many women find men attractive, and therefore like looking at them, particularly without their clothes on."[28] It's not complicated! Unless you decide to make it complicated. Neville goes on to suggest that even her ostensibly straight subjects "are reading the world with queer eyes, and engaging in a perverse form of interpretation."[29]

I see how she arrives at this place, trying to honour her subjects' own understandings. She interviews one woman who "believes that 'though only engaging in heterosexual sex with a male-identified partner' she identifies as 'queer, and by queer I mean what I have just talked about: humanness.'"[30] I want to find this woman and let her know that straight people are also a subset of humanity.

The queerness angle just seems like a reach, particularly Neville's claim that "heterosexual women producing smut for other women is something that can arguably be seen as queer."[31] Would anyone suggest this of straight male pornographers?

Yes, it's gender non-conforming for women to fantasize about two men together. But if you take this to its logical conclusion, and what's subversive is not the two-men-together aspect but the woman in active / gazing role, then ultimately all active desire women have for men is "queer." But is it, though?

Let's put this in *really* simple terms: If a woman asks a man on a date, is she queering heterosexuality? Or if anything, is she *more* of a straight woman than the lady who might say yes if a man asked, but maybe her yes will be about doing what society expects of her? This matters, not because it's important that as many people as possible *get to be straight* (it's not!) but because calling phenomena the very thing they're not only confuses matters.

So no, there is no secret queer world of women fantasizing about men. What Neville finds is a deeper truth about female heterosexuality. That it is about looking at men, lusting after men, and being a full-fledged human being while doing so. She backs up the commonsense truth that our society is full of sensual images of beautiful naked women, while male nudity gets treated as comedic. It's like the women who go on a gay male hookup app not in search of *nicer* men but to get men stripped down—as it were—and without the baggage of traditional gender roles. Neville's findings indicate—to me, if not to her—that women's supposed preference for gazing at women is a sign not of female sexual fluidity but rather of a sexist and homophobic society that's wary of letting anyone admire male beauty, least of all allowing women to do so. The book left me more suspicious of claims that all women are naturally aroused by the female form. I realize this may not have been Neville's intent, but learning just how robustly women are into the naked, sex-having dudes only further confirmed, for me, that straight women are real.

WHY NOT BOTH?

It is my contention, then, that straight women are simple creatures, same as everyone else. When a straight woman fantasizes about two men together, she does not need a new Pride flag invented in her honour. It's just straight-lady stuff. As for how it came to be understood as aberrant or warranting explanation, that *is* a bit complicated.

That women, but not men, are reputed to be sexually fluid has all kinds of implications. One is that in an opposite-sex marriage, if the wife comes out as bisexual, the husband classically thinks, *Excellent, three-ways!* (This can be a problem if what she really means is, she is a lesbian letting him down gently.) Switch the genders and the wife assumes her husband has soft-launched the information that he and his boyfriend are keeping a place across town, and also—crucially—that he has never once for even a fleeting moment been sexually attracted to her or any other woman. One situation is a sexual dream come true, the other a domestic tragedy.

The assumption that women do not want their husbands running off with other men is, broadly speaking, unassailable. But if the default assumption of the presumed-hetero man announcing attraction to men were bisexuality, rather than homosexuality—or if the possibility that *he's bi* were even more commonly entertained—who's to say women wouldn't be *into it*?

This is the admittedly outlandish premise of a couple episodes of the 2018 Netflix series *Insatiable*. Bob, a flamboyant, is-he-or-isn't-he middle-aged Southern lawyer, cheats on his wife, Coralee (Alyssa Milano as a Southern Belle), with his nemesis, a macho, chiselled-of-torso lawyer, also named Bob. When she learns what's going on, Coralee is first devastated, as you'd expect. But there's this strange scene where they're all three in tears and she sees the two Bobs kissing and suddenly the music becomes what might be called *sexy and ominous*. Something clicks in her mind, and she lets them know that she's not jealous in the way she'd imagined. She approaches the Bob who isn't her husband, a man she's had a crush on for years, and starts kissing him. He kisses her back, thus beginning (in "Winners. Win. Period.") a short-lived throuple. There is no polyamorous happily-ever-after for these characters (the Bob whose gayness was hinted at all along turns out to be bisexual, but the ripped Bob comes to realize he only likes men), but it's incredible that this is even brought up as a possibility.

There are bisexual men out there, and—see Jane Ward's *Not Gay*—sexual fluidity among straight-identified men may be greater than commonly assumed. But yeah, most of the time, a man's consistent sexual interest in other men means what you'd think it does: he's gay. And gay men's enthusiasm for being of sexual interest to women is, understandably, rather limited. Men—if I may generalize—are uncomfortable with being objectified by people they're not interested in. Women, of any sexual orientation, are more used to dealing with this. A lesbian may not *like* that straight men are *into lesbians* (by which they mean girl-on-girl porn), but she's unlikely to see this as a taste she can argue them out of having. She might consider the very fantasy an invasion of space, but the most she can do is try to reclaim "lesbian" as something that exists outside of male-oriented porn categories.

Ah, one might say, but *gay* men are fine with being objectified, right? Yes and no. By other men, sometimes. But there can be something invasive, *appropriative*, about the very idea of straight women having man-on-man fantasies.

In the 2007 *Girls Who Like Boys Who Like Boys*, the friendship-anthology one, several of the gay men's contributions include some wincing regarding the women who catch feelings. In "Welcome to My Dollhouse"—the title presumably a reference to the 1995 Todd Solondz film *Welcome to the Dollhouse*, about an ugly and unpopular middle-school girl—nightlife journalist (and *Violet Tendencies* cameo-haver) Michael Musto describes the appeal of female friendships for a gay male teen: "Without the hint of sex—which can make things so messy and complicated, after all—we were able to explore our friendships with a minimum of game-playing and an absence of hidden motives." Musto then addresses the "hint of sex" that there is, just never on the boy's side. "Of course, sometimes the girl will develop a friendship-paralyzing crush on the gay, but that's when you simply move on to another, less complicated fag hag."[32] For all the talk of straight women tokenizing their gay male friends, this instance reminds that callousness can go in both directions. Although I suppose one could look at this more generously and say that in a society that does (or did; Musto was born in 1955) its darndest to make boys date girls, any added pressure to do so would feel oppressive.

Simon Doonan's essay is harsher still: "There was a boring girl in a duffle coat called Leslie who used to pounce on me and tell me she was madly in love with me and that she was ready to leave her boyfriend. She was a specific genre, a gal who, out of the blue, randomly fell in love with a gay man and pined for him and stalked him. I never thought of these girls as fag hags. I thought of them as idiots."[33] Doonan thus distinguishes between the "fag hags," fun-loving eccentrics who might incidentally have sex with an ostensibly gay man, and pathetic, badly dressed "boring" straight women who "fell in love."

Doonan describes the London 1970s scene, where functional bisexuality abounded. "Some fag hags had a knack for getting gay boys, even nellie cross-dressers, to shag them. Alcohol seemed to play a big part in these dodgy couplings. I never shagged a fag hag or a female of any description. No amount of alcohol would have been enough." He adds, hinting at the existence of male sexual fluidity, that "this probably puts me at the far end of the straight-fag continuum."[34] Doonan never seems to consider that the "gay boys" sleeping with women may have been bi, or maybe even cross-dressing straight men. This comes up elsewhere in the anthology as well, the notion that when a man who has sex with men goes to bed with a woman, something nefarious is afoot. The existence of bisexual men—more than that of bisexual women—poses a problem for a book about the special relationship between gay men and straight women, because it leaves open the possibility that a girl could like a boy who likes boys, *and he could like her back*.

Poor Leslie, though! There's a sense in which a frumpy straight woman is taken to task—not just by gay men, but generally—for doing female heterosexuality wrong. She isn't playing the role of the desired. She's going around in her duffel coat, thinking of herself as a sexual being, unmoved by the fact that the men she wants don't reciprocate. Gay or straight, men see women like that coming and the wincing begins.

"THE SAFE DISTANCE OF BOOKS"

Remember the bisexual lady who wrote in to *Slate* to complain about her predilection for gay men having sex? "I even seek out media featuring gay men, like books, movies, and music," she admits, "although I do it secretly because I don't want to come off as some kind of weirdo. I feel guilty for fetishizing gay men, but it also feels like I can't help it—the more I try to resist, the more it turns me on." Why guilt? She recalls going to a "woke" therapist, and that "after I tearfully confessed my fetish she shamed me for fetishizing gay men and making their lives harder, and called me a homophobe while I sat there and sobbed."[35]

It might seem a bit ridiculous—and does, to the advice columnist—to think that a woman horny for *representations* of gay men is somehow harming actual gay men in the process. It's not as if she's asking them to go to bed with her, let alone doing so and not taking no for an answer. But as in so many areas, sexual fantasy is one where women are held to a higher standard.

I have for years been mildly obsessed with a 2018 *Electric Literature* think piece by Claire Rudy Foster entitled "Why Are So Many Gay Romance Novels Written by Straight Women?" Subtitle: "Stay Out of My Queer Romance, Sharon."[36] (This was before "Sharon" became "Karen.") It is a problem for Foster—who identifies as queer, but not as a gay man—that most male-male romance fiction is "written by women. White women. Straight, white women." Basic ones, even, Foster suggests, giving examples of the hobbies they list in their author bios.

Foster takes straight-lady authors of two-dudes romances to task for "controlling queer bodies . . . to make money and titillate the audience of straight women who buy her books." This essay has stuck with me because of how its author has the strangest idea of *what fiction is*, erotica or otherwise. Novelists do in fact fully 100 per cent control the "bodies" of their fictional creations. There is no other way this could work. Foster's essay reads as a demand that novelists set their characters free, as though these are autonomous people.

Foster insists that straight women are free to privately fantasize about whatever but should not be winning accolades for *queer representation* for writing unrealistic books about hot men having sex. That much seems fine, if a little 2018-brained to worry about. But can you apply cultural-appropriation analysis to masturbatory aids? Foster suggests that women who find man-on-man a turn-on shouldn't merely avoid harming actual gay men in the process but also need to go above and beyond. That upholding real-life gay men ought to be the *purpose of their activities*—when plainly it is that these women get off on a certain type of content. "If a straight writer is really that devoted to queer progress," writes Foster, they should cease publishing gay-themed erotica.

Neville, the gay-erotica scholar, also addresses the cultural appropriation angle, albeit in more scholarly terms. She is less prescriptive than Foster, but does also point out, approvingly, that appreciation of things man-on-man "can play an important role in . . . moving people towards playing a more active role in community activism."[37] Thirst, but for a good cause.

Something about this does not sit right, and that *something* becomes immediately clear when you remember that men who fantasize about two women are neither expected nor assumed to be *allies of the lesbian community*. The idea that straight women's sexual desires would ever need to be in service of the marginalized reeks of the thing where women are expected to put others first at all times. When men jerk off, one can only hope that what they're looking at onscreen didn't involve anyone being sexually assaulted. But women reading a novel about two made-up dudes getting it on need to check their straight privilege and take a cold shower? I think not.

A MAN'S WORLD

There is an additional question at stake: the idea that there is something inherently inaccessible to straight women about *real* gay sex, and indeed about male sexuality more generally. There's this oddly prevalent notion that we have *no idea* what sordid things straight men are thinking about when they look at us. As for gay men—and this comes up both in Foster's ranticle and Neville's study—there's a pervasive belief (one Foster shares and Neville rejects) that straight women's understanding of man-on-man is limited by the PG nature of our fantasy lives. A woman might think she wants in on gay masculinity but if she understood what it is gay men do, sex-wise, she would lift her petticoats and run screaming.

The tameness question is explored in a 2023 podcast interview critic Blake Smith and writer James Kirchick did with Daniel Oppenheimer, "The Fall of the White American Gay," about the status of white gay men in today's queer and ostensibly intersectional progressivism.[38] They discuss the presence of trans men in gay clubs, but also the impact on gay men of a shift from gay male spaces to queer ones. A #MeToo-type feminism, one wary of inappropriate touching between strangers, changed the culture of certain environments. Men, after all, can grope one another without anyone getting pregnant, and without this harkening back to millennia of sexism. There's this rough-and-tumble *man's world*, and if you let in women, or anyone who isn't a cisgender man, things get a bit too . . . civilized.

If the straight man with a "lesbian" fantasy is presumed guilty of imagining women doing things more sordid than what actual lesbians are up to, the straight woman with the "gay" one is probably picturing longing glances and not anything involving bodily fluids or orifices. I always wonder about the ignorance angle, though, given that women in our society have access to the internet. Even if we did not, the human body and the physical world are things known to us, and we are not without imaginations. I have trouble imagining any full-fledged adult learning about any commonplace sex act—one not involving complicated props that can only be purchased at one store in Berlin—and reacting with a stunned: *They do* WHAT*?*

ENTERING THE CLUB

"Gay Nude Resort Must Allow Women, Judge Declares" is the headline of a 2023 *Advocate* story about "a 38-year-old cisgender woman who identifies as part of the LGBTQ+ community," who took action against "at least two nude resorts" in Florida for their all-male policy in nude areas.[39] The easy interpretation here is that this is a woman trying to enter sexual spaces others have not consented to have her in. This I wouldn't dispute, but there is *also* an element of something else. It also evokes things like the exclusive "eating clubs" of Princeton University, some of which were men-only until student Sally Frank sued them for sex discrimination.

Ostensibly the purpose of a social club at an Ivy League college is different from that of a nude resort in Key West. But is the distinction as great as all that? A place where men and only men are gathered is going to have homoerotic elements and corridors-of-power ones as well. Lucy Neville cites a woman named Jill Nagle, who in 1997 wrote that she found "'female'" limiting, because she sought entry to both "'the clubhouse'" and "'the hot house.'"[40] This falls between wanting entry to an eating club and demanding access to a nude space at a hotel. Neville writes that some of what intrigues women about gay male spaces is the way their elusiveness relates to that of other traditionally all-male environments, like certain schools and professions. A woman can sue her way into a manly retreat, but once she's in, it is an all-male space no more.

The inherent impenetrability of *the club* is challenged by the existence of gender transition. Not new, but newly recognized. It wasn't part of the conversation in 1998 or 2010, not the way it is in the 2020s. Gay manhood really was, for straight women, the quintessential *club that wouldn't have you as a member*. New conceptions of gender fluidity changed the limits of possibility. It is now possible—to a point—to identify into gay manhood, and to demand your place in the proverbial club not as a bachelorette, nor even as a well-behaved ally like Violet, but as a gay man yourself.

Blake Smith once remarked, as an aside in a 2023 *Tablet* essay[41] about theorist Eve Kosofsky Sedgwick, that "nerdy, mousy, and frumpy sweater-wearing" women, not content with fag-haggery, "increasingly purport to *be* gay men, and pursue surgery in an attempt to make themselves so," calling this "a mystery for another time." Well, there's no time like the present!

While my sweater-wearing self is making no such claims, I don't find the draw itself mysterious, though I will admit to having found the whole how-it-actually-plays-out bit confusing. Even a plain-looking straight woman is going to have better luck on the man-getting front than a post-sex-change version thereof. Right? Not necessarily, and also, not everything everyone does is about maximizing potential romantic partners.

A 2024 essay in *Quillette*, "I Thought Being a Gay Man Would Save Me From Womanhood (It Didn't),"[42] offers a cautionary tale. Laura Becker recalls emerging from a troubled childhood with "the specific fantasy . . . of inhabiting gay masculinity as a straight woman." She—as the title (and the "Laura") suggest, Becker returned to identifying as female—didn't ever exactly feel like a man but fell in with a clique in which queerness functioned as a form of escape from conventionality. She convinced herself she could live as a gay man, but found this untenable. She writes that her "delusion" is "not as uncommon as some readers might think. While many who identify as trans are homosexual teenagers grappling with same-sex attraction, many straight girls are now calling themselves 'gay boys.' Based on my online experiences, I'd say that more teens who adopt a trans identity are heterosexual than homosexual."

Becker recalls having a bunch of miserable casual hookups via gay apps, only to determine, at twenty-two, that she was not a gay man after all. Nor was she even queer: "I gradually accepted my heterosexuality."

Detransition narratives appeal to the skepticism many have that it would be possible for an awkward young girl to "glow-up" into an out-and-proud gay man, and are therefore fraught within trans-activist circles, and more likely to pop up in conservative or heterodox publications. On paper, I might share the skepticism. But I have just enough anecdotal evidence of happily transitioned FTMs that I know such things have been known to happen. And testimony from trans gay men attests to the fact that regret is by no means universal.

Harry Nicholas's 2023 memoir *A Trans Man Walks into a Gay Bar*[43] traces the then-mid-twenties author's unusual journey from lesbian to straight man to gay man. Nicholas knew from a young age that he was attracted to men, but because he presented first as a masculine-looking young woman, people assumed he was a lesbian, and he went along with that. This meant that when he first transitioned, he was ostensibly a heterosexual man. It took a while for him to put together that his attraction to masculine self-presentation didn't automatically come with a desire to be with women.

Nicholas calls one chapter "The Lesbian to Straight Man to Gay Man Timeline," suggesting that he, a person assigned female at birth, who *likes men*, somehow managed to live as a member of every (binary) sexual identity group apart from the obvious one for someone in that situation. It's not as if taking testosterone woke up some previously untapped interest in dudes, as can apparently happen. The orientation towards men was there all along. So why skip over *straight woman* as a possibility?

Nicholas addresses this, kind of:

> I have at times wondered if it would have been easier to continue hiding as a girl and simply tried to squash down any dysphoria and live life as a straight woman as best I could. In fact, at 17, that's exactly what I decided to do. But in the end, none of us can deny our true selves.[44]

In other words, there were a few moments, as a teenager, when he lived as a straight girl, but this didn't stick.

Sometimes you have to put a book down and look at someone's Instagram, and Harry Nicholas . . . yes might read as a trans man to a trained eye, but absolutely presents as male. Not everyone into men would be into him (nor would this be true of anyone), but people into *women* aren't going to be asking for his number. This is a person who has chosen to take hormones that bring about body hair and a receding hairline, not because this maximizes the number of male partners available to someone with an otherwise female body (he has had top surgery, but would not pass in all ways as a cisgender man), but because he understands himself to be a man, and would be miserable living as a woman.

By transitioning, Nicholas gains access to a type of man-liking and man-pursuing that is simply not available to women. He visits gay bars and saunas, finds more men on apps than he knows what to do with, and makes repeated reference to how freeing it is to be queer and thus not part of the heteronormative constraints that lead people to settle down with a partner. He has nevertheless, by the book's end, settled down with another man.

Nicholas writes in strangely confident tones about things he believes straight people are incapable of noticing: the rainbow flags on a gay bar, or the longing look of a man in a David Hockney painting. For Nicholas, being a gay man, rather than a straight woman, means more than just getting to live as the man he knows himself to be while having the male partners he desires. It's also membership in an in-group. It's access to a *sensibility.*

Is someone with a vagina arriving at a gay male space—or in a gay man's bed—a transgender pioneer, or are they disrespecting gay men? Opinions evidently differ. When Nicholas uses "we" and "our" to speak of gay male history, there is a part of me that questions whether he really ought to be including himself in the history of—how else to put this?—men into dick. But I'm a cishet woman, right? So I'm not meant to question such things. But you know who has questioned them? Some cis gay men.

Nicholas is no bachelorette. He nevertheless writes about the backlash he's experienced from within the gay male community. "As a publicly out trans gay man I have been labelled a 'sex tourist,' accused of 'committing rape by deception' and told that I am appropriating gay culture."[45] He rejects this interpretation. But at the end of the day, this is less about his persuasiveness than his *lived experience*. He writes about falling into the trap of having too much casual sex . . . with men, via Grindr. I can sit here saying that a gay man should have every right to demand that his partners have penises, but if some gay men themselves aren't bothered (he writes that some are, some aren't; Becker, the detransitioner, evidently had no trouble finding men on these same apps), who am I to say they should be?

"MY" GAY MAN

There's a late-middle-aged gay man in my neighbourhood who appears like a mirage, jogging or biking by—alone, or with his even fitter, younger partner—whenever I'm doing something like hauling the no-longer-baby up a hill from the supermarket, a week's worth of groceries stashed in the stroller's undercarriage compartment. The shabbier I feel, the more cumbersome the snack-and-toy-filled tote bags I'm carrying, the more likely he is to appear in my line of vision.

I don't know this man personally and have only a hunch (and, OK, the existence of the boyfriend) to go on where his orientation's concerned. I have no doubt he has his own inner monologue, his own challenges, maybe even makes his own projections about random people he sees on the street. He's just as *real* as I am. But this is not about him.

This man represents, for me, a parallel track, where the decades can go by and nothing holds you back from simply being a wealthier version of your early-twenties self. Gay men can seem unencumbered and free. They face homophobia but are not beaten down by life into haggard *womanhood*. Even the ones with kids did not personally *birth* those kids. Gay men get to age into, fine, maybe a different type than they were when young, but they will still have their male admirers, along with the usual male perks of greater professional success and status along with age.

I think of a line in a viral excerpt from Maggie Smith's divorce memoir, where she describes her appearance as that of "one of the least visible creatures on earth: a middle-aged mother."[46] There's something about the paraphernalia of parenting young children that immediately marks a woman—whether twenty-five or forty-five—as *out of the game*. (I do however recommend the music video for the Rufus Wainwright song "Out of the Game" in which a sexy librarian played by Helena Bonham Carter fantasizes about three Rufuses making out with each other.) Sure, there are the trillion men putting "milf" into their porn searches, but when you on-the-ground *are* a mom, you're outside of the spaces where adult things are happening. As for women who reach midlife without kids, society wants to know why. Where childless gay men are concerned, the *why* rather answers itself.

NO, STRAIGHT WOMEN ARE NOT GAY MEN

A part of me has always liked the idea that I might be *different from the other straight girls*, a bit more like a gay man. Gay men have said this about me, unprompted, and whenever they have, I've thought, smugly, *yes, I suppose I am*. But when I stop and think what it is about this that I find flattering, I realize it's my fear of being a basic straight lady. Which is wrong on my part. The straight woman who sees herself as the protagonist, who experiences genuine desire for men, who has fantasies that go beyond a *romantic dinner*, is not an exception to the rule, let alone a creature so confusing that she needs to be defined as something other than a straight woman. This *is* who straight women are. It's not often who we're written as when other people write about us, but it is largely true to our own experience of things.

If an enthusiastic, exclusive interest in men and a perhaps excessive appreciation of male beauty makes me queer, fantastic, let me into the club of all things interesting and modern. I was never going to get in on the basis of attraction to women, so my only hope would be if something in *how* I liked men made me not-a-woman. But the very thought of labelling my forty-year-old self, who has been with my now-husband since we were twenty-three, as "queer" seems dismissive of actual queer people. I may not be what "cishet" implies, but it's the implication itself that's the problem.

Casting all straight women with affinities for gay men as oblivious bachelorettes—and reclassifying these same people as righteous the moment they hint at being not entirely straight or cis—misses something key about what attracts straight women to gay male spaces to begin with. What bothers me about the "trapped in a gay man's body" line of thought is that it represents a misunderstanding of female heterosexuality, and indeed of women. How wild it is that sexual attraction to men, something experienced *primarily by women*, a trait that is maligned as feminine when it exists in men, is only fathomable as a male urge! To say that man-desiring women are tantamount to gay men treats straight womanhood as an aberration, when it is anything but. It might be transgressive—or subversive, or unusual, or not—for women to desire men in the straightforward manner associated with gay men. But it's bizarre to label it as *queer.*

SIX

The Himbo Plot

AMY, CHASING

There are few premises less erotic than the one I'm about to recount: At the 2023 Minnesota state fair, U.S. senator Amy Klobuchar, a sixty-three-year-old Democrat and one-time presidential candidate, posed for social media with some public-sector employees under a sign that read, "Union Workers Are Essential."[1] Wholesome enough, but what relevance could this possibly have to a book about straight women?

In the photo, Klobuchar is sandwiched between four beefy-looking firefighters, of whom three are shirtless. All the men are toned and tattooed, the shirtless ones revealing six-pack abs. Klobuchar herself is substantially more covered up, in an open light-purple button-down, a white T-shirt underneath. These she paired with flat-front belted khakis and something in the sneaker family. Perfectly presentable. She looks every bit the suburban mom. And she's beaming. Klobuchar's accompanying text contains just a hint of a wink: "State Fair pro tip: You don't want to miss the Minnesota firefighters at the @MNAFLCIO." Who might be the "you" she's addressing?

I could make some on-brand remark about how I hardly noticed Klobuchar in the picture, what with all the hunks. But it wouldn't be true. Her presence is essential to the image. Photographs of fit, shirtless men are a dime a dozen. No, what's special here is the lady in the middle, grinning in a way that suggests—inasmuch as a smile from a politician ever can suggest this—authentic enjoyment.

Some spoil-sport detractors online pointed out that it would be received rather differently if a male politician posed with scantily clad young women. To them I would ask: Your point being? When a congresswoman ogles a fireman, there's no implication that only women can be politicians. For all that's said about men these days falling behind, they're still holding their own in the corridors of power.

The Klobuchar-and-firemen image not only fails to offend me but also delights me because of what it represents. I like the way the gaze—the metaphorical gaze; she's looking at the camera—is so unambiguously in one direction. (Well, in four directions, what with the four firemen.) It is not a sexy image *of* Amy Klobuchar. It is a sexy image *featuring* Amy Klobuchar. She is the protagonist, the only one named, the one whose words we're reading, who's at the centre of the image, and who stands out for being fully clothed. Where Amy Klobuchar herself would rank in a beauty contest is immaterial. The image subverts gender roles without claiming to be *queering heterosexuality*. It's quite simply a woman appreciating some firemen, as we are wont.

WHAT THE HIMBO PLOT IS NOT

Not every sitcom has a himbo-plot episode, but enough of them do that narrowing things down for this chapter proved a challenge. If you have watched your share of sitcoms, you will be familiar with the scenario: A hunk makes a one-episode appearance, leading the women characters to swoon and the male ones to mutter, *He's not all that*. The question of how a lesbian or asexual woman would react to a himbo never arises, because we are in the realm of cartoonish mid-to-late twentieth-century sitcom. The comedy comes from a simple gender role reversal: What if a bimbo, but a man? *What then?*

The himbo, a dim (or just *chill*) and good-looking man, is himself a trope, but the himbo *plot* is something more. It's a narrative structure based around the effect a spectacular-looking man has on the women around him. Everything's going along the way it normally does, the regular characters doing their usual thing, when suddenly there is a handsomeness situation afoot. A man's beauty, and nothing else about him, sets forth plot developments, romantic or otherwise.

To avoid trying to discuss all the pretty men of sitcom, I'm restricting the himbo-plot explorations that make up this chapter to these one-episode wonders. If you're expecting analysis of Ashton Kutcher's character on *That '70s Show*, or Ted Danson's on *Cheers*, or Josh Chan on *Crazy Ex-Girlfriend*, or Joey from *Friends*, I'm sure to disappoint. Yes, Idris Elba's character on *The Office* utters the line "I am aware of the effect I have on women," itself now the go-to meme for conveying when a man's allure is generally agreed upon by the opposite sex. The *line* is very himbo-plot, but Charles Miner appears in multiple episodes and isn't a himbo.

The himbo plot crumbles the moment a himbo character is given complexity. It is for this reason I must also exclude seductive bicurious Spanish bartender Mateo from *Benidorm*. Mateo offers the British ladies (mostly the ladies) visiting the all-inclusive resort a chance to experience a *Latin lover*, albeit not one with the best memory. (He sleeps with an unhappily married Englishwoman, then—much to her horror—hits on her again, as though meeting her for the first time.) The show ran for a decade, allowing Mateo to age into the role of ex-himbo, with all the vanity and beauty treatments that implies. It's all glorious fun, but not a himbo plot.

I can't even include Jung from *Kim's Convenience*, which is a sacrifice when you consider that doing so would have meant that I could image-search Simu Liu for legitimate work purposes. Jung may be a himbo—which is to say, he is a total himbo, and his dynamic with his painfully uncool female boss, who is eventually his girlfriend, is *very* man-as-the-pretty-one—but Liu is a star of the show, playing a character with an inner life. Himbo-plot himbos don't have those.

That said, the himbo is a man, so he requires a profession. He is permitted a fitness-intensive career: He's a rock climber, golf pro, tennis coach, ski instructor, a gardener. (Or, why not, a firefighter.) The himbo need not be stupid, but his brawn needs to be more in evidence than his brains. If the himbo has a white-collar job requiring an advanced degree, you're no longer in the realm of the himbo plot, even if other boxes are ticked. The 1998 *Frasier* episode "The Perfect Guy," about a man so beautiful every woman wants him, so stunning even the men take note (although this is *Frasier* and thus to be expected), makes its himbo a physician. This adds up in the context of the show (how could Frasier Crane envy a man who lacks *credentials*?) but takes it outside the himbo-plot bounds.

Apologies in advance if your own preferred himbo plot is missing. There was only room for so many, but I am aware that there are more—from shows I've seen and the ones I've regretfully missed.

I've omitted the *30 Rock* that paired Tina Fey with Jon Hamm—I know, *I know*, but press on I must.

"HE JUST HAPPENS TO HAVE A PERFECT FACE"

Seinfeld is not where the himbo plot originated, but its 1994 "mimbo" (Jerry's shorthand for "male bimbo") episode, "The Stall,"[2] is the one most associated with the concept, though himbo plots were already well established by the 1990s. In it, Jerry accuses Elaine of dating a man named Tony just for his looks, which is indeed what she is doing. She throws the accusation back at Jerry. Doesn't he have a new gorgeous girlfriend each episode? Jerry explains that it's fine for men to date women based on their looks alone because it's just assumed that men are "superficial." Elaine doesn't challenge the double standard. She insists she's dating Tony for nobler reasons (which the viewer knows to be ridiculous; he's a ditz) and that his "perfect face" is mere coincidence.

The truth comes out near the end, when Tony the Mimbo falls while rock climbing. This leads Elaine to despair. "Did something happen to his face?" *Seinfeld* is a show with only one core female character, so its himbo plot can only allude to Tony's general effect on women: waitresses apparently give him "free pie." In the role of smitten schoolgirl, adult heterosexual man George forms a dorky platonic crush on Tony, agreeing to go rock climbing with him. Rock climbing is about the least of potential George Costanza leisure pursuits. It is on that expedition that Tony meets his face-crushing fate, when George prioritizes offering him an array of sandwiches over harness safety.

"THE MOST GORGEOUS PERSON OUT THERE I HAVE EVER SEEN IN MY ENTIRE LIFE"

The mimbo may be 1990s, but there is something 1970s about the himbo plot. Was it the rise of the contraceptive pill, and its legal accessibility from 1972 onwards to American women no matter their marital status? The way polyester clings to a male torso? The 1972 "Tennis, Emily?" episode from *The Bob Newhart Show*[3] offered a template for decades of himbo-plot shenanigans, as well as one of the less-clothed himbos. Chicago psychologist Bob's schoolteacher wife

Emily, played by Suzanne Pleshette, is listless at home during her summer break. (In Pleshette, slothfulness is more languid than dirtbag.) Bob finds Emily's new attitude a real turnoff and wants her to find something to occupy herself. By way of context, Bob, played by Newhart, is a nondescript middle-aged man while Emily is a perfect-looking woman with cleavage that could make Emily Ratajkowski jealous. This is necessary information for what follows.

Emily stuns Bob by coming home giddy, with shopping bags. She's now taking tennis lessons and wants to dress the part. Bob asks her where the racquet is, and she says she forgot to get one of those. (Women!) She also lets Bob know that her tennis pro is a wonderful but troubled man, whom she has cheerily referred to Bob for psychotherapy, because why not.

At this point you can probably guess who the himbo is going to be. But the himbo *plot* announces itself indirectly, via Carol, Bob's receptionist. She bursts into the room where Bob is with his friend Jerry, and says, "There is the most gorgeous person out there I have ever seen in my entire life." Jerry, terminally single and hopeful, or just confused about the existence of male-directed lust, misses the tenor of Carol's announcement, asking, "Who is she?" Carol corrects: "He." Carol tells them that a man named Stan has an appointment with Bob. "That must be Emily's pro," says Bob. Carol responds, full of 1970s innuendo, "I bet he is." Later in the episode, Bob specifies that Stan is Emily's "*tennis* pro," with "pro" on its own suggesting there are other services on offer.

Here's where we at last meet Stan, who has shown up for therapy in tiny shorts, his work attire. He steels himself before letting Bob know what the lifelong problem is that he's come to Bob to address: "Bob, you have no idea what it's like to be incredibly good-looking." Bob, more amused than insulted, agrees he doesn't. Stan's complaint is that women hit on him incessantly and he can't get himself to say no to any of them. He's afraid he'll realize, on his deathbed, that there was "one girl I've missed."Stan asks Bob to guess his proverbial belt-notch number. His answer is that he'd already lost track at nineteen. Bob: "That's about the time I started counting."

Bob is his usual even-keeled, deadpan self about this man's revelations, but does take issue with the fact that Don Juan here is his wife's new tennis instructor. Stan first insists he's not attracted to Emily but later says she's "one of the most beautiful women I've ever seen," an ambiguity necessary for the himbo plot to ensue. Is Emily going to have an affair with Stan? Will she admit to wanting to do so, even if she doesn't go ahead with it? Is their marriage strong enough to survive the arrival of this most alluring and seductive man, who has already made it clear that Emily has caught *his* eye?

At home, Bob tries to process this with Emily, asking her if she thinks Stan is good-looking. Her answer—"Oh, yes"—isn't what he'd hoped. He presses on, asking her if she prefers Stan to her own husband, and this she denies. Emily then produces a monologue sure to please every man who imagines that the likes of an early-1970s Suzanne Pleshette is around the corner, and that he's just her type. She reminisces about how, when her high school friends dated handsome athletes, she went for "the second trumpet player in the school band." She spells out, "I just never went for those big, good-looking guys like Stan. That's why I married you." Bob is at first on the defensive, insisting that in his own high school days, he was nothing to sneeze at, but soon comes around and accepts the fact that Suzanne Pleshette, I mean Emily, has chosen him as the win that it is: "You just explained that you're not attracted to attractive men. That's why you like me."

Bob and Emily have sorted things out enough that a party they've invited Stan to in their apartment can proceed. Stan shows up in a pair of slacks that, if they were 2010s athleisure, would be recalled for excessive transparency. Carol again swoons, amazed he's remembered her name. Emily gives Stan a tour of the apartment, and the other women at the party leap up to join, even though they've just had one. Then, crisis! Stan pulls Bob aside and says he must stop their therapy sessions because Emily is hitting on him. Bob doesn't believe him, but Stan insists that something in her eye contact has told him this. Emily denies it, and Stan is forced to admit that this might have been in his head. This leads Stan to understand that maybe his sister-in-law wasn't ogling him during her wedding ceremony, either. Maybe women are not all after him, after all! Maybe he's just a narcissist in short-shorts! Then Howard's date asks him seductively for tennis lessons, asking him if he "takes beginners," at which point Bob and Stan have to conclude that *some* of this isn't in Stan's imagination.

Classically a himbo-plot episode needs one scene where women gather and admire the himbo. "Tennis, Emily?" squeezes in a second one. Stan emerges from Bob's therapy office in *the shorts*, paired with an unzipped jacket with nothing under it. A bunch of women follow him downstairs. Bob remarks to Jerry, who had been chatting with the women until they saw Stan and bolted, "It's amazing how most women find him attractive." Jerry disagrees: "Women don't go for good-looking guys like that anymore." Bob then spells out to Jerry that the women had been waiting for Stan, not hanging around to talk to *him*. Jerry and Bob are forced to conclude that women are attracted to gorgeous men. That is, *most* women. Emily is impervious to the himbo, because her type is Bob. This is as much of a male fantasy as a Bob Newhart snagging a Suzanne Pleshette.

"THE MOST GORGEOUS HUNK OF FLESH I HAVE EVER SEEN"

Wifely loyalty does not withstand the force of the himbo quite so readily in the 1974 *Mary Tyler Moore Show* episode "Not Just Another

Pretty Face."[4] Mary Richards, a single-but-social news producer in her thirties, has a new boyfriend, Paul Van Dillen, played by Robert Wolders. Now Wolders doesn't do it for me, but his real-life partner was Audrey Hepburn, making it somehow plausible that he'd have been the rare man *out of Mary's league* on the looks front, and I mention this because boy does this come up in the episode. Before we meet Paul, we see Mary telling neighbour Phyllis and Phyllis's sensible teenage daughter Bess about him. Phyllis admonishes Mary for letting a strange man pick her up, and Mary clarifies, "I picked *him* up." Paul arrives, Phyllis opens the door, looks at him, and says, dreamy-eyed, "Oh." Bess: "Man, was he good-looking." Phyllis: "Oh, did you think so?" Mother and daughter giggle in rare agreement.

Mary brings Paul to a party with her colleagues. Sue Ann Nivens, the show's sex-crazed cooking-show host played by Betty White, at first seems uncharacteristically oblivious, chit-chatting with Mary, but then turns to Paul and says, "Incidentally, Mr. Van Dillen, you are the most gorgeous hunk of flesh I have ever seen." Ted Baxter, the newscaster whose birthday it is, immediately registers that Paul is a beautiful man, not because he's interested in *dating* Paul—it's not a given in the show's universe, but Ted is straight—but because he's intensely vain and needs to be the prettiest man in the room. "I'd give my right arm to have dimples like yours," Ted tells him.

Gruff, no-nonsense newsroom boss Lou Grant is less convinced. "I wonder what she sees in *him*." Apart from Ted, the men make a show of not getting Paul's appeal. Lou says, "I wouldn't have figured he was Mary's type." News writer Murray—like Lou, a bald, normal-looking middle-aged man—asks, "In what way?" Lou explains that he'd assumed Mary "likes guys with more character, more intelligence." Ted asks, as if insulted on behalf of beautiful men, "What makes you think a guy who's handsome can't have brains and character too?"

Murray responds, putting his arm around Lou's shoulders, "Because if we didn't believe it, I don't think we could go on living." Lou nods. He gets it. He nevertheless disapproves of the relationship, later asking how Mary would act if he had taken up with a "bimbo," and says that she's doing the equivalent. He doesn't coin "mimbo," but this is the gist. Lou bluntly informs Mary that Paul is "prettier than" she is.

But it's not just the men in her life who feel the need to question why Mary would date a man for his looks. Mary asks Phyllis what makes her think she's only dating Paul for that reason, then is seen walking away, a naughty smile on her face. Precocious Bess seems to get it. She makes an impassioned feminist speech about the right of women to objectify men the way men have women, but then backtracks and says if women did this, they'd be no better than men. Bess always was a bit of a killjoy.

But the grown women know where Mary is coming from. Phyllis tells Mary about the time when her now-husband Lars—an off-screen character—proposed to her. She wasn't sure what to do, which for some reason led her to take a solo trip to Paris. "On the plane, seated next to me was the most fantastic-looking man I have ever seen in my life, I can't tell you how beautiful this man was." Phyllis recalls weighing marrying Lars against an affair with this man and tells Mary she's ashamed that she wasn't sure which to pick. The punchline: "Fortunately I was spared the decision when I called his hotel room and he wasn't there."

There are many wonderful things about this scene, delivered flawlessly by Cloris Leachman, but one of them is that Phyllis summons, for Mary and the viewer, the image of a man *even better-looking than Paul*.

Contrast Phyllis's story with Emily, on *The Bob Newhart Show*, reassuring Bob that she never did go for hunks. The difference this says about the two shows' perspectives. This is what Emily is telling *Bob*. Is it what she'd say to a female friend, if the show had allowed her those?

Everyone assumes Paul is an airhead from looking at him, and appearances turn out not to be deceiving. His only interest is skiing, and he needs Lou's help to figure out how to eat dip at the party. Mary resolves to break up with him because the two have nothing in common. But then he gazes into her eyes, and she just goes for it. Their relationship doesn't last beyond this episode, but this is because it's a single-episode himbo plot—on a show that, like *Seinfeld*, assumes its single stars get new dates each week—not because she's learned a lesson. Unlike the nefarious himbo Emily rebuffs on *The Bob Newhart Show*, Mary's Paul is a neutral presence. His good-natured, Golden Retriever–esque charms give Mary and the viewer permission to relax and enjoy.

"LUCKY MUM"

Not every himbo episode announces itself as such via an actor's own self-evident handsomeness. The 1979 *Fawlty Towers* episode "The Psychiatrist"[5] is more of a slow burn. It starts with hotel co-owner Sybil Fawlty (Prunella Scales), in Torquay, England, drooling over a sleazy, open-shirted hotel guest, Mr. Johnson (Nicky Henson). A rewatch reminded me that in addition to the Bernard-Henri Lévy–style décolletage, Mr. Johnson wears tight leather pants, to which the viewer is offered a lingering view from behind.

To say that Sybil is all over Mr. Johnson would be an understatement. He tells an unfunny joke (the punchline is someone saying, "Pretentious? Moi?") and she can't stop laughing. She compliments him on his chain necklaces and alludes to the many women who must be after him. Mr. Johnson tries to make a phone call at the front desk, and Sybil makes use of the captive audience to tell a meandering story about her mother's phobias, the purpose of which is seemingly to emphasize her own relative youth. He tells her his mother will be sharing his hotel room with him, prompting Sybil to utter the definitely not weird at all line "Lucky Mum," followed by maniacal laughter.

Basil comes up with a passive-aggressive response to Sybil's fawning, making remarks alluding to his belief that Mr. Johnson resembles an "ape." This does not put Sybil off. Quite the contrary! "I suppose the reason you confuse them with monkeys is that monkeys have fun. They know how to enjoy themselves. That's what makes them sexy I suppose." Yes, decades before scientists were publishing the results of how women's genitals respond to images of bonobo copulation, Sybil Fawlty had her well-manicured finger on the pulse of what women want. (The notion that monkey-like men are women's preference is reprised in a 1993 episode of *One Foot in the Grave*, "The Pit and the Pendulum," in which the not-un-Basil-like retiree Victor Meldrew contends with a hairy-backed gardener who charms everyone from local schoolgirls to Victor's own hyper-practical sixtyish wife.)

Having established that Basil dislikes Mr. Johnson, the episode turns to Basil overhearing a woman laughing in the ape's room, in response to his same "Pretentious? Moi?" anecdote. Basil becomes preoccupied with enforcing a hotel rule against having overnight guests "of the opposite . . ." and Basil can barely get himself to say the word "sex." This is the tightness level to which he is wound. The ape insists he's in the room by himself, and Basil spends the rest of the episode trying to get confirmation there's a lady with him. But Basil can't get proof, despite his best efforts, which include spying with a ladder on what turns out to be the room of a married fiftyish couple, both doctors, the man the titular psychiatrist. By the time Basil does get *the woman in Mr. Johnson's room* to appear, the date has already left, and now the woman in with him really is his mother.

"The Psychiatrist" may not show any women apart from Sybil lusting after the ape (although I guess the young woman he's snuck into his room for the night likes him enough), but the way she presents her attraction to him suggests this is emblematic of how women generally find men of his sort. She's nominated herself as representative of womankind and as demystifier, for Basil and the audience, of *what women want*.

As you will have guessed—or known from seeing the episode—who should arrive at the hotel front desk but a stunning young blonde Australian in a tight, cleavage-baring top. The parallel is emphasized with Basil admiring the Australian's necklace, just as Sybil did with the ape. But there is no equivalent analysis of what Basil sees in the Australian, no investigation of *what men want*. It's immediately obvious when you look at her. When I watched this episode as a kid in the 1990s, it was clear to me that the Australian was meant to be attractive. It was only with later rewatches that I understood that the ape was supposed to be hot, and that Sybil was flirting with him for this reason versus because she's batty like that.

"The Psychiatrist" might not seem a perfect himbo-plot episode, given that the himbo is sort of witty, not to mention clever enough to have snuck a female guest into his hotel room. The Australian, meanwhile, is pure bimbo, looks without brains. But it's the himbo whose sex appeal drives the plot. Basil is obsessed, but not, as Sibyl presumes, with the pretty young woman he keeps inadvertently groping. (She's a little *too* understanding at first, not out of any interest in Basil, but because she's not sharp enough to see what's happening.) Sybil misinterprets all of Basil's shenanigans as an attempt to get close to the Australian. He clearly does find her attractive, but this is not what's motivating him.

Seeing how Sibyl reacts to the ape, and contemplating how all women would, is what sets Basil off. It's what inspires Basil to fixate on the hot, forbidden, premarital, hotel-rule-violating sex he's convinced the ape is having, and that he himself is not. It's Basil's sexual insecurities propelling this episode. He's convinced that the psychiatrist guest is obsessed with sex, and more specifically, with how much sex Basil himself is having, something that does not appear to be remotely on this man's radar. But even if the episode is more about male anxieties than female desire, it's Sybil's attraction to the ape that sets all this in motion. If Mr. Johnson had no effect on Sybil, there'd be no episode.

BUT WOMEN AREN'T VISUAL CREATURES!

In theory, the himbo plot makes no sense. Beauty exists in men as well as women, as well as in flowers and oceans and whatnot. But it isn't meant to be all that important to women that some men are better looking than others. One hears this all the time, how *men are visual creatures*, women more preoccupied with a man's sense of humour or his title at the office, maybe with his height or fitness, but certainly not with how *pretty* he is. And yet in the world of living, breathing women, somehow male beauty matters a great deal. The himbo plot explores that dissonance, but in a way *so* much more enjoyable than a dry phrase like "explores that dissonance" suggests.

As a woman who has always cared what men look like, I have long been fascinated by the truism about men—and men alone—being visual creatures. It's science! It's testosterone! What motivates me to refute it isn't a 1990s-feminist belief that men and women are identical in the aggregate (we're not, though differences within each set are substantial), but rather a hunch that this visual-creatures divide *just isn't true*. Women with sufficient eyesight to do so absolutely *are* looking at men, even at inappropriate moments, categorizing them as *woulds* and *wouldn'ts*.

The myth that women aren't visual creatures relates to another: that we have no specific visual (or physical) requirements, and could therefore be with a man, a woman, or no one at all. But even those who accept that most women want sex with men will nevertheless describe female desire as less looks-based than male desire, or maybe even not about appearances at all. This is a narrative reinforced in best-man speeches about dorky men and their drop-dead gorgeous brides—a convention meant to flatter, and that evades the reality of assortative mating, wherein people are usually approximately as good-looking as their partners. You see it in wedding announcement articles, in which the groom inevitably knew from the moment he saw her that the bride was The One, but where the bride had to get to know him for a while as a friend before considering anything more. Was this actually how the relationship played out, or is this just what reads as *romantic*?

In a *Variety* profile, the then-twenty-one-year-old pop star Billie Eilish held forth about beauty and double standards. "Nobody ever says a thing about men's bodies," she told her interviewer. "If you're muscular, cool. If you're not, cool. If you're rail thin, cool. If you have a dad bod, cool. If you're pudgy, love it! Everybody's happy with it. You know why? Because girls are nice. They don't give a fuck because we see people for who they are!"[6]

Eilish is right that there's no male equivalent to her experiences as a young girl who developed early, while in the public eye, and whose large bust has been a source of much commentary. She's wrong that men's bodies are never commented on, although on this, one could forgive her for speaking hyperbolically. Men's bodies are unquestionably *less* commented on than women's, as three seconds considering who typically gets cosmetic surgery or has eating disorders will attest. None of this is complicated or interesting. What *is* of interest is this idea of "girls" being "nice" and therefore not caring what men look like.

It is, of course, not true that women are above caring how "people" look. Even if most body-shaming targets women, there are (she types, having attended middle school) more than a few ladies engaged in that shaming. But let's say that "people" in this context refers to men, which is the more logical reading. Is Eilish saying that women "don't give a fuck" how men look, or that women give fucks aplenty, but are too "nice" to voice their opinions publicly? Because these are two different claims. Is it that women *don't* notice what men look like, or that we know better than to say? Where does one stop and the other begin? That is, at what point does the idea that *women just don't objectify men* become ingrained as something women understand to be true about their own sexuality?

"AH SUFFER"

The most curious thing about the myth that women aren't visual is that *no such myth exists* where teen girls are concerned. They write lists of cute boys in their notebooks and screenshot photos of teen idols. The cultural icon for that life stage, for my generation, was earnest Angela Chase, pining for floppy-haired slacker Jordan Catalano (Jared Leto), on the 1994 one-season teen drama *My So-Called Life*. The show is a fine illustration of *why* this is permitted of (attractive) teen girls. Jordan may not know Angela's alive (until he does; they eventually get together), but the audience is watching a pretty, young Claire Danes. Not only is the actress herself good-looking, but the dorky boy next door has a huge crush on her. The young girl with a crush on a pop star or fit athlete exists on two registers at the same time. She is at once the pathetic desirer and the cute girl who's easy on the male-gaze audience's minds. That, and society (outside the most traditionalist fringes) is not trying to get teen girls to settle down with husbands.

The effect a beautiful man has on teen girls is known. But grown women don't suddenly develop blinders that make them only able to see whether a man is *reliable*. Where, then, does the idea that women are less visual come from? Elderly women, like teen girls, are permitted visual attractions, but they're all kitsch and Blanche on *The Golden Girls*. The thirsty post-menopausal woman is harmless, fodder for patronizing humour, but not a cause for concern. But for women between, say, twenty-five and forty, there's prescription posing as description. A woman that age very well might want to sleep around like a college student, but society will warn her that doing this uses up dwindling husband-catching time. "How long can I go on chasing these hunky 25-year-olds that are all looks and no substance?" Roz asks Frasier in a 1995 episode of *Frasier.* He responds, "Exactly, Roz," relieved that she sees the error of her ways. She *is* a bit long in the tooth to be acting like a horny coed. She sets matters straight, so to speak, with her next line: "No, I'm serious. I'm asking, how long? Three, four years?"[7] The thirty-ish woman who prioritizes hunkiness is a threat. The clock is ticking, if not on having kids (maybe she doesn't want any, or already has some) then on her own eligibility. *Women* absolutely care what men look like, but women *of marriageable age* are socialized into obfuscating this rather central facet of attraction.

The 1963 musical *Bye Bye Birdie*[8] is not a sitcom, but it follows the himbo plot, in that all the action is fallout from a spectacular-looking man's destabilizing effect. The play is a performance classic in high schools, but in case it didn't swing through yours, here's the gist: Elvis Presley stand-in Conrad Birdie comes to Sweet Apple, Ohio, to bestow a symbolic "one last kiss" before he enlists in the U.S. Army. The presence of a hard-livin' rocker in the wholesome town is bad enough, but he is there to *kiss one of the girls*, a girl who happens to have a serious boyfriend to whom she is "pinned" (pre-engaged). Conrad's hunkiness throws everything in the town off-balance.

Conrad Birdie, the character, is a celebrity, which I realize cuts against it being pure himbo-plot, same as Burt Reynolds on *The Golden Girls*. I don't want to be inconsistent in my himbo-plot classifications, heaven forbid. But what exactly is Conrad famous *for*? This becomes clear when Conrad performs a song at the town hall. "Honestly Sincere" is an ironically titled ode to how it is to "really feel that girl," which he sings in a skin-tight gold bodysuit. The title and lyrics ostensibly speak to an innocent teen-girl fan base, the audience for chaste love songs about feelings and eye contact. Girls like the ones who throng The Beatles in *A Hard Day's Night*. But he's also thrusting his hips and oozing sex in a deeply adult way, not least because he's in his early thirties himself. If you conclude from this scene that women don't like looking at nude men, then I suppose you'd think men's appreciation of women in lingerie is evidence that they're put off by entirely naked women.

The "Honestly Sincere" scene culminates in all the teen girls from the town fainting, and then with the entire crowd collapsed, the girls having knocked over the tsk-tsking boys like dominos. Rewatching the movie as an adult, I noticed that the first to tumble is not a teenager at all, but rather the mayor's wife, standing next to her husband in a ceremonial capacity. Primly attired in a below-the-knee purple dress, white gloves, and a middle-aged-lady hat with a bunch of flowers on it, she collapses into a seated position, her legs spread, the moment Conrad begins the song, with the lyric "You gotta be sincere." Her husband struggles to close her legs, and sort of rearranges her skirt over her, for decency. There's no point. The lyrics have Conrad flirting with the teen girls in his audience, asking them to "hug" him. He then turns to the mayor's wife and adds, "Ah suffer." The refrain repeats, with "ah suffer" again accompanying Conrad gesturing towards the mayor's limp wife. She tumbles three times before Kim—the girl selected to give Conrad his last kiss—and then the remaining girls, follow suit.

The mayor's wife isn't the only old lady suffering for lack of Conrad. During a rehearsal scene, later in the film, Albert Peterson, Conrad's songwriter, is trying to get him to relax. Albert's domineering mother, a stern presence in a fur coat, a histrionic martyr of the old school, who does things like stick her head in the oven to make a point, is hanging around mainly to meddle in Albert's life. But she is still, underneath it all, *a woman*. She's reassuring Conrad, ostensibly to help her son, but then the tone becomes less maternal. Patting Conrad's arm and then stroking it, she asks him to drive with her "in the country." He looks at her, clocks what's happening, and turns her down not-so-gently: "Man, I hope I never get *that* tense." By the end of the movie, Mrs. Peterson is announcing her engagement to a same-age widower, so she's not all that hard up. Conrad was a reach, but you can't blame a girl for trying.

The mayor's wife fainting. Mrs. Peterson planning a hot date that's never going to happen. What are these things doing in a movie about smitten teenagers? To some extent, it's about conveying just how hot Conrad is supposed to be. The moments are there for comic effect. Isn't it hilarious that *elderly women* have the same reaction as teen girls to a gorgeous rock star in tight trousers? (The actresses in question were both in their thirties at the time, but thanks to good acting, costuming, and context, they read as ancient.) Unlike the girls, whose collective crush is meant to read as charming, theirs is just pathetic. After all, where the girls are concerned, Conrad reciprocates! (Audiences today would know to object to this, and it poses its share of issues even in the 1963 context.) When it's grown women, *older* ones, even, responding sexually to a same-age-as-they-are male pop star, it's unexpected and unseemly. A behavioural equivalent of mutton-dressed-as-lamb.

But there's one woman in *Bye Bye Birdie* immune to Conrad's charms: Rosie DeLeon, Albert's girlfriend, played by Janet Leigh. She, unlike everyone else in the movie's universe, inhabits a marriage plot rather than a himbo plot. Rosie recalls, in role and physicality, Emily from *The Bob Newhart Show*. That's because Rosie, like Emily, inhabits a marriage plot, nestled within a broader himbo plot. Emily's loyalty to Bob, like Rosie's to Albert, takes precedence, keeping them from bothering about a tennis pro and a pseudo-Elvis, respectively. The himbo plot treats a Rosie or Emily—a woman so devoted to her husband or husband-to-be that she simply wouldn't care if the world's best-looking man crossed her path—as an exception to the rule. Within the closed universe of a himbo-plot episode, the himbo is this *force* whose hold over women makes no allowances for variations in taste, type, relationship status, or, indeed, sexual orientation. The himbo is *what women want* personified. The broader culture, meanwhile, assumes all women, barring a few "sickies," are like Rosie and Emily. Neither the marriage plot nor the himbo plot accurately describes *womankind's true nature*, because no such thing exists. Arguably, both could be about instructing women in what's expected of them, in *inculcating heteronormativity*, I suppose, but in such radically different ways. Because the vast majority of women don't need to be *told* to notice beautiful men. They might however benefit from permission to speak more openly about the thing they are already doing.

VISUAL CREATURES

When it is said that men are visual creatures, what's meant? What it is that women are thought *not* to experience? Is it that all men are connoisseurs of the female form, and if so, how does this square with men's rumoured eagerness to have sex with any woman who'd have them? If it matters so much more what women than men look like—and goodness knows it does in many everyday situations—why is it *also* a truism that even the plainest-looking woman could have a man in her bed in no time? Is a visual creature someone who's up for sex upon seeing a blurry photo of anatomy, and if that's the case, where does the myth of male superficiality come from?

Some of the perception of men as "visual" emerges from demonstrable differences in male and female sexuality. Men are bigger porn-watchers than women, although the exact breakdown varies by study. Women are also, for all kinds of reasons, more discreet in our gazing. The himbo plot offers a window into the mind of the female ogler, but in life as lived, when a handsome man in a business suit (or shirtless and in jogging shorts) passes by, he is not typically catcalled.

When we speak of men liking beautiful women, it is assumed that consensus exists about who, exactly, these women are. This comes through in a letter a man sent to the *Dear Sugars* advice podcast.[9] The letter-writer explains that when he met his girlfriend, "I didn't feel as much of a physical attraction to her as I thought I should, but I decided that my attraction to her on all other levels was deep enough to overcome that." But he can't. He then heads off in a different direction, mentioning that his friends think he could snag a hotter woman. The way he sums up his problem is incredible in the way it illustrates that this man's sexual response to his girlfriend is *altogether inseparable* from how hot he believes his buddies find her. He asks, "Am I doing the right thing in pursuing a relationship with this wonderful person and ignoring what I perceive to be totally invented standards of beauty? Or is physical chemistry the first and most important part of a real relationship?"

The author Cheryl Strayed, one of the Sugars, asks him to separate these two pieces: what he wants and what he thinks his friends are seeing. Strayed is right, or rather, she ought to be, but I'm not sure straight male desire works like that. For heterosexual men, perceptions of a woman's sex appeal sometimes really do seem to be "conflated" with the status it would confer on the man to be with that woman. His buddies' perceived appreciation of his girlfriend is, for him, *part of sex.*

Male and female beauty are equally of interest to straight women and men, respectively, in intimate contexts and in day-to-day appreciations, but have different functions in society. Outside of himbo-plot sitcom episodes, there's no notion that a man could be so beautiful that he'd be of interest to all women, let alone that he'd be able to parlay this into a more generally enviable life. There is a kind of beauty, accessible only to women, that is about power. The objectively hot woman, on a man's arm, brings clout. Her presence signifies to other men—to other *people*—that this is a man with exceptional qualities. All the more so if he himself isn't much to look at. It's not by chance that Henry Kissinger came to be known for his quip about power being the greatest aphrodisiac. And yet, for all the media attention paid to important older men with young wives, most couples are similar to each other in looks and age. There are only so many consensus-approved supermodels to go around, and most men want female companionship.

Perhaps less consensus exists among men about female beauty than is imagined, but more among women about male beauty very well might. That the himbo is immediately recognized as such suggests that we do have some shared conception of which men are hot. Words like "hunk," "beefcake," or "handsome" would be otherwise incomprehensible. But there's no status boost to being a plain-looking woman with a conventionally attractive man. This is something you do *for you.*

COMPULSORY HIMBOSEXUALITY

My own interest in the himbo plot is not thirst-derived, or not as straightforwardly as it might seem. I don't think my taste in men is that unusual, but it's idiosyncratic enough that I am not attracted to the majority of even beautiful men. The television actors who most do it for me (a list topped by John Castle as Inspector Craddock in two 1980s episodes of noted erotica series *Miss Marple* and Steve Pemberton as layabout Mick on *Benidorm*) are reasonable-looking, but not ones who'd get cast in a beefcake role. What I like about the himbo plot is the way it focuses on women *finding* men beautiful. The episodes feature women doing the desiring, and unable to stop themselves from becoming blushing, stumbling messes. Showcasing a man who is obviously attractive is the only way to visually represent how giddy a woman gets around a man who's painfully attractive *to her*.

Himbo-plot episodes may celebrate and normalize female hetero lust, but they only make sense in a culture that treats this form of desire as suspect. The non-himbo men shaking their heads in disapproving incomprehension are stand-ins for how society views women's visually based attractions. These episodes set up a tension between how women are supposed to act—*supposed to* in the dual meaning of, what's assumed and what's demanded—versus how they do. You watch a himbo-plot episode and, however absurd the specifics, the dynamic itself rings immediately true as a thing in the world.

In the *Mary Tyler Moore Show* himbo episode, there's a scene where a group of women surround Mary's ski-instructor beau. Paul makes some banal remark about how cold it is in Minneapolis, and they all react as though he's told a great joke. One of the women says, "Doesn't he have a wonderful sense of humour, Sue Ann?" Sue Ann, still laughing at his witticism, says, "No, but who cares?"

CONCLUSION

Frumpy-but-horny

"WHEN A WOMAN WHO IS SEXUAL TAKES OFF HER TOP"

In July 2016—pre-Trump-presidency, pre-#MeToo—*Harper's Bazaar* ran an interview with the headline "Emily Ratajkowski's Naked Ambition."[1] They weren't kidding. At the top is a large photo (by Mona Kuhn) of the model, then twenty-five. It's quite something. She is nude, bareback astride a white horse. Her thick, flowing brown hair barely covers the nipples of her famously perfect breasts.

Along with modelling, acting, and having her own line of swimwear, Ratajkowski is perhaps the foremost theorist of the sexiness-positive branch of feminism, defending at every turn the right of women to look fabulous in a bikini, profit from the same, and not be thought less of for that. This may sound catty on my part, the sneering of a jealous woman who does not look like that. To which I can only say, *everyone* wishes they looked like that. This is no gotcha. And up to a point, she's not wrong. Sex appeal doesn't imply shallowness. Nor does a woman's choice to be a lingerie model excuse sexual assault or abuse. What I object to isn't that equity-of-outcome hasn't come for bikini modelling, but rather the way Ratajkowski conflates sexiness and sexuality. She doesn't just want to be professionally gorgeous and unmolested, as is her right. She wants to present her career as an empowering example of sex-positive feminism. It's there that she's on shakier ground.

Knowing this is her thing, the interviewer prompts Ratajkowski to discuss "the fear and contempt of female sexuality and the just intolerable cultural reaction when women take ownership of their sexuality and their bodies." Ratajkowski obliges, sharing what she sees as a double standard in how female nudity is received: "When Lena Dunham takes her clothes off, she gets flack, but it's also considered brave . . . But when a woman who is sexual takes off her top, it plays into something."

Consider the phrasing: "A woman who is sexual."

Ratajkowski is using "sexual" to mean sexually desirable. The implication is not that Dunham, an accomplished writer and actress who didn't get where she is based on her looks, is asexual or celibate or a form of moss. It's that being "sexual" requires being the sort of woman whose shirt-removal makes the average person (man) want sex. All this would be news to the legions of women who look more like Dunham, yet who have sex, even while naked, even with the lights on.

It's here that Ratajkowski's interviewer cuts her off, saying, "I'll just jump in and say that any woman is sexual," leading to a partial backtrack from the called-out subject.

It's no coincidence that the interviewer has the insight she does. She is none other than *The Beauty Myth* author Naomi Wolf. In that iconic 1990s feminist manifesto, Wolf writes incisively about the way girls are socialized to view sexuality in terms of a straight male gaze:

> What little girls learn is not the desire for the other, but the desire to be desired. Girls learn to watch their sex along with the

> boys; that takes up the space that should be devoted to finding out about what they are wanting, and reading and writing about it, seeking and getting it. . . . Women come to confuse sexual looking with being looked at sexually.[2]

Hear, hear!

But sometimes a messenger overshadows her message. Wolf has been known in recent years for Covid conspiracy theories, and for inadvertently tarnishing the good name of leftist intellectual Naomi Klein, with whom she is (per Klein's 2023 book *Doppelganger*) often confused. It has been chic to be dismissive of Wolf, to claim that because she's become a crank, because one of her later books turned out to be riddled with errors and even *The Beauty Myth* required some corrections, her output was nonsense from the get-go. But her insights about female heterosexual desire, and the way women are socialized into self-objectification, and out of judging men on their physical attributes, are sound, as well as sorely lacking in contemporary discussions. Who better to push back against sexiness-positive feminism?

The conversation we ought to be having is the one about all the ways women are nudged away from straightforwardly appreciating male beauty and towards obsessing over our own looks. Instead, one hears about how heterosexuality itself is a heteronormative imposition. It's meant to be freeing for women generally (versus for the handful who actually want this) to have a sex life that excludes men. We're meant to believe the supermodel naked on a horse in the women's magazine is there because women are inherently sexually fluid and get some kind of pleasure out of gazing at it, because it is hardwired into us to find attractive naked men uninteresting. The grim reality is that, as a rule, photos of flawless women inspire us normal-looking ones to feel crap about our own appearance and wonder if we bought the eye cream or whatever that's advertised on page 210 we'd look just like her. And it's *grim* we are now about to flee from.

Sexual desire is complicated, a mess of motivations. It is not possible to fully decouple wanting another person and wanting that person to want you, or even from hoping, in some bigger sense, to be desirable. This is true across age, gender, or sexual orientation. The problem isn't that desirability is a part of human sexuality, but the centrality it takes on in what people imagine female heterosexuality entails. What does it look like when a straight woman is sexual, *very* sexual, but sits firmly in the role of the one doing the desiring?

It looks like a category of sitcom character I call frumpy-but-horny. These are heterosexual women characters who care deeply about the visual, just not as it pertains to themselves. They'd rather drool over a beautiful man than check their own teeth for spinach. The shows will mock them for this, laugh tracks will leave no room for doubt, but it'll be refreshing to see them all the same. It's not like the himbo plot, where the woman's own looks are beside the point, but she's allowed to be pretty, and the subversiveness can come from her beauty being overshadowed by a man's. And the man (or men) the frump is drawn to need not be objectively handsome. He need not register to anyone other than the frump as a sexual object. The presence onscreen of a frumpy-but-horny character is the opposite of the naked-on-horse photo. It's sex-positive, in its way, but has the effect of decoupling sexual desire from a woman's own sex appeal. And this is not something you see much of, unless you're looking for it.

While cultural representations of heterosexuality could hardly be called scarce, the woman who's hot for men but not particularly hot *to* them is a rarely seen figure in contemporary North American pop culture. The closest you'll get will be something like Taylor Swift, back when she had the persona of the high school girl passed over for a miniskirt-wearing classmate. She may have sung a song of unrequited love, but she looked awfully cute while doing so. American actresses generally have to be good-looking, even the ones playing plain. The character of Liz Lemon on *30 Rock* is homely. Is Tina Fey herself? (Don't answer this; I look enough like her that someone once thought I *was* her.) Dunham may be the rule-proving exception.

The frumpy-but-horny archetype is better represented in British comedy. British actresses tend to be more ordinary-looking than their white-toothed American counterparts. Cross the Atlantic, go back a few decades, and examples abound of women in unflattering cardigans and no makeup, who simply cannot get enough of men. I'm thinking of characters like Selina Cadell's Mrs. Tishell on *Doc Martin* (2004–22), the Cornwall pharmacist whose crush on the titular doctor hovers somewhere between inexplicable, unrequited, and terrifying.

My aim with *The Last Straight Woman* is to shift the focus onto what female heterosexuality is at its core: wanting men. The point of this book isn't that straight women have been straight-womaning incorrectly, or that the world has too few (or too many!) of us, but that our society has gotten female heterosexuality all wrong. The more emphasis we put on the man-wanting aspect of things, the less on being generically attractive to men, the better place we land. But this is too abstract, which is where frumpy-but-horny enters into it.

THE HORNY-FRUMP CANON

In an early *The Golden Girls*, "Rose the Prude" (1985), Blanche, the not-prude one, tries to interest one of her roommates in "a night on the town with two handsome, eligible bachelors."[3] Rose demurs, "I'm not that interested in dating anymore." Blanche cuts through the BS: "Now you know that's not true, honey, or you'd let your hair go natural." Fifty-something Rose is a perfectly coiffed blonde, suggestive of some artifice. And in this episode and subsequent ones, Blanche will be proven right—Rose, like Blanche, is still in the game. Not as *game* as Blanche—few are—but a participant all the same. And a woman's participation on the hetero dating scene is traditionally indicated with signifiers—hair dye, high heels, a push-up bra, whatever it is, the specifics varying according to age and subculture. The effort itself matters as much as the result.

And then there's Dorothy. Taller and deeper voiced than the others, she dresses in drapey, no-nonsense clothes, with grey hair untouched by the dye bottle, and is ever ready with a wisecrack or a judgmental look. She judges Blanche for being a "slut," Rose for ditziness. Dorothy, for her part, is serious, dignified, practical. The one left home on a Saturday night. "Mannish" is the word for this type of woman, and yes you do need an out-of-date, vaguely derogatory term to describe what Dorothy is, because this is not a type that fits in 2020s gender understandings. The lone divorcée in a house full of widows, she views men with suspicion.

Despite being played by Bea Arthur as something of a continuation of strident Maude from *Maude* and, before that, *All in the Family*, Dorothy is a bit sappy. She goes weak in the presence of a man she's attracted to. Not cute and swooning weak but awkward and prone to freezing, giggling, or making an inappropriately blunt sexual request. The most excruciating of her many romantic humiliations is when she forms a crush on a colleague who is—her roommates learn before she does, after she's asked him over to her place for dinner with hopes of *dessert*—a Catholic priest ("Forgive Me, Father," 1987). That on its own would be nothing to take personally. But a misunderstanding leads Dorothy to think this man is on the cusp of leaving the priesthood for her. She tries to tell him gently that he shouldn't do this, not that she isn't intrigued, and he *laughs*. The joke is not that a priest would never do such a thing, but how hilarious it would be for a man to renounce a vow of celibacy *for Dorothy Zbornak*. But even Dorothy had a heyday (there was a Mr. Zbornak, who still sometimes comes a-knockin') and to some extent has just aged out of love-interest territory earlier than her friends.

The character I see as embodying frumpy-but-horny is mousey retirement-home worker Jane Edwards, who pines after her boss Harvey Bains on 1990s Britcom *Waiting for God*. This is an ongoing secondary plotline on a largely forgotten (if still streaming) series but could not be more central to my own understandings of female heterosexuality. Jane describes herself as a thirty-seven-year-old virgin—decades before the show *Jane the Virgin*—and her love persists across all five of the show's seasons, despite Harvey's preference for Scandinavian aerobics instructors and sullen aristocrats. Jane is all drab brown clothes with the hairstyle to match, projecting whatever is the opposite of sex. But unlike fifty-something Miss Flood, her closest "spinster" counterpart, on legal sitcom *May to December* (1989–94), something simmers within Jane. Miss Flood just sort of goes about her business, unmoved by males or females, until in a later season she's for some reason granted a boyfriend. Not so, Jane. She is as horny as she is frumpy, and she's as frumpy as they come. That Jane is relatively young makes the frumpiness that much more notable, a testament to whatever the mix of casting, acting, and makeup-and-costume departments. Watching the show, Jane comes across as genuinely repulsive to men.

But it's not men Jane wants. It's Harvey. And Harvey is a sleazy would-be Trump, a man of the flashy 1980s stuck in the dismal 1990s, fancying himself a tycoon but working as the manager of a retirement community in coastal England. That Harvey is played by Daniel Hill, a British actor with no physical resemblance to the Donald, means that even though the *show* treats Jane's crush like some sick quirk of hers, it is, to the viewer—at least, to this viewer—no great mystery. One episode has the residents pulling a trick on him, leading to some unexpected but unobjectionable from-the-rear male nudity, another thing British shows seem less fussed about than their U.S. equivalents. Daniel Hill as Harvey Bains is hot. But within the universe of the show, Harvey's a ridiculous person to have fixated on.

The crush renders Jane a doormat employee, a submissive *yes Harvey* always at the ready. But not sexy-submissive, at least not to Harvey. She's a pious Catholic and a romantic, more pre-sexual than asexual, and strongly disapproves of some of the residents' non-marital relations. She wants her fairy tale, but also—some of the more plugged-in elderly residents point out—*wants* Harvey in a more immediate sense. Teasing her about having possibly gotten somewhere with him, something they well know she has not, they ask Jane, "Was he any good?," and in a carpets-match-drapes reference, "Is he a genuine brunette?"[4] Jane is played as someone who understands just enough of what's being alluded to for her to know she should be flustered and disturbed.

If Harvey and Jane were real people, both would be removed from their workplace for sexual misconduct, Harvey for inappropriate discussions of his (desired) sex life and Jane for all that touching. Jane finds any possible opportunity to comfort Harvey, rather transparently taking advantage of the occasion to pat him on the shoulder. Harvey says, so often it's his catchphrase, "Jane, you're touching me." To which Jane responds, meekly, "Sorry, Harvey," but you know she's not. Jane is in no way put off by Harvey's indifference bordering on revulsion towards her. It would seem to be if anything the source of his allure.

Janine Duvitski, who plays Jane, is not one to be typecast. On *Benidorm*, Duvitski plays Jacqueline, a married, heteroflexible swinger. The anti-Jane, really, but with the common ground of also being something of a frump. The humour there comes from the fact that this still-mousey, now-fifty-something woman is the one having the most and wildest sex of anyone at the all-inclusive Spanish resort, beyond what the younger and hotter guests could dream. Jacqueline regularly shoots and misses, too, but doesn't take it personally.

As a rule, frumpy-but-horny is a visual medium. Pauline Park from comedian Victoria Wood's 1997 song "Reincarnation"[5] is an exception. Wood sings (tongue-in-cheek) this list of everywoman characters she'd like to be in her next life, and Pauline is one of them. We don't learn very much about Pauline, beyond her penchant for low-heeled footwear and TV dinners. She merits a mention, though, for how her thirst intermingles with the unwillingness or inability to go on dates with real-life men: "I'll sit and I'll fantasize / about cruel men with piercing eyes / then I'll microwave two mince pies and have them with a cup of tea." Pauline isn't home having her mince pies out of indifference to sex. She appears sexless to the outside world, but her inner life is as steamy as the inside of her microwave.

IS FRUMPY-BUT-HORNY . . . HOT?

All the characters I've classified as frumpy-but-horny share a tendency to not just tolerate but also eroticize men's unkindly expressed lack of interest in them. Their turn-ons include, or at least don't preclude, being stood up, being referred to as ugly, and getting passed over in favour of a different woman. The (rare) man who makes himself straightforwardly available is not of much interest.

All of this makes me wonder to what extent frumpy-but-horny is itself . . . if not a *fetish*, exactly, then a subtype of female desire, one rendered invisible in the culture but commonplace enough in the world. The closest examples I can think of to nameable things would be a humiliation fetish or negging, though neither is quite it. The phrase "humiliation fetish" suggests a latex-clad female dominatrix telling a business tycoon he's a worm. It doesn't generally refer to a woman getting off on thinking she's unattractive, a scenario understood to be so outside the bounds of female sexuality as to make no sense. A man wincing when you look at him *that* way is meant to send you running in the other direction. There is no script according to which a man might, with a woman's persistence, come around. And even if he did change his mind, a woman would be plagued by the knowledge that he hadn't been immediately blown over by her beauty.

Negging, meanwhile, is the pick-up-artist technique of insulting a beautiful woman so as to knock her off her pedestal. She's told she's gorgeous all the time; distinguish yourself as a suitor, they say, by choosing a different approach, one that makes her a bit insecure, and then the next thing you know you're in bed with a supermodel. So that can't be it, either.

Neither humiliation nor negging, though, is what I'm talking about. And they're not quite "femcels" either—a term that sounds like it would refer to involuntarily celibate women but is more used to describe women who've gone off men in favour of celibacy and hyperfemininity.

So maybe I've unearthed a new category, some subset of women who get off on being called repulsive? Or maybe not. My hunch is, this is more mundane. In other areas, we recognize unattainability as an alluring quality. We get that women are sometimes attracted to bad boys who won't commit, or to married men, and that their unavailability contributes to their appeal. We just don't have language for the woman who gets a thrill from being around a man more beautiful than she is, and who revels in that dynamic. We can only describe this in terms of a woman sitting around waiting for a man to notice how pretty *she* is. Maybe she prefers to be around someone pretty than to be the pretty one herself!

Frumpy-but-horny, then, is a subversive role swap, but one that involves the woman in the role of hopeless pursuer, not as some kind of sex-positive go-getter alpha. Stories of women obsessed with a man tend to have, as their origin, a time when the woman had concrete, real-world affirmation of this man's interest. The touchstone for the unhinged rejected woman, Glenn Close's "bunny-boiler" in the 1987 movie *Fatal Attraction*, is jilted after an affair. The TV show *Crazy Ex-Girlfriend* (2015–19) is, as the title suggests, about a woman's inappropriate attempts at rekindling a past relationship. These narratives explore the pain of rejection, but never question that the rejected woman was, at least at one time, of interest to the man she's chasing. Chris Kraus's autofiction *I Love Dick*, about a married woman's obsession with a male acquaintance, begins as Chris "notices Dick making continual eye contact with her."[6] The two do not have *an affair*—nearly the whole thing is in Chris's head—but the two do consummate things.[7] Frumpy-but-horny, in its purest form, allows for no reciprocation, however fleeting or inadequate. It's not a woman nostalgic for a time when she felt her allure was affirmed. Her indifference to a man's reciprocation isn't healthy or anything like that—do not try this at home—but there is something intriguing about it conceptually.

THE MEN WHO "BRISTLE"

All things being equal, men want sex more than their wives do. The thing is: All things are not always equal. If the frumpy-but-horny single woman is the bizarro version of the lusted-after young women posting #MeToo (Chapter 1), then the sexually frustrated wife is the counterpart to the women of Chapter 2, the ones who've had it up to here with their (ex-)husbands. There's a variant of frumpy-but-horny that's about the women who cannot get enough of their husbands, much to these husbands' dismay.

The most sexually frustrated wife of sitcom is almost certainly unkempt, late-middle-aged Daisy on *Keeping Up Appearances*. Daisy is snobbish, striving Hyacinth Bucket's embarrassingly lowbrow sister, a living reminder of Hyacinth's grimy origins. Unlike Hyacinth, Daisy has not kept up a single appearance in her life. Her hair is lank and grey, sometimes put up with a couple plastic butterfly hairclips. She wears a dreary cardigan over shapeless loungewear over a larger body, in contrast to a third sister who lives with her, the man-hungry, figure-retaining Rose.

Daisy, forever with a romance novel in hand, is convinced that her slovenly husband Onslow is an Adonis, irresistible to womankind. Apart from an episode where a crotchety elderly lady makes some remark about his *size* (he's a big fella), the show gives no reason to think Onslow is of interest to women who aren't Daisy. He's unemployed and immobile by choice, committed as a matter of principle to a life of utter sloth. He has the easy confidence of the supremely unbothered, which makes him a likeable television character, but not, in romantic terms, a catch.

Daisy spends a part of just about every episode trying to convince Onslow to choose an intimate moment with her over such activities as sleeping, drinking beer in his armchair, and watching horse racing on a television set that—unlike Daisy—needs to be slapped on the top to get turned on. Many scenes have her lying next to Onslow in bed, a headboard-less situation with a greasy wall behind them. Daisy makes some crack about how Onslow never gets excited anymore (excitement has just come up in a non-sexual context), and he responds, defensively, "I got excited on your birthday!"[8] A running gag is that the only thing that snaps Onslow out of his inertia and gets him out of bed for the day is when Daisy propositions him.

Speaking of propositions, consider the following 2024 *Daily Mail* headline: "Head chef at country hotel wins another £8,000 after his boss sexually harassed him by singing Victoria Wood's classic 'Ballad of Barry and Freda' to him—after judge ruled £80k wasn't enough."[9] This told the apparently all-too-real story of a man who came on to an underling by "serenad[ing]" him with the comedy song in question and making "disconcerting gestures." The 1986 Cole Porter–spoofing song tells the story of a woman's failed attempt at seducing her husband.[10] Like Wood's above-mentioned song character, Pauline Park, Freda is sexual without sex appeal. But Freda, unlike Pauline, is not content to stew in her own unmet desires. Does Freda want Barry in particular, or is he just what's on hand in the man department? That it's the latter is established in Freda's opening lines, when she describes her "appetite" by singing, "I could handle half the tenors in a male voice choir." As those men are not sat listening to *Gardeners' Question Time* with her, Barry will have to do.

Wood sings the song from three perspectives: as Freda (in a normal voice), as Barry (in a whiny-man voice), and as a third-person narrator in her usual singing voice. Freda's demands, all prefaced by a "let's do it," mix domesticity with sexual ravenousness. My personal favourite of her demands lies elsewhere: "Wear your baggy Y fronts with the loose elastic." As indicated by the state of the man's underpants, this is a heterosexual couple of a certain vintage. It's a funny line because worn-out straight-guy underwear isn't imagined to be sexy. But of course, if you stop and think about it a moment, this is what many straight women are going to associate with sex. Not the abs-having, new-pair-wearing man on the underwear package.

On paper, Freda shouldn't exist. Barry, perhaps. If men's sexual peak hovers around twenty—one of those things that is *said*, but that's too subjective to be proven or disproven—then this sort of thing would happen all the time. Maybe his testosterone's on the wane. So, too, if men of all ages are wired to demand twenty-year-old women. But what explains Freda? Is it just that her sexual peak is later than his? Here's a woman whose horniness is spontaneous, unprompted, and directed not at a new lover but at her own dreary husband. And her interest is, if anything, piqued by her husband's evidently ongoing refusals. (The word "dread" is used.) If female sexuality is inherently narcissistic, what's in it for a woman who knows the man she's with doesn't find her ravishing, but who nevertheless wants a deed done?

A woman pestering her husband for more sex is the stuff of comedy. Whether it's that men are typically hornier than women, or that women get bored more quickly in long-term relationships, the assumption is that a husband wants more sex than his wife comes through with. "Wifely duties" and all that. Even if libido-mismatched couples follow certain patterns, there are enough exceptions to the rule that we're not talking about an obscure phenomenon. Moreover, the lustful, pent-up wife comes across as harmless. What's she going to do? The husband who wants sex his wife isn't up for might force things. The reverse is not a comparable threat. She screams *do me* and he says *not this again* and the audience laughs. It's unexpected but innocuous.

When sexually frustrated wives like Daisy and Freda plead for sex from their husbands, they're not engaged in any kind of second-order thinking. It's not about affirming their sex appeal generally. They're just red-blooded women, with needs. Their tragedy is that their urges exceed their own desirability. When Onslow announces yet another headache, it's a punchline. But the joke isn't that Onslow isn't virile.

It's that Daisy herself is—per the show—so thoroughly unfuckable, and the audience is meant to be on Onslow's side. He's doing what any man would, if a Daisy threw herself at him.

Perhaps owing to the straight-woman creator, "The Ballad of Barry and Freda" seems rather more on the wife's side. The song isn't trying to shame Barry into having sex he doesn't want, or not quite. It's that Barry's inability to come through for Freda is presented less as an insult to her appeal than as evidence that there's something up with *him*. Not all Wood characters are in the frumpy-but-horny mould (her best song, "Pam," is sung from the perspective of a woman who's what would now be called asexual), but there's something about her oeuvre that is uniquely attuned to this dynamic.

LETTING HERSELF GO

In her 2017 essay "Notes on Frump,"[11] writer Emma Copley Eisenberg defines "frump" as a form of feminine self-presentation that "rejects and denies the male sexual gaze." The article is an explanation of what constitutes frump, but also a reclamation of a derogatory term: "The dominant sensibility of femininity, which we will call Sexy Adult Woman (SAW), values flattering-ness, attractiveness above all else—pleasing the eye. In common parlance, 'frump' is the defective result when a feminine person tries and fails to achieve SAW." Indeed, the *Britannica Dictionary* defines "frump" as "a woman who wears unattractive clothes or does not make an effort to appear attractive." Eisenberg posits a different understanding: "Frump is a whole sensibility in and of itself, entirely distinct from, and in [sic] valid alternative to, SAW." Exactly how opt-in frumpiness is, I cannot determine. Women have far more leeway than men do in deciding whether to look conventionally attractive. A man cannot will himself tall, broad-shouldered, and thick-haired, and cosmetics only serve to make a man look gender non-conforming. Women have countless ways to shift things in whichever direction. Hair, makeup, eyelashes, or even just . . . I mean there is *no such thing* as sexy clothing for a (straight) man. (Counterpoint: surfers in partially unzipped wetsuits.) It is not an agreed-upon concept. Whenever a woman chooses bowl cut over balayage, potato-sack-style dress over sleeveless Lycra mini, she has decided something. Or has she?

Do Jane and Dorothy reject the male gaze out of feminist principles, or do they try and fail to live up to them? Asking this question about these characters is uncomfortably close to asking it about myself. Do I opt against ongoing head-to-toe refurbishment because I would rather spend the time watching sitcoms and the money on expensive cheese, or is it that I suspect such efforts would be futile? I am within-normal-limits looking, and probably more interested in fashion and style than most, but always feel faintly ridiculous when I try to *look good*. If I put on an overtly sexy outfit, I feel like I'm in a costume. Heavy makeup comes across, on me, less as *slut* (in the sex-positive sense of course) and more as clown.

When, in one particularly hard-to-watch *Keeping Up Appearances* scene, Daisy trades her grey cardigan for lingerie to seduce Onslow, he rebuffs her as usual, if with a bit more horror. She's still Daisy, just with a wardrobe change. The effect is silly, not sexy. When Mrs. Tishell does herself up in the hopes of catching Doc Martin's eye, he looks at her as if she's come down with an unusual rash. There's the time on *Waiting for God* when Jane, learning that Harvey likes "beauty queens," dresses up as one.[12] At least this is what she imagines she's doing. Harvey interprets the bad-bridesmaid-dress situation as a "grotesque charade," a comical getup she's put on to entertain the residents, and literally spits out coffee when she explains the intended effect. *Poor Jane*.

Dorothy's gesture at glamour on *The Golden Girls* leads to humiliation in a somewhat different form but amounting to the same. She returns home dressed up for what turns out to have been a date with her ex-husband Stan. She doesn't want her mother knowing she has lapsed in this manner, but realizes her mother needs to find out eventually, and dramatically reveals that under her bathrobe, she's wearing her *going-out outfit*, some kind of loose, drapey black sequinned jacket. Sophia has no clue this is what Dorothy is trying to indicate. She thinks Dorothy has accidentally left the house in pyjamas. *Poor Dorothy.*

It's possible to age into frumpiness, but not all thirsty older women are frumps. Consider the aging-nymphomaniac trope: sister Rose on *Keeping Up Appearances* or Roz on *Frasier* or Marion on *Waiting for God* or Patsy on *Absolutely Fabulous*. Or the classics, Blanche and Samantha. I appreciate these characters, obviously I do. They're horny, all right, but where's the frump? They're too vain, and too put-together, to represent the decoupling of desire and desirability. One does not see Patsy's long legs swung over a young lover's motorcycle and find it surprising she'd be in that situation.

The phenomenon I'm getting at isn't simply a matter of, here is a woman who is not a twenty-year-old lingerie model and yet she is being portrayed in a heterosexual romantic context. This isn't about MILFS or sexy librarians. It's not about the newer phenomenon, made possible by cosmetic injectables, of older actresses playing sexy older-but-smooth-skinned temptresses. It's about women's desire for men being portrayed in a way that is in no possible interpretation *for* men, as in for men's sexual gratification. Lusting in ways that are awkward and strange, not arousing or titillating. In ways that cause a man to grimace uncomfortably and try to leave the room. Jane, Dorothy, and Daisy are heterosexual women characters, but as far as it gets from *straight women* in the comedy sense of the *straight man*. Their desire is unseemly and absurd, not something these shows celebrate. I wouldn't even say they act in ways that I endorse! What matters is that the characters exist at all. Their presence establishes women like this as a part of the human experience worth recording.

SENSIBLY SHOD BUT STRAIGHT

Frumpy-but-horny is about women being sexual in a way one wouldn't anticipate. But is it a *queering of heterosexuality*? Frump, according to Eisenberg, is associated with queerness. And if you take female heterosexuality to mean Carrie Bradshaw in her Manolos, or Rose Nylund dyeing her hair, or—if I must live in the present moment—some trad influencers trying to sell a mediocre-looking rayon sundress based on the fact that it will allegedly lead your husband to impregnate you (it seems to have a push-up bra built into it), you could conclude that subversion on the beauty-standards front implies a sexuality other than straight. You could conclude this, on paper, but then you'd look around at the world of actual women—most are straight and few resemble Barbie dolls or are making great efforts in that direction—and have to wonder exactly how linked female heterosexuality really is with a compulsion to look gorgeous. It is easy enough to buy an Onslow wardrobe in the women's department.

Frump, as I understand it, is primarily a hetero phenomenon. It's not that a frumpy lesbian is unfathomable (they're fathomable, entirely fathomable!) but that there's a whole terminology for the various ways lesbians and bisexual women deviate from conventional, male-gaze-oriented femininity. *Frump* is something else. Sometimes, at least, it's when a woman who might inadvertently read as gay or asexual, who wears *sensible shoes*, is at least nominally straight, and is therefore registering as a sexual nonentity to the very people she might wish to attract. She's not going out of her way to repulse men. She's just not cinching herself into anything uncomfortable.

Dorothy is the epitome here, a hetero character so lesbian-coded it is even spelled out on the show that she reads this way. But she's far from alone. Daria Morgendorffer, from MTV's *Daria* (1997–2002), is sometimes reclaimed as a lesbian icon, this despite her mega-crush on her best friend's older brother. But the pinnacle for me is Diana Trent on *Waiting for God*, a retired war photojournalist—never married, no kids—with a Katharine Hepburn swagger. Initially, Diana has a friendship dynamic with widower neighbour Tom that's less flirtatious banter and more confirmed-bachelorette with diva-obsessed male friend.

So when the two do consummate things midway through the series you'd be forgiven for thinking some heteronormative 1990s sitcom force swung in and swapped a charmingly eccentric, queer-coded friendship for a banal will-they-won't-they plot. It feels a bit out-of-the-blue, but moments in earlier episodes allude to the possibility. Diana drops hints of an unbothered promiscuous past: fighter pilots she slept with as a cohort, and a man who died making love to her. Tom makes an offhand comment to Diana about his still being "capable." The capabilities are confirmed in 1992's "Scandal."[13]

One night, drunk, Diana stumbles into Tom's room by accident. She wakes up naked (not pictured) in what she realizes is his bed. Diana accuses Tom of having taken advantage of her, which doesn't sound like gentle Tom, and indeed was not what happened. Tom clarifies that she's the one who came on to him. He'd seen her in his bed and done the gentlemanly thing of sleeping in his armchair. She propositioned him, Tom explains, with a monologue about the need to "grab" life "by both hands." As Tom recalls, this was, literally, Diana's next move. "My eyeballs nearly popped out."

Tom and Diana are henceforth a couple, but it's a conflict-filled relationship. Tom wants cohabitation, marriage. Diana loves Tom but cherishes her independence. He's a neat freak and she's a slob. She can't cook to save her life. She is, in other words, *the man*. The show's finale is set up to be their wedding, but Tom has overheard Diana saying how miserable she is at the thought of marriage. He gallantly refuses to marry her, right there at the altar. This is their alternative happily ever after, a grand romantic gesture that is, in keeping with the show, the opposite of what you'd expect.

We can look at a character like Diana as someone from a bygone age who really should have been *permitted* to be their true queer self, but who was shoehorned into their era's only viable option. But sometimes a woman is a little more assertive, a little less made up, and also into dudes. And sometimes things even work out in her favour.

HAPPY ENDINGS

For most of *The Golden Girls* and *Waiting for God*, Dorothy and Jane, respectively, are stand-ins for the phenomenon of wanting without getting. These are women who can't/won't change themselves for a man, but whose pent-up lust is all-consuming. "If ever there was a spinster, it's you," Tom tells Jane, in an uncharacteristic moment of frankness.[14] Harvey seems out of bounds, but so too do men generally. And so it goes for Dorothy as well: A man calls the house and asks to speak to Dorothy, and Blanche tells him he has the wrong number, so implausible she finds it that a *man* would have called she who is without men.

Yet each series concludes with its frump getting her happily-ever-after in the form of a good, old-fashioned sitcom-finale wedding. As a culmination of the ever-more-improbable twists that make up the show's final season, *Waiting for God* plops Jane at the altar with

Harvey. Dorothy's is more of an out-of-the-blue Prince Charming situation. The show brings in a new male character—Blanche's uncle Lucas—and through similarly unrealistic circumstances (Dorothy and Lucas play a trick on Blanche, claiming they're in love and want to get married, only to realize moments later that this is true), there they are at the church. In this case, there's a certain symmetry with the pilot episode, wherein Blanche is on the cusp of marrying and thereby breaking up the household.

I know the thing here would be to dismiss these wedding-scene end-of-series episodes as clichéd and heteronormative. Wedding as sitcom finale, does it *get* any more basic?

In the shows' defence, neither treats its finale wedding as the natural end point for all characters. On *Waiting for God*, Tom and Diana don't go through with their much-anticipated nuptials. Rose of *The Golden Girls* is conventional and has a boyfriend, yet she stays with her "girls." And Rose's reaction when she learns Dorothy is getting married makes clear this match is not about Dorothy betraying feminist principles: "Oh I think it's romantic, it's like something out of a '40s movie. Strong, handsome, daring. And now she's got a man!"[15] The unsubtle joke is that you first assume Rose is talking about Lucas. Dorothy doesn't wilt into hyperfeminine passivity. She has quite simply met her match.

Jane wants Harvey; she shouldn't but she does. The show doesn't have Jane nobly triumphing over her severe case of Harvey-itis, nor the conservative, church-wedding-bound form it takes. It takes at face value that Jane's goal is becoming Mrs. Harvey Bains and, rather than (further) judging her for this, allows her that outcome. Dorothy—not a virgin like Jane, but a bit of a second-virginity situation—wants incredible sex and the show gives her this, in the form of a *Naked Gun*–era Leslie Nielsen, playing very much the same character. And somehow it makes sense, the two of them, similarly grey-haired and deadpan. Dorothy is blunt about why she is marrying this man: The sex is *that good*. So good, she explains on several occasions, that they "named it."

The Golden Girls ends on a tearjerker note, with Dorothy's departure breaking up the chosen family, and with the three remaining "girls" comforting one another after she's left for her honeymoon. But as modern and noble as it might have been had they kept the alternative family structure going, and as much as one might want to gently suggest that Dorothy take things more slowly with Lucas, the fact of the matter is, Dorothy absolutely did want a man. That, or they already knew that the spin-off wasn't going to have Bea Arthur in it, so she needed to be written out of the story. I'd suppose the best sex of her life is a much better send-off than death by a ten-ton weight on her head.

MRS. SLOCOMBE'S PUSSY, REVISITED

Mrs. Slocombe, she of the pastel beehive on *Are You Being Served?*, is plain and middle-aged but too colourful in all ways to qualify as a frump. Despite the matronly Grace Brothers department store uniform, she looks a bit like a drag queen (and drag queens have taken her as inspiration). Her outlandishness may suggest an indifference to the (straight) male gaze, but everything in her look and demeanour says *please notice me*. Whatever she's aging into, it isn't invisibility.

Classic Mrs. Slocombe would be an anecdote she tells Miss Brahms about a recent evening out.[16] "Young man, I said, if you don't take your hand off my knee at once, I'm getting off this barstool and going home." Miss Brahms asks if he did so. Mrs. Slocombe answers, in a tone suggesting her honour was violated, "He did not." Miss Brahms, again: "So you went home?" Mrs. Slocombe, sultry this time: "Eventually."

Mrs. Slocombe goes on, explaining that they're going out again, this time to the movies, so that he can "apologize," adding, with a coquettish giggle, "I do hope he behaves himself on the back row." Miss Brahms, the (comedic-sense) straight woman, asks Mrs. Slocombe how she knows where they'll be seated. Mrs. Slocombe, in with the punchline: "I've *booked*."

Mrs. Slocombe's thirst isn't solely a part of the alluded-to, off-screen world that makes up so much of that show. She's also seen flirting with the men's counter employees, including the odd ill-fated attempt to catch the eye of Mr. Humphries, who prefers Mr. Walpole from the Sports department. Mrs. Slocombe isn't letting herself fade into the background, but nor is she fussed with looking nubile, as if such a thing were possible. The closest Mrs. Slocombe comes to emulating youth is in the *Are You Being Served?* himbo-plot episode, 1983's "Memories Are Made of This," wherein an accident involving a Walpole the Himbo and a golf ball sends her into a concussion (or so it first seems), leading her to suddenly present herself as a little girl. (A *very* good episode, by the way, and a rare himbo plot that lets a gay male character join in the himbo appreciation.)

It is impossible to discuss Mrs. Slocombe without bringing her pussy into the equation.

Mrs. Slocombe, as you may recall, lives alone with her cat, Tiddles. Tiddles is her family, really, so she mentions him a lot at work. Thus the moment in each episode (BritBox has a great YouTube compilation[17]) where she starts holding forth about "my pussy," much to everyone else's momentary confusion. Her what now? Every "my pussy" anecdote works both ways. Often, it hinges on the creature's loneliness, a problem when she's asked to work late: "If I'm not home at the stroke of six, my pussy goes mad." In a rainstorm, Mrs. Slocombe struggles to make it to work on time, explaining, "My pussy got soaking wet, I had to dry it out in front of the fire." The one that gets the best reaction from other characters: "Mr. Humphries, leave my pussy alone!" There will be this moment before the other characters realize it's Tiddles she's referring to. These allusions to the genitalia of a character with over-the-top sexuality and no conventional sex appeal is, in the misogynistic universe of the show, hilarious. It is also, in the world of this 2020s rewatcher, hilarious. Mollie Sugden knew what she was saying, even if Mrs. Slocombe did not.

The "my pussy" double entendres point to a duality of Mrs. Slocombe herself. Is she a pathetic cat lady? Or is she a sexually voracious, full-force *woman*, pussy-forward and proud, doing what those hipper and less boringly hetero than myself might call *serving cunt*?[18] What *are* we being served? Unlike the frumpy-but-horny characters, Mrs. Slocombe isn't wallowing in the tragedy of her situation. Her man-liking exceeds men's liking of her, but she's not bothered; she gets on with it. She's not hopelessly pining after any particular man—not over the course of more than one episode, that is—and isn't sitting around in the vain hope that some loser of a husband she married when young and cute will rise to the occasion. Like most women, Mrs. Slocombe somehow manages to exist as a sexual entity without winning any beauty contests, without any women's magazines inviting her to pose naked on a horse. "My pussy" over *My Body* any day.

There is one last Victoria Wood comedy-song character I need to introduce you to. It's Vera, a lady "of a certain age" whose "libido would defeat a rabbit's."[19] She bears a significant, though I suspect inadvertent, resemblance to Mrs. Slocombe. (It's just a type of woman, one I have absolutely met in real life.) But the lyric I must draw your attention to is where Wood sings that Vera would "never change the duvet."

Why that detail? Some of Wood's comedy is so distinctly English that it goes over my Canadian-American head. Who cares about this character's laundry habits? It was only after countless relistens that I remembered that "slut" has a double meaning in British English. According to the *Cambridge Dictionary*, "slut" can refer to "a woman who has sexual relationships with a lot of men without any emotional involvement" or "a woman who is usually untidy and lazy." It's right there in the English language that female heterosexuality unchecked is about desiring men, and has less than nothing to do with keeping house.

ACKNOWLEDGEMENTS

The Last Straight Woman owes its existence to my editor at the *Globe and Mail* Opinion section, Mark Medley, introducing me to this book's editor, Doug Pepper, and to both of them believing I had another book in me. I'd also like to thank my agent, William Callahan, for help with the mysterious world of publishing contracts, and the book's copyeditor, Eleanor Gasparik, for immense patience and for getting what the project is about. Thank you to anyone who in any capacity said yes to this book happening and helped get it out.

It is also impossible to imagine this book existing without the on- and offline conversations over the years with my friend and *Feminine Chaos* podcast cohost, the novelist and culture writer Kat Rosenfield. So too my friend Marc Weisblott, who as my editor at *The Canadian Jewish News* and beyond has known exactly which new (and not-new) books and stories to send my way.

My sincerest appreciations to Blake Smith, for a too-kind profile in the ever-evolving publication that is *Tablet*, and to my fellow Torontonian Lydia Perović, for inviting me to do a public dialogue with her about #MeToo.

I'd like to thank everyone who has podcasted with me on the topic of female heterosexuality: Katie Herzog, Leigh Stein, Jessa Crispin, Tara Henley, Meghan Daum, Dan Savage, Daniel Oppenheimer, Jon Kay, and others I may be forgetting, it has been a lot of podcasting. Thank you to everyone who reads anything I write or listens to anything I podcast and responds in a non-revolted manner. Thank you especially to Sophie Scott, and others who may wish to remain nameless, for sending me old video clips of the British actor John Castle, the one who made *Miss Marple* so unexpectedly steamy.

Thank you most of all to my family: to my daughters Annabel and Francesca, to my mother, Ellen Hymowitz, and to (yes, I know, whodathunk, in a book about straight women) my husband, Jo Bovy. I live my values so will mention here that I chose him for his looks; what a perk that he has so many other great qualities as well.

NOTES

Epigraphs

1. *As Time Goes By*, season 4, episode 4, "The Affair," aired Mar. 26, 1995.
2. "The Ballad of Barry and Freda (Let's Do It)," by Victoria Wood, from *Victoria Wood: As Seen on TV*, season 2, episode 1, aired Nov. 10, 1986.

Introduction: Mrs. Slocombe's Pussy

1. *Are You Being Served?*, season 2, episode 5, "Hoorah for the Holidays," aired Apr. 11, 1974.
2. *Are You Being Served?*, season 7, episode 3, "The Apartment," aired Nov. 2, 1979.
3. Maya Salam, "For Online Daters, Women Peak at 18 While Men Peak at 50, Study Finds. Oy," *The New York Times*, Aug. 15, 2018, https://www.nytimes.com/2018/08/15/style/dating-apps-online-men-women-age.html.
4. Jeffrey M. Jones, "U.S. LGBT Identification Steady at 7.2%." Gallup, Feb. 22, 2023. https://news.gallup.com/poll/470708/lgbt-identification-steady.aspx.
5. Andrew R. Flores and Kerith J. Conron, *Adult* LGBT *Population in the United States*, Report (The Williams Institute, UCLA School of Law, Dec. 2023), https://williamsinstitute.law.ucla.edu/publications/adult-lgbt-pop-us/.
6. Lisa M. Diamond, *Female Sexual Fluidity: Understanding the Diversity of Women's Sexual Responses* (Harvard University Press, 2008).

7. Robin Respaut and Chad Terhune, "A Gender Imbalance Emerges Among Trans Teens Seeking Treatment," Reuters, Nov. 18, 2022, https://www.reuters.com/investigates/special-report/usa-trans youth-topsurgery/.
8. Moises M. Patel, "How Generation Z Is Redefining Gender and the Rise of Gender Identities," *Time*, May 1, 2023, https://time.com/6275663/generation-z-gender-identity/.
9. Nona Willis Aronowitz, *Bad Sex: Truth, Pleasure, and an Unfinished Revolution* (Plume, 2022). Accessed online.
10. Suzannah Weiss, "12 Things People Get Wrong About Being Non-Binary," *Teen Vogue*, May 20, 2022, https://www.teenvogue.com/story/9-things-people-get-wrong-about-being-non-binary.
11. Julia Wright, "I Shouldn't Have to 'Look' Non-Binary for My Identity to Be Respected," CBC *First Person*, Aug. 8, 2023, https://www.cbc.ca/news/canada/montreal/i-shouldn-t-have-to-look-non-binary-1.6903041.
12. Phoebe Maltz Bovy, "Ban Men? If Only It Were That Easy," *The Globe and Mail*, Mar. 7, 2020, https://www.theglobeandmail.com/opinion/article-ban-men-if-only-it-were-that-easy/.
13. Anna Sussman, "How Girls Are Shaping the Internet—and Each Other," *The New York Times*, Sept. 10, 2023, https://www.nytimes.com/2023/09/10/style/girls-internet-gender.html.
14. Katherine Angel, *Tomorrow Sex Will Be Good Again: Women and Desire in the Age of Consent* (Verso, 2021), 62.

Chapter 1: Sex After Trump

1. The Bumble apology Instagram post (https://www.instagram.com/p/C67U1nyuZNI/?img_index=1) is no longer available.
2. Gina Cherelus, "Bumble to Users: You Need Sex. Users to Bumble: Get Lost," *The New York Times*, May 14, 2024, https://www.nytimes.com/2024/05/14/style/bumble-celibacy-ad-apology.html.

3. Marisa Charpentier, "Why I'm Boysober: Choosing Celibacy for Mental Health," *The New York Times*, Feb. 3, 2024, https://www.nytimes.com/2024/02/03/style/boysober-celibacy-hope-woodward.html.
4. Jonathan Chait, "'White Women Voted for Trump' Is the Worst Election Trope," *New York Magazine*, Dec. 1, 2020, https://nymag.com/intelligencer/article/did-white-women-vote-for-trump-no.html.
5. John Burn-Murdoch, "A New Global Gender Divide Is Emerging," *Financial Times*, Jan. 26, 2024, https://www.ft.com/content/29fd9b5c-2f35-41bf-9d4c-994db4e12998.
6. Blythe Roberson, *How to Date Men When You Hate Men* (Flatiron Books, 2019), accessed online.
7. R.O. Kwon, "On Being a Woman in America While Trying to Avoid Being Assaulted," *The Paris Review*, Jan. 7, 2019, https://www.theparisreview.org/blog/2019/01/07/on-being-a-woman-in-america-while-trying-to-avoid-being-assaulted/.
8. Sasha Weiss, "The Power of #YesAllWomen," *The New Yorker*, May 26, 2014, https://www.newyorker.com/culture/culture-desk/the-power-of-yesallwomen.
9. A 2022 *Washington Post* article offers a good overview of where the men wound up: "A few went to prison. Some have disappeared. But many are rebuilding their careers. And some were barely affected." Ashley Fetters Maloy and Paul Farhi, "Five Years On, What Happened to the Men of #MeToo?," *The Washington Post*, Oct. 16, 2022, https://www.washingtonpost.com/lifestyle/2022/10/16/metoo-men-what-happened/.
10. Marie Le Conte, "On Tits and Ghosts," Medium blog post, Oct. 12, 2017, https://youngvulgarian.medium.com/tits-or-ghosts-12ef2491308b.
11. Willa Paskin, "Greta Gerwig's 'Barbie' Dream Job," *The New York*

Times Magazine, July 11, 2023, https://www.nytimes.com/2023/07/11/magazine/greta-gerwig-barbie.html.

12. https://twitter.com/LynzyLab/status/1049215347025465344.
13. Rosa Sanchez, "'Emily Ratajkowski Says She's Bi and Doesn't 'Believe in Straight People,'" *Harper's Bazaar*, Nov. 2, 2022, https://www.harpersbazaar.com/celebrity/latest/a41846870/emily-ratajkowski-comes-out-bisexual-doesnt-believe-straight-people/.
14. Lauren Christensen, "Emily Ratajkowski Is a Work in Progress." *The New York Times*, Oct. 19, 2021, https://www.nytimes.com/2021/10/29/books/emily-ratajkowski-my-body.html.
15. William Deresiewicz, "Unfuckable Hate Nerds," *Tablet*, June 27, 2023, https://www.tabletmag.com/sections/arts-letters/articles/unfuckable-hate-nerds-william-deresiewicz.
16. *The Dick Van Dyke Show*, season 3, episode 32, "Teacher's Petrie," aired May 13, 1964.
17. *Keeping Up Appearances*, season 2, episode 4, "Golfing with the Major," aired Sept. 22, 1991.
18. Ashley Hupfl post responding to Mayor Eric Adams's public comment, X, Aug. 16, 2023, https://twitter.com/AshleyHupfl/status/1691855751529070657.
19. This is from a May 31 tweet (https://twitter.com/lameypilled/status/1663907223544774657) by suspended account @lameypilled, whose bio offered a detailed self-portrait indeed: "19 | evil femcel | Journalist | Half-Jewish | Libertarian | D1 Soccer | DC Native | Criminal Justice Reform | Langley, Virginia."
20. Alexandra Alter, Jonah Engel Bromwich, and Damien Cave, "The Writer Zinzi Clemmons Accuses Junot Díaz of Forcibly Kissing Her," May 4, 2018, https://www.nytimes.com/2018/05/04/books/junot-diaz-accusations.html.
21. Katie Way, "I Went on a Date with Aziz Ansari. It Turned into the

Worst Night of My Life," Babe, Jan. 13, 2018, https://babe.net/2018/01/13/aziz-ansari-28355.

22. Jamie Kahn, "Inside the Secret Facebook Group Where Women Review Men They've Dated," *Glamour,* Oct. 26, 2022, https://www.glamour.com/story/are-we-dating-the-same-guy-facebook-group.
23. Courtney Sender, "He Asked Permission to Touch, but Not to Ghost," *The New York Times*, Sept. 7, 2018, https://www.nytimes.com/2018/09/07/style/modern-love-he-asked-permission-to-touch-but-not-to-ghost.html.
24. This is journalist Helen Lewis's term, collectively, for these thinkers, based on phrasing by Mary Harrington. Lewis, "The Feminists Insisting That Women Are Built Differently," *The Atlantic*, June 8, 2023, https://www.theatlantic.com/ideas/archive/2023/06/reactionary-feminism-differences-between-sexes/674447/.
25. This phrase is in the headline of an article by Christine Emba, "Consent Is Not Enough. We Need a New Sexual Ethic," *Washington Post*, Mar. 17, 2022, https://www.washingtonpost.com/opinions/2022/03/17/sex-ethics-rethinking-consent-culture/. It is also included in the title of a chapter in Louise Perry, *The Case Against the Sexual Revolution* (Polity, 2022).
26. Kat Rosenfield, interview with author, Sept. 7, 2023.
27. "Pam" by Victoria Wood, on *Real Life: The Songs*, produced by Ovation Records, released Jan. 19, 1997.
28. Jancee Dunn, "Watch Out for this Common Intimacy Killer," *The New York Times*, Sept. 29, 2023, https://www.nytimes.com/2023/09/29/well/family/relationships-intimacy-bristle-reaction-sex.html.
29. *Seinfeld*, season 6, episode 15, "The Beard," aired Feb. 9, 1995.
30. Dan Savage, host, *Savage Lovecast*, podcast, episode 916, "Wet & Messy," May 14, 2024, https://savage.love/lovecast/2024/05/14/8686/.

Chapter 2: Soap Dispenser Husbands

1. Hanna Rosin, "The End of the End of Men," The Cut, Feb. 1, 2021, https://www.thecut.com/2021/02/hanna-rosin-end-of-the-end-of-men.html.
2. Sophie Vershbow, Twitter (now X), May 16, 2023, https://twitter.com/svershbow/status/1658469717429071872.
3. On the origins of modern wedlock, the classic remains Stephanie Coontz, *Marriage, a History: How Love Conquered Marriage* (Penguin Books, 2006).
4. Maggie Smith, *You Could Make This Place Beautiful: A Memoir* (Atria/One Signal Publishers, 2023), accessed online.
5. Oli Coleman, "Famed Author Emily Gould Asks Newsletter Readers to Fund Her Divorce," *The New York Post*, Oct. 12, 2022, https://pagesix.com/2022/10/12/author-emily-gould-asks-newsletter-readers-to-fund-her-divorce/.
6. Amy Shearn, "A 50/50 Custody Arrangement Could Save Your Marriage," *The New York Times*, Oct. 8. 2022, https://www.nytimes.com/2022/10/08/opinion/married-divorce-parent.html.
7. In lieu of the no-longer-active hyperlink (for the internet archivists, it's this: https://twitter.com/robinschaer/status/1109096787682492417), Kat Rosenfield and I discussed the then-new tweet on the *Feminine Chaos* podcast, Apr. 3, 2019, https://bloggingheads.tv/videos/56116?in=56:51.
8. Lyz Lenz, *This American Ex-Wife* (Crown, 2024), 4.
9. Philippa Perry, "My Husband Won't Lift a Finger to Help Me. Should I Stay or Go?," *The Guardian*, Apr. 3, 2023, https://www.theguardian.com/lifeandstyle/2023/apr/30/my-husband-wont-lift-a-finger-to-help-me-should-i-stay-or-go.
10. Jancee Dunn, "Watch Out for this Common Intimacy Killer," *The New York Times*, Sept. 29, 2023, https://www.nytimes.com/2023

/09/29/well/family/relationships-intimacy-bristle-reaction-sex.html.

11. Anne Helen Petersen, "Why Are (White) Men So Unambitious?," Culture Study, Mar. 29, 2023, https://annehelen.substack.com/p/why-are-white-men-so-unambitious.
12. Maggie Smith, "My Marriage Was Never the Same After That," The Cut, Mar. 28, 2023, https://www.thecut.com/article/book-excerpt-you-could-make-this-place-beautiful-maggie-smith.html.
13. As is often the case with tweets from the pre-X era, the link leads nowhere, but it's this: https://twitter.com/isabelkaplan/status/1641111964062564353.
14. Isabel Kaplan, "My Boyfriend, a Writer, Broke Up with Me Because I'm a Writer," *The Guardian*, Dec. 5, 2022, https://www.theguardian.com/lifeandstyle/2022/dec/05/my-boyfriend-a-writer-broke-up-with-me-because-im-a-writer.
15. Maggie Smith, "I Suddenly Became a Hit Writer—but I felt My Husband Treated My Career Like an Interruption of My Domestic Work," *The Guardian*, Sept. 2, 2023, https://www.theguardian.com/lifeandstyle/2023/sep/02/i-suddenly-became-a-hit-writer-but-i-felt-my-husband-treated-my-career-like-an-interruption-of-my-domestic-work.
16. Petersen, "Why Are (White) Men So Unambitious?"
17. Smith, *You Could Make This Place Beautiful*. The most we are told is that a doctor, learning that Smith was splitting from her husband, spontaneously suggested she get tested for sexually transmitted infections, in case he'd been cheating and, in doing so, passed something along to the wife he might (*might*) still be sleeping with. This passage segues into an artful version of what we non-poets call changing the subject. It's clear that she turned down the test but is ambiguous whether there'd have been a need for it to begin with.

18. Lyz Lenz, "Women Are Divorcing—and Finally Finding Happiness," *The Washington Post*, Feb. 28, 2024, https://www.washingtonpost.com/opinions/2024/02/28/lyz-lenz-this-american-ex-wife-divorce/.
19. Judy (Brady) Syfers, "I Want a Wife," reprinted on The Cut in peak #MeToo (Nov. 22, 2017) under the headline "'I Want a Wife,' the Timeless '70s Feminist Manifesto," https://www.thecut.com/2017/11/i-want-a-wife-by-judy-brady-syfers-new-york-mag-1971.html. The author's byline exists as different variations of Brady and Syfers or just one or the other name; for consistency's sake, and at the possible expense of feminist point-making, I'm going with her legal name.
20. Taffy Brodesser-Akner, "Stuff Your 'Rules,'" *The New York Times Magazine*, May 14, 2019, https://www.nytimes.com/2019/05/14/style/the-rules-book.html.
21. Emily Gould, "The Lure of Divorce," The Cut, Feb. 14, 2024, https://www.thecut.com/article/marriage-divorce-should-i-leave-my-husband-emily-gould.html.
22. Meghan Flaherty, "So Your Kid's a Tornado. Now What?," *Slate*, June 7, 2022, https://slate.com/culture/2022/06/keith-gessen-raising-raffi-review.html.

Chapter 3: "Are Straight Women Okay?"

1. This is the title of a section in Jane Ward, *The Tragedy of Heterosexuality* (New York University Press, 2020), but Ward cites a 2017 *Autostraddle* essay by that name. Further searching reveals a 2019 Buzzfeed book review where "Okay" is abbreviated as "OK." The expression is commonplace online.
2. Sara Glass, *Kissing Girls on Shabbat* (One Signal Publishers/Atria, 2024), 229.
3. Glass, *Kissing Girls*, 182.

4. Phoebe Maltz Bovy, "Straightness Studies," *The Hedgehog Review*, Spring 2021, https://hedgehogreview.com/issues/who-do-we-think-we-are/articles/straightness-studies.
5. Abstract from James Dean and Nancy Fischer, eds., *Routledge International Handbook of Heterosexualities Studies* (Routledge, 2019), https://www.taylorfrancis.com/books/edit/10.4324/9780429440731/routledge-international-handbook-heterosexualities-studies-james-dean-nancy-fischer.
6. Ward, *Tragedy*, 7, and Lisa M. Diamond, *Female Sexual Fluidity: Understanding the Diversity of Women's Sexual Responses* (Harvard University Press, 2008).
7. Ward, *Tragedy*, 8.
8. Ward, *Tragedy*, 121.
9. Ward, *Tragedy*, 6.
10. Ward, *Tragedy*, 12.
11. *Absolutely Fabulous*, season 1, episode 2, "Fat," aired Nov. 19, 1992.
12. On the AskWomen subreddit, Dec. 17, 2021, https://www.reddit.com/r/AskWomen/comments/ric1lh/lesbians_what_do_you_think_about_straight_women/.
13. Shockingly, I'm not the person to go to for explanations of TikTok, but there is a section of the platform with videos of women who wish they were lesbians: https://www.tiktok.com/discover/woman-who-wishes-she-was-a-lesbian.
14. Julie Bindel, "Why Are Boringly Straight Women Claiming to Be Lesbians," *The Spectator*, June 5, 2019, https://www.spectator.co.uk/article/why-are-boringly-straight-women-claiming-to-be-lesbians.
15. Ward, *Tragedy*, 135.
16. Jane Ward, *Not Gay: Sex Between Straight White Men* (New York University Press, 2015), 1, 203.

17. Asa Seresin, "On Heteropessimism," *The New Inquiry*, Oct. 9, 2019, https://thenewinquiry.com/on-heteropessimism/.
18. Leeds Revolutionary Feminist Group (multi-authored pamphlet), *Love Your Enemy?: The Debate Between Heterosexual Feminism and Political Lesbianism* (Onlywomen Press, 1981), 5. The pamphlet is a collection of mainly untitled letters, back-and-forths, and so on; authors are named in text with endnotes alerting where in the book each is found.
19. *Love Your Enemy?*, 34–35.
20. *Love Your Enemy?*, 8.
21. *Love Your Enemy?*, 14. Cloutte is the co-author of *How to Assert Yourself* (MIND, 1995). https://www.goodreads.com/work/editions/8485472-how-to-assert-yourself.
22. *Love Your Enemy?*, 25.
23. Adrienne Cecile Rich, "Compulsory Heterosexuality and Lesbian Existence," *Journal of Women's History* (Johns Hopkins University Press) 15, no. 3 (Autumn 2003): 11–48.
24. *Love Your Enemy?*, 21.
25. *Love Your Enemy?*, 23.
26. *Love Your Enemy?*, 28.
27. *Love Your Enemy?*, 61.
28. Tranna Wintour, "My Guilty Pleasure: A Morbid Curiosity for *Say Yes to the Dress*," *The Walrus*, Aug. 22, 2023, https://thewalrus.ca/say-yes-to-the-dress/.
29. The post and comments are at a May 10, 2023, post on the Are the Straights OK? subreddit, "Is This Actually Normal in Straight Relationships?"
30. Ward, *Tragedy*, 32.
31. Ward, *Tragedy*, 126.

32. Ward, *Tragedy*, 126.
33. Ward, *Tragedy*, 127.
34. Seresin, "On Heteropessimism."
35. Ward, *Tragedy*, 163–164.
36. Anna Marks, "Look What We Made Taylor Swift Do," *The New York Times*, Jan. 4, 2024, https://www.nytimes.com/2024/01/04/opinion/taylor-swift-queer.html.
37. Marks, "Look What We Made Taylor Swift Do."
38. Forum post by Reddit user Motor_Resource_9143, Sept. 5, 2023, https://www.reddit.com/r/Gaylor_Swift/comments/16axq40/comment/jzbokwz/.
39. Marks, "Look What We Made Taylor Swift Do."
40. "I Knew You Were Trouble," by Taylor Swift, produced by Max Martin and Shellback, Big Machine, released Nov. 27, 2012.
41. Twitter (now X) user @reegnkay, Feb. 3, 2022, https://x.com/reegnkay/status/1489256611138785287.
42. Seresin, "On Heteropessimism."
43. *Love Your Enemy?*, 48.
44. *Love Your Enemy?*, 29.

Chapter 4: Are Straight Women Real?

1. Lloyd Evans, "My (Surprisingly) Decent Proposal," *The Spectator*, Apr. 20, 2024, https://www.spectator.co.uk/article/my-surprisingly-decent-proposal/.
2. Stephen Marche, "The Unexamined Brutality of the Male Libido," *The New York Times*, Nov. 15, 2017, https://www.nytimes.com/2017/11/25/opinion/sunday/harassment-men-libido-masculinity.html.
3. Rosa Sanchez, "Emily Ratajkowski Says She's Bi and Doesn't 'Believe in Straight People,'" *Harper's Bazaar*, Nov. 2, 2022, https://www

.harpersbazaar.com/celebrity/latest/a41846870/emily-ratajkowski-comes-out-bisexual-doesnt-believe-straight-people/.

4. Magdalene J. Taylor, "In Defense of Negging," The Cut, Aug. 23, 2023, https://www.thecut.com/article/negging-flirting.html.
5. Sarah Barmak, "The Misunderstood Science of Sexual Desire," The Cut, Apr. 28, 2018, https://www.thecut.com/2018/04/the-misunderstood-science-of-sexual-desire.html.
6. Katherine Angel, *Tomorrow Sex Will Be Good Again: Women and Desire in the Age of Consent* (Verso, 2021), 65.
7. Tammy La Gorce, "An 'Indoor Kid' Falls in Love with Nature, and an Actress," *The New York Times*, Oct. 14, 2022, https://www.nytimes.com/2022/10/14/style/ellie-macpherson-lucas-mcmahon-wedding.html.
8. Linda Marx, "Saying 'Yes' Before a Studio Audience," *The New York Times*, Apr. 4, 2014, https://www.nytimes.com/2014/04/06/fashion/weddings/saying-yes-before-a-studio-audience.html.
9. Sadiba Hasan, "Art Was an Easy Topic. Defining Their Relationship Was Not," *The New York Times*, Apr. 7, 2023, https://www.nytimes.com/2023/04/07/style/amy-cheng-robert-hall-wedding.html.
10. Angel, *Tomorrow Sex Will Be Good Again*, 62.
11. Angel, *Tomorrow Sex Will Be Good Again*, 62–63.
12. Andrea Long Chu, *Females* (Verso, 2019), 6.
13. Jane Ward, *The Tragedy of Heterosexuality* (New York University Press, 2020), 18.
14. Beth Eck, "Men Are Much Harder: Gendered Viewing of Nude Images," *Gender & Society* 17, no. 4 (2003): 691–710.
15. Eck, "Men Are Much Harder," 698.
16. Eck, "Men Are Much Harder," 699.
17. Eck, "Men Are Much Harder," 705.
18. Eck, "Men Are Much Harder," 705–706.

19. Kirsten Roupenian, "Cat Person," *The New Yorker*, Dec. 4, 2017, https://www.newyorker.com/magazine/2017/12/11/cat-person.
20. Sarah Beauchamp, "This Story About a Really Bad Date Is Painfully Relatable," *Nylon*, Dec. 10, 2017, https://www.nylon.com/articles/new-yorker-cat-person-story-relatable.
21. Amanda Petrusich, "The Photographer Behind the 'Cat Person' Image on Capturing a Bad Kiss," *The New Yorker*, Dec. 13, 2017, https://www.newyorker.com/culture/photo-booth/the-photographer-behind-the-cat-person-image-on-capturing-a-bad-kiss.
22. Constance Grady, "The Uproar over the New Yorker Short Story 'Cat Person,' Explained," *Vox*, Dec. 12, 2017, https://www.vox.com/culture/2017/12/12/16762062/cat-person-explained-new-yorker-kristen-roupenian-short-story.
23. Roupenian, "Cat Person."
24. Charles Moser, "Autogynephilia in Women," *Journal of Homosexuality* 56, no. 5 (July 8, 2009): 539–547.
25. Esther Perel, interviewed—no date or interviewer named, but in approximately 2020 per web archive—on the Goop website ("Esther Perel on Sex, Monogamy, and Who Really Gets Bored First"), https://goop.com/wellness/relationships/esther-perel-on-sex-monogamy-and-who-really-gets-bored-first/.
26. Daniel Bergner, *What Do Women Want?: Adventures in the Science of Female Desire* (HarperCollins Publishers, 2013), 126.
27. Bergner, *What Do Women Want?*, 127.
28. *The Golden Girls*, season 1, episode 17, "Nice and Easy," aired Feb. 1, 1986.
29. Daisy Alioto, "The Desire Question: Is It Better to Desire, or Be Desired?," *Dirt*, Feb. 8, 2024, https://dirt.fyi/article/2024/02/the-desire-question.
30. Bergner, *What Do Women Want?*, 15.

31. Daniel Bergner, "What Do Women Want?," *The New York Times*, Feb. 3, 2009, https://www.nytimes.com/2009/01/23/health/23iht-25desiret.19636765.html.
32. Jenny Morber, "What Science Says About Arousal During Rape," *Popular Science*, May 31, 2013, https://www.popsci.com/science/article/2013-05/science-arousal-during-rape/.
33. Kelly D. Suschinsky and Martin L. Lalumière, "Prepared for Anything? An Investigation of Female Genital Arousal in Response to Rape Cues," *Psychological Science* 22, no. 2 (2011): 159–165, https://doi.org/10.1177/0956797610394660.
34. Lisa M. Diamond, *Female Sexual Fluidity: Understanding the Diversity of Women's Sexual Responses* (Harvard University Press, 2008), 79.
35. Diamond, *Female Sexual Fluidity*, 79.
36. Diamond, *Female Sexual Fluidity*, 88.
37. Diamond, *Female Sexual Fluidity*, 74.
38. Peter Tatchell, "Sex Beyond Labels," Queer Majority, Jan. 5, 2022, https://www.queermajority.com/essays-all/sexbeyondlabels.
39. Matt Flegenheimer, "Bill de Blasio and Chirlane McCray Are Separating," *The New York Times*, July 5, 2023, https://www.nytimes.com/2023/07/05/nyregion/de-blasio-marriage-chirlane-mccray.html.
40. *Sex and the City*, season 3, episode 2, "The Cheating Curve," aired July 11, 1999.
41. Jane Ward, *Not Gay: Sex Between Straight White Men* (New York University Press, 2015), 1.
42. "The College Try," by Garfunkel and Oates, produced by No One Buys Records, released on album *Secretions*, Sept. 10, 2015.
43. Nona Willis Aronowitz, *Bad Sex: Truth, Pleasure, and an Unfinished Revolution* (Plume, 2022), accessed online.
44. Aronowitz, *Bad Sex*.
45. Aronowitz, *Bad Sex*.

46. Aronowitz, *Bad Sex*.
47. Molly Roden Winter, *More: A Memoir of Open Marriage* (Doubleday, 2024), 181–182.
48. Winter, *More*, 182.
49. Winter, *More*, 182.
50. I will add, as a caveat, that apparently this term *is* used in public health settings, in reference to the subset of gay men who are more risk-taking than their peers, but the meaning is different.
51. Meghan Daum, "Honorary Dyke," in *The Unspeakable: And Other Subjects of Discussion* (Farrar, Straus and Giroux, 2014), 93.
52. Daum, "Honorary Dyke," 93.
53. Daum, "Honorary Dyke," 107.
54. Kimberly Zapata, "I'm a Queer Woman and I'm Married to a Man," Scary Mommy, Dec. 20, 2020, https://www.scarymommy.com/queer-woman-married-man.
55. "I'm So Lost," archived post on the Actual Lesbians subreddit, Nov. 25, 2023, https://www.reddit.com/r/actuallesbians/comments/183leyp/im_so_lost/.
56. Comment on "Are Straight Girls Actually Physically Attracted to Guys?," archived post on the Actual Lesbians subreddit, May 3, 2023, https://www.reddit.com/r/actuallesbians/comments/13grboq/are_straight_girls_actually_physically_attracted/.

Chapter 5: Are Straight Women Gay Men?

1. *The Nanny*, season 3, episode 3, "The Dope Diamond," aired Sept. 25, 1995. Fran Drescher's real-life husband at the time, *The Nanny* co-creator Peter Marc Jacobson, would come out a few years later, itself the inspiration for their 2011–2013 sitcom *Happily Divorced*.
2. Dan Savage, host, and Buck Angel, guest, *Savage Lovecast*, podcast, episode 577, "Get Thee to a Therapist, Go. With Buck Angel," Nov. 14,

2017, https://savage.love/lovecast/2017/11/14/get-thee-to-a-therapist-go-with-buck-angel/.

3. Rich Juzwiak, "I'm a Heterosexual Woman Who's Politically Opposed to Heterosexuality: Who Do I Date?," *Slate*, Jan. 27, 2020, https://slate.com/human-interest/2020/01/straight-woman-dating-on-grindr.html.
4. leiaj (community contributor), "18 Girls Looking for Gay Friends on Grindr," BuzzFeed, Nov. 28, 2012, https://www.buzzfeed.com/leiaj/girls-on-grindr-5xwk.
5. Hallie Lieberman, "Straight Women Are on Grindr Now. Some People Don't Want Them There," BuzzFeed, May 12, 2022, https://www.buzzfeednews.com/article/hallielieberman/women-on-grindr.
6. Chadwick Moore, "Bridal Party Problems: How Bachelorettes Are Ruining Gay Nightlife," *Out*, Apr. 11, 2016, https://www.out.com/lifestyle/2016/4/11/bridal-party-problems-how-bachelorettes-are-ruining-gay-nightlife.
7. Chadwick Moore, "What the Heck Is a 'Queer' Anyway?," OUTspoken, Nov. 15, 2022, https://getoutspoken.com/alphabet-soup/what-is-a-queer.
8. Thomas Rogers, "Why 'Sex and the City' Is Bad for the Gays," *Salon*, May 28, 2010, https://www.salon.com/2010/05/28/sex_and_the_city_bad_for_gays/.
9. Lee Siegel, "Relationshipism," *The New Republic*, Nov. 18, 2002, https://newrepublic.com/article/66593/relationshipism.
10. James P. Pimkerton, "The Hypersexualization of Culture," *The Ledger*, July 19, 1999, https://www.theledger.com/story/news/1999/07/19/the-hypersexualization-of-culture/26592581007/.
11. See Louise Perry, critiquing the Sexual Revolution and SATC alike, in a Free Press debate, in the following Oct. 5, 2023, post on X: https://twitter.com/TheFP/status/1709986801757065727.

12. Germaine Greer, *The Beautiful Boy* (Rizzoli International Publications, 2003), 22.
13. Greer, *The Beautiful Boy*, 228.
14. "The Art Teacher," by Rufus Wainwright, produced by Marius de Vries, Geffen Records, released June 29, 2004.
15. The edition I read is the long-subtitled original: Melissa de la Cruz and Tom Dolby, eds., *Girls Who Like Boys Who Like Boys: True Tales of Love, Lust, and Friendship Between Straight Women and Gay Men* (Dutton, 2007). The title itself references a lyric from the 1994 Blur song "Boys & Girls."
16. Anna David, "Love in Other Lifetimes," in de la Cruz and Dolby, eds., *Girls Who Like Boys Who Like Boys: True Tales*, 124.
17. David, "Love in Other Lifetimes," 125.
18. Rich Juzwiak, "Only One Kind of Sex Turns Me On—and I Can Never Have It," *Slate*, Sept. 2, 2020, https://slate.com/human-interest/2020/09/woman-with-gay-sex-fetish-advice.html.
19. Lucy Neville, *Girls Who Like Boys Who Like Boys: Women and Gay Male Pornography and Erotica* (Palgrave Macmillan, 2018), 242.
20. *Violet Tendencies*, directed by Casper Andreas, released Apr. 24, 2010.
21. Brandon Voss, "Mindy Cohn: No Shrinking Violet," *Advocate*, July 8, 2010, https://www.advocate.com/arts-entertainment/film/2010/07/08/no-shrinking-violet.
22. Neville, *Girls Who Like Boys Who Like Boys*, 2.
23. Neville, *Girls Who Like Boys Who Like Boys*, 3.
24. Neville, *Girls Who Like Boys Who Like Boys*, 14.
25. Neville, *Girls Who Like Boys Who Like Boys*, 66.
26. Neville, *Girls Who Like Boys Who Like Boys*, 32.
27. Neville, *Girls Who Like Boys Who Like Boys*, ix.
28. Neville, *Girls Who Like Boys Who Like Boys*, 50.

29. Neville, *Girls Who Like Boys Who Like Boys*, 73.
30. Neville, *Girls Who Like Boys Who Like Boys*, 232.
31. Neville, *Girls Who Like Boys Who Like Boys*, 233.
32. Michael Musto, "Welcome to My Dollhouse," in de la Cruz and Dolby, eds., *Girls Who Like Boys Who Like Boys: True Tales*, 183.
33. Simon Doonan, "Fag Hags: the Laughter, the Tears, the Maribou," in de la Cruz and Dolby, eds., *Girls Who Like Boys Who Like Boys: True Tales*,15–16.
34. Neville, *Girls Who Like Boys Who Like Boys*, 15.
35. Juzwiak, "Only One Kind of Sex," *Slate*, Sept. 2, 2020, https://slate.com/human-interest/2020/09/woman-with-gay-sex-fetish-advice.html.
36. Claire Rudy Foster, "Why Are So Many Gay Romance Novels Written by Straight Women?," Electric Literature, Mar. 20, 2018, https://electricliterature.com/why-are-so-many-gay-romance-novels-written-by-straight-women/.
37. Neville, *Girls Who Like Boys Who Like Boys*, 275.
38. Daniel Oppenheimer, host, with Blake Smith and James Kirchick, guests, *Eminent Americans*, podcast, "The Fall of the White American Gay," May 30, 2023, https://danieloppenheimer.substack.com/p/the-fall-of-the-white-american-gay.
39. Neal Broverman, "Gay Nude Resort Must Allow Women, Judge Declares," *Advocate*, July 3, 2023, https://www.advocate.com/business/gay-nude-resort-allow-women.
40. Neville, *Girls Who Like Boys Who Like Boys*, 139–140.
41. Blake Smith, "Eve Kosofsky Sedgwick's Big Fat Nonbinary Mistake," *Tablet*, Jan. 12, 2023, https://www.tabletmag.com/sections/arts-letters/articles/eve-sedgwick-non-binary-mistake.
42. Laura Becker, "I Thought Being a Gay Man Would Save Me from Womanhood (It Didn't)," *Quillette*, Nov. 18, 2024, https://quillette

.com/2024/11/18/i-thought-being-a-gay-man-would-save-me-from-womanhood-trans/.

43. Harry Nicholas, *A Trans Man Walks into a Gay Bar: A Journey of Self (and Sexual) Discovery* (Jessica Kingsley Publishers, 2023), accessed online.
44. Nicholas, *A Trans Man*.
45. Nicholas, *A Trans Man*.
46. Maggie Smith, "My Marriage Was Never the Same After That," The Cut, Mar. 28, 2023, https://www.thecut.com/article/book-excerpt-you-could-make-this-place-beautiful-maggie-smith.html.

Chapter 6: The Himbo Plot

1. Amy Klobuchar, X, Aug. 25, 2023, https://twitter.com/amyklobuchar/status/1695052478264258707.
2. *Seinfeld*, season 5, episode 12, "The Stall," aired Jan. 6, 1994.
3. *The Bob Newhart Show*, season 1, episode 2, "Tennis, Emily?," aired Sept. 3, 1972.
4. *The Mary Tyler Moore Show*, season 5, episode 2, "Not Just Another Pretty Face," aired Sept. 21, 1974.
5. *Fawlty Towers*, season 2, episode 2, "The Psychiatrist," aired Feb. 26, 1979.
6. Katcy Stephan, "Billie Eilish Was Made for This: 'Being a Woman Is Just Such a War, Forever,'" *Variety*, Nov. 13, 2023, https://variety.com/2023/music/features/billie-eilish-body-shamers-sexualized-barbie-oscar-buzz-1235787860/.
7. *Frasier*, season 2, episode 24, "Dark Victory," aired May 23, 1995.
8. *Bye Bye Birdie*, directed by George Sidney, released Apr. 4, 1963.
9. Steve Almond and Sheryl Strayed, hosts, *Dear Sugars*, podcast, "Rapid Fire: Love In Doubt," Jan. 6, 2017, https://www.wbur.org/dearsugar/2017/01/06/dear-sugar-episode-eighty-one.

Conclusion: Frumpy-but-Horny

1. Naomi Wolf, "Emily Ratajkowski's Naked Ambition," *Harper's Bazaar*, July 7, 2016, https://www.harpersbazaar.com/culture/features/a16417/emily-ratajkowski-interview/.
2. Naomi Wolf, *The Beauty Myth: How Images of Beauty Are Used Against Women* (Perennial, 2002), accessed online.
3. *The Golden Girls*, season 1, episode 3, "Rose the Prude," aired Sept. 28, 1985.
4. *Waiting for God*, season 2, episode 9, "Young People," aired Oct. 31, 1991.
5. "Reincarnation" by Victoria Wood, on *Real Life: The Songs*, produced by Ovation Records, released Jan. 19, 1997.
6. Chris Kraus, *I Love Dick* (Semiotext(e), 2006), 19.
7. Kraus, *I Love Dick*, 159–162.
8. *Keeping Up Appearances*, season 5, episode 1, "The Senior Citizens' Outing," aired Sept. 3, 1995.
9. Gemma Parry, "Head Chef at Country Hotel Wins Another £8,000 After His Boss Sexually Harassed Him by Singing Victoria Wood's Classic 'Ballad of Barry and Freda' to Him—After Judge Ruled £80k Wasn't Enough," *Daily Mail*, Nov. 10, 2024, https://www.dailymail.co.uk/news/article-14065961/chef-tribunal-boss-sexual-harassment-Victoria-Woods.html.
10. "The Ballad of Barry and Freda (Let's Do It)," by Victoria Wood, from *Victoria Wood: As Seen on TV*, season 2, episode 1, aired Nov. 10, 1986.
11. Emma Copley Eisenberg, "Notes on Frump," *Hey Alma*, Aug. 10, 2017, https://www.heyalma.com/notes-on-frump-a-style-for-the-rest-of-us/.
12. *Waiting for God*, season 2, episode 5, "Tell the Truth," aired Oct. 3, 1991.
13. *Waiting for God*, season 3, episode 6, "Scandal," aired Oct. 15, 1992.
14. *Waiting for God*, season 2, episode 5, "Tell the Truth," aired Oct. 3, 1991.

15. *The Golden Girls*, season 7, episode 23, "One Flew Out of the Cuckoo's Nest," aired May 9, 1992.
16. *Are You Being Served?*, season 3, episode 3, "Up Captain Peacock," aired Mar. 13, 1975.
17. "Mrs. Slocombe's Hilarious Pussy Cat Moments | Are You Being Served?," BritBox channel on YouTube, https://www.youtube.com/watch?v=d-i523Gie9Q.
18. From Know Your Meme, this slang term means "to be powerful in an unapologetic and feminine manner." https://knowyourmeme.com/memes/serving-cunt.
19. "Reincarnation" by Victoria Wood, on *Real Life: The Songs*, produced by Ovation Records, released Jan. 19, 1997.